SURRENDERIN

PATRICK LAUDE

Surrendering to the Self

Ramana Maharshi's Message for the Present

دامعة جورجتاون قطر
GEORGETOWN UNIVERSITY QATAR

Center *for* International *and* Regional Studies

HURST & COMPANY, LONDON

Published in Collaboration with
Center for International and Regional Studies
Georgetown University-Qatar

First published in the United Kingdom in 2022 by
C. Hurst & Co. (Publishers) Ltd.,
New Wing, Somerset House, Strand, London, WC2R 1LA
© Patrick Laude, 2022

Printed in Great Britain by Bell and Bain Ltd, Glasgow

The right of Patrick Laude to be identified as the author of this publication
is asserted by him in accordance with the Copyright, Designs and Patents
Act, 1988.

A Cataloguing-in-Publication data record for this book
is available from the British Library.

ISBN: 9781787385382

www.hurstpublishers.com

CONTENTS

INTRODUCTION

WHY WRITE ABOUT RAMANA MAHARSHI?

Ramana Maharshi is no doubt one of the most widely known Indian spiritual figures of the last century. It is testament to the Maharshi's worldwide renown that *Life Magazine*,[1] in May 1949, carried an eleven-pages-long article by Winthrop Sargeant devoted to the sage of Arunachala, accompanied by splendid photographs taken by Eliot Elisofon.[2] Since then, beyond this anecdotal albeit significant reference, the truth is that dozens of books on Ramana Maharshi have been published in many languages. Most of them—collections of interviews and anthologies, evocations, meditations and biographies—are works composed by devotees, or by people who have been deeply inspired by the Maharshi's personality and teachings. A visit to the bookstore of Ramanasramam in Tiruvannamalai, the geographical center of his global radiance where he lived the latter years of his life, reveals the wealth of the output devoted to the sage both in Indian and European languages, and the availability of numerous translations of kindred books in a wide spectrum of languages, from Telugu and Malayali to Spanish and Korean.

Ramana Maharshi himself, however, was definitely not an author out of vocation, and did not undertake his few instructional and poetical ventures into writing of his own accord. Instead, his works were composed in response to inquiries or requests from his devotees. The paucity of Ramana's writings is no doubt one of the reasons why academic books on the Maharshi are relatively few. Indeed, in one of these rare scholarly studies, John Grimes quotes the Maharshi warning against the dangers of the mind when writing and reading become illusory substitutes for spiritual realization: 'the more the mind expands, the farther it goes and renders Self-Realization more difficult

1

and complicated.'³ One may question, therefore, the opportuneness of writing about the Maharshi, at least from a spiritual point of view. There might even appear to be something misplaced, or even seemingly presumptuous, in studying a sage whose perspective deliberately and explicitly transcends the domain of discursive expression, and points to the primacy of spiritual introspection beyond concepts, words and images. To wit, the Maharshi actually compares to a gramophone those who do not seek beyond the mental script of the doctrine.⁴ Furthermore, 'as has often been said, only a *mukta* [a liberated soul] can truly understand another *mukta*.'⁵ Let us take this reminder as an introductory warning that any mental or discursive understanding remains perforce on the surface of the matter at stake since it presupposes a duality—that of the mind and its object—that only Self-realization dispels. This does not mean, however, that the mind cannot play a preparatory role in the emergence of spiritual realization: 'through knowledge by description we may succeed in gaining knowledge by identity.'⁶ In a way, if it were not so there could not be any passage from ignorance to knowledge: there has to be in between, as it were, a knowledge that is ignorance, but leads to full knowledge. It is in keeping with this need for a transition that the traditional formal disciplines of the *Advaita Vedānta*, the Hindu school of Vedāntic non-duality, assign specific functions to the reading of scriptures and the meditation of the doctrine as also to the pondering concentration of the mind on the ultimate object of knowledge, which is referred to as *nididhyāsana*.⁷

Ramana's experience was, by contrast, seemingly unmediated, and this is a key to understanding many features of his teachings. In keeping with the mode of his realization, the Maharshi tended to limit the benefit of the mind to its capacity to cancel itself out, as it were. In other words, the only activity of the mind that is truly worthwhile lies with relentlessly raising the question 'who am I?', and delving deep—beyond the mind itself—into the Self, or *Ātman*, that is the Self of all selves. This pursuit is *vichāra*, or investigation into the Self, the point of departure of which is the mind, while its outcome lies beyond the mind. Interestingly, Ramana identified his *Ātmā-vichāra* or Self-investigation with *nididhyāsana,* the intense intellectual concentration considered to be the crux of Advaitin discernment; this is because it constitutes a thorough examination of the 'I', which is the principle of reality, and in a sense like the peak of meditational activity. Considered from another point of view, however, *vichāra* pertains to a dimension altogether different from mental meditation, since it points to that which is the very condition of meditation, and that no meditation can reach. It consists in delving into the

2

very source of 'I'-consciousness. As Michael James puts it quite felicitously: 'Self-investigation is not any action or activity of our mind, but is only the practice of keeping our mind perpetually subsided in our real self, that is, in our own essential and ever clearly self-conscious being.'[8] Thus, discourse as based on mind activity cannot but be a straying away from the Self, and from that point of view only the silence of the *muni*, the silent sage who reached realization on the exclusive basis of his own inner experience, can do justice to its non-dual reality. Yet, the Maharshi himself broke the silence that he had kept since his arrival in Tiruvannamala in September of 1896. First, in the early 1900s, this was merely in response to questions, but opening the doors of expression out of compassion meant that he entered the world of conceptual cross-relations. By the same token, he paved the way for opportunities to meditate his own words, a paradoxical if not perilous involvement of the mind in the very work of passing beyond the mind. It is clear, however, that from his own vantage point speaking or writing was in no way jeopardizing his abiding in the Self, meaning that verbal expression was no different from silence.

Why add another book to an already wide array of works devoted to the Maharshi? While the purpose of this book is in some way parallel to that of most books written on the subject, in that it is offering a presentation of one of the greatest sages of our times, its outlook is significantly distinct from most other such attempts. In common with most, if not all, contemporary books devoted to the Maharshi, the immediate objective of the following study is to offer an introduction to Ramana Maharshi's life and teachings to contemporary readers who may be unaware of their major significance. Within this perspective, this book must involve an examination of the non-dualistic teachings of the Maharshi as expressions of the Hindu philosophy and spiritual path of *Advaita Vedānta*, the *Vedānta* of non-duality whose main expositor was the great eighth-century Shankarāchārya. In this regard, the current manuscript adds its own contributions, with distinctive focuses and inflections, to the vein of scholarly works such as John Grimes' *Ramana Maharshi: The Crown Jewel of Advaita*,[9] and T.M.P. Mahadevan's *Ramana and His Philosophy of Existence*.[10] However, the specific intent of this book reaches beyond a merely introductory endeavor to the metaphysical and spiritual lessons to be drawn from the Maharshi's teachings. Here, it does not only, or primarily, situate the Maharshi within the non-dual tradition of Hinduism, but it also delves into themes and questions that are particularly relevant to the contemporary spiritual crisis and search for meaning.

Needless to say, the concerns and questions that are brought to the fore in this book reflect its author's personal interests and perspective. Thus, it can be read, in a way, as an exploration of the Maharshi's life and teachings in light of the latter. During my visits to the ashram of Sri Ramana in Tiruvannamalai, I have been consistently intrigued by the diversity of devotees and visitors, diversity of origins, searches and backgrounds. One element of this diversity lies in the contrast—illustrated by the mingling of Hindu devotees and Western seekers, betwen the traditional modes of 'religious' ways and the postmodern styles of 'spiritual' quests for the Self. These contrasts raise the question of what is at stake in the Maharshi's message, and how this message may prove to be most relevant to contemporary seekers without losing its authentic spiritual grounding and being diluted into the general mood of neo-spiritual individualism and informality.

A sage for the contemporary world

One of the most fruitful ways of introducing the Maharshi's spiritual message is to do so in the critical contexts of modernity and postmodernity. I do not imply that these teachings are in any way conditioned by contemporary predicaments, since—as will be quite apparent—the Maharshi's claims know no time and no location. However, even from a traditional Hindu perspective, the very fact that the Maharshi lived and taught in the twentieth century must mean that his presence had a certain karmic resonance with the modern world. For the purpose of this study I characterize modernity by three fundamental phenomena: the rise of individualism, the secularization of culture, and the advent of a pluralistic concept of truth. Individualism can be defined with Louis Dumont as a set of historical and cultural representations in which the value is primarily placed on the individual, by contrast with holistic societies in which the value is placed on the whole, or the group.[11] The latter would certainly include the type of social ambience in which the young Ramana grew up in Tamil Nadu. The organic context of a Brahmin family and a small Hindu community, with its formal norms and communal values, makes for a very different kind of upbringing than does the cultural ambience in which most contemporary Westerners have been raised. Notwithstanding, the concept of Self-realization undoubtedly rings a bell with the individualistic ethos that is prevalent in the modern world. Confusion may therefore arise as to what is at stake in the spiritual odyssey traced by Ramana Maharshi. This is why it bears stressing that, in relation to modern individualism, the Maharshi's message amounts to a kind of spiritual revolution. In a cultural context in which the individual self is deemed to be of ultimate value, the sage invites one to realize the true Self by transcending the limitations and illusions of the individual. Thus, the Maharshi's words and presence take us beyond the realm of individual psychology. They immensely exceed the primacy of the core value of modern culture, and must actually be characterized as utterly supra-individual in scope.

At the same time though, by contrast with traditional holistic perspectives, the Maharshi's teachings do not arise from an explicitly and specifically religious outlook. This may be deemed to be both an opportunity and a potential pitfall. The seemingly areligious starting point of the Maharshi's Self-realization may be free from associations that would hinder its radiance in a *de facto* secular context, and therefore resonates *a priori* beyond its civilizational and spiritual land. In this regard, it is worth highlighting that Ramana's teachings take a non-conventional view of the Hindu religious tradition, and of religious tradition in general, one that is deeply consistent with its spiritual heights while being independent of its formal limitations. In a sense the Maharshi's point of view is akin to that of the traditional Hindu renunciate, the *samnyāsin*. The latter forgoes his social and family duties to focus on the spiritual goal of life, *moksha* or spiritual deliverance, thereby transcending the traditional caste system without subverting it. And indeed Ramana Maharshi became a *samnyāsin* from the day of September 1886 when he arrived in Tiruvannamalai, where he would spend the rest of his life: he signaled his renunciation of all worldly possessions and social duties by being shaved and throwing the little money he had left from his trip in the Ayyankulam Tank.[12] Moreover, as Gabriele Ebert has noted, it is significant that the first place visited by the young sage on his initial day in Tiruvannamalai was the Arunachaleshwara Temple.[13] For him, the spiritual awakening and the religious context were intrinsically connected. Thus, inasmuch as it is situated at the intersection of the horizontal universe of Hinduism and the vertical axis of universal inner emancipation, the Maharshi's perspective may provide one with a renewed sense of religion that redefines its meaning and end in terms of Self-knowledge.

In an age in which truth is split and presence elusive, the Maharshi's vision opens the way to a different kind of pluralism, one that does not entail relativism but allows one to envisage multiplicity in light of a single source and a single goal. In this regard, the Maharshi taught a kind of 'relativistic absolutism,' if one may say so. Arvind Sharma has characterized Ramana's

Hinduism as 'absolutistic.'[14] This is quite an adequate characterization in the sense that the Maharshi's life and teachings were exclusively centered on the Self as the Absolute, or the Absolute as the Self. On the religious plane, however, this absolutism with respect to the goal of life led him to recognize the relativity of religious paths, a recognition that may strike a chord with the contemporary ethos of pluralism. Indeed, as several sections from this book will illustrate, the Maharshi was not only adamantly conscious of the one ultimate Absolute, but he was also keenly aware of the diversity of needs and the paths leading to it. However, the pluralism of the Maharshi, if one may call it this way, has no meaning except in relation to his absolutism, which is the core element of his teachings and indeed his life.

The first chapter of this book provides biographical orientations that highlight, in the Maharshi's life, the areas of relevance and consonance that have just been sketched. Many biographies of the Maharshi have been written, and there appears to be little need for new biographical forays. This being said, our intent in including a biographical section in the current book is not only to provide readers unfamiliar with the Maharshi with a few landmarks that may help them better understand the living background of his teachings, but also to lay the groundwork for some of the major focal points of our study.

Religion and spirituality: Beyond an opposition

The distinction, often couched as an opposition, between the religious and the spiritual has become almost stereotypical in the twentieth and early twenty-first century. On the one hand, religions have become increasingly understood in terms of identity—mostly collective and communal, and in the ways of beliefs and practices that crystallize such identities. They therefore provide individuals and communities with a strong sense of being and belonging. The contemporary emphasis on this dimension of religion has most often been to the detriment of the theological and spiritual aspects of religious phenomena. It is as if the incapacity to be fed by the spiritual treasures of one's tradition, or the very widespread ignorance thereof, needed to be compensated by an emphasis on collective, social, or even political substitutes that end up being identified with religion as such. Or else, as if it was imperative that religion be translated into extra-religious categories. The transformation of religion into ideology is one of the extreme outcomes of this displacement of religious identity.

In a curious contrast that is actually in many ways but the other side of the formal and collective sedimentation of religious life, spirituality has been claimed, particularly in the modern West, as an individual search for meaning that seeks to be independent from so-called 'organized religions,' when it does not assert antagonism toward them. The reason for this lies in a culturally pervasive sense that nothing external must hamper the freedom of the quest for oneself, and that the dogmatic, ritual and institutional structures are in fact obstacles to such a search, given their fixed and prescriptive nature, if not their deleterious historical circumstances. When perceived in this negative light, the most external manifestations of religion appear in fact profoundly at odds with any sense of inner quest.

It is in such a setting that one must situate part of the fascination exercised by the Maharshi in the contemporary Western world. Accordingly, many works devoted to the Maharshi have tended to emphasise the trans-religious dimension of his life and teachings. Indeed, the perspective of Self-inquiry that he has repeatedly taught does not rely on any religious 'mythology.' It is couched in the most simple and direct language, and appears to be independent from any creed or metaphysical presuppositions. A closer examination discloses, however, that this apparent independence does not amount to making religion irrelevant or disposable. It is one of the main intents of this book to argue how and why this is not so. One of the difficulties lies in the fact that the very concept of religion may be understood in different ways, or on different levels. Thus, it is serviceable to distinguish, in this regard, between four distinct dimensions: religion as a way, religion as a set of practices, religion as a collective tradition, or as a 'cumulative tradition,' to make use of Wilfred Cantwell Smith's terminology, and, finally, religion as an exclusive belief system in contradistinction with others. The first two aspects of religion are intrinsically connected: by 'way' I mean a living relationship between the faithful and their divinity—arguably the essence of religion as a sacred bond. This relationship is established and deepened through particular acts, the most central of which relates most directly to the transcendent Object of worship, and is none other than prayer. The third and fourth aspects are also related: tradition is the outcome of a growth that has sustained and enriched a religious identity while contributing to making it distinct from others. These four aspects of religion are considered in different chapters of this book, as sketched in the following pages.

The religious way and the meaning of prayer

The religious way is often primarily defined in terms of devotion and grace, human worship and divine gift. I have come to realize that this common understanding of religion raises a number of important questions when it is related to the Maharshi's perspective. Thus, at face value, the Maharshi's teachings may be equated with a psycho-spiritual technique of self-inquiry. The latter appears to be quite foreign to any notion of a divine grace, as it emphasises a personal search for the source of one's own being. Indeed, it appears to be akin to a methodical exercise in which the human practitioner is the only, or at least the main, agent, independently from any divine power. Understood—or rather misunderstood—in this way, the Maharshi's teachings would seem to strike a chord with both the individualist and secular bents of modernity.

Moreover, the quest for the Self, the realization of which is *moksha*, is typically associated, in the context of traditional Hinduism, with the way of knowledge, or *jñāna*. It is therefore normatively distinguished from the path of love, or *bhakti*. The latter is intrinsically dualistic, or at least akin to so-called qualified non-dualism, whereas the former is focused on the non-dual essence of Reality, i.e., the one and single *Brahman* or *Ātman*.[15] A close examination of Ramana's life and words reveal, however, that the two elements of devotion and grace play an important role in the spiritual economy of his realization. These considerations are very significant for all those who do not see religion as disjointed from spirituality; while being fascinated by the spiritual radiance of the Maharshi, they may be at a loss to situate his teachings within a religious framework, given the sovereign independence of his Self-realization from all forms. After all, monotheistic traditions do not explicitly equate the search for God with Self-knowledge. Thus, it may be difficult to recognize, when reviewing the Western literature on the Maharshi, how the relational reality inherent to religious life—and epitomized by devotion and grace—is indeed relevant to Self-inquiry. In order to address these crucial questions a chapter of this book is focused on highlighting the ways in which devotion and grace must be understood as integral parts of the Maharshi's way.

Another essential aspect of religion is prayer, since the latter relates most directly to the very object of worship, the Divine Reality, as the transcendent 'interlocutor' of mankind. In the context of a discussion of the Maharshi's perspective one question is therefore likely to arise: what is the relationship between Self-realization and prayer? The relevance of this question dwells with the very essence of the religious practice. It arises from a basic recognition that prayer is intrinsically dualistic since it presupposes the bond between the human agent of prayer and a divine object or interlocutor. Whether conceived in the form of a simple conversation with God or as a ritual activity of worship, any type of prayer appears to be consubstantial with relationship. By contrast, Self-realization is not. This is not so on account of a presumed 'spiritual egoism' that would exclude a consideration of others. The fact of the matter is not subjective in the individual sense of the term, but it pertains in fact to the ontological and epistemological ground of reality. Thus, as will be made more explicitly plain in the pages of this book, Self-realization— in the sense in which the Maharshi understands it—is non-dualistic since it amounts to realizing that the Self is in essence the only Reality. No duality can be ultimate, and the Ultimate knows of no relationship, being the common essence of everything. As a consequence of this recognition, one may wonder whether the Maharshi's non-dualistic view does not undermine the very reality of prayer, but also, in a way, religion in general—since both appear to be intrinsically relational. Such a consideration is particularly important in our day and age, when various forms of 'self-help spirituality' choose to bypass or reject any relationship with the Divine, and may all too conveniently discern in the Maharshi's teachings a further reason to do so. In response to these interrogations and queries the third chapter of this book is devoted to the Maharshi's understanding of prayer as *japa yoga* or *mantra yoga*, the invocation of a divine name or formula, and its relationship with Self-knowledge. As will be developed further, this particular practice, which is most widespread in the Hindu world, constitutes a kind of bridge between the perspective of Self-knowledge, *jñāna*, and devotion, *bhakti*.

Religion as tradition

Tradition is rarely contemplated in a positive light in today's world. The word itself is fraught with ambiguities and pitfalls. This is particularly the case in the domain of spiritual search, one in which traditional forms and institutions are routinely deemed to obstruct the liberty of the spirit. In fact the term 'tradition' is most often used as a misnomer, since, far from denoting the fossilized or repressive forms with which the modern mind tends to equate it, it actually entails the meaning of transmission, and therefore the living reality of a communication between humans. As Henry Corbin put it: 'a tradition transmits itself as something alive, because it is a ceaselessly renewed inspiration, and not a funeral cortège or a register of conformist opinion.'[16] For sure, the risks that such a living transmission may lose its creative impetus are always present in any religious universe, and the sedimentation, or even fossilization, of tradition is a destiny that no religious civilization can entirely escape. Christ's admonition to the Jewish traditional authorities of his time rings as a warning in this regard: 'But woe to you, scribes and Pharisees, hypocrites! For you shut up the kingdom of heaven against men; for you neither go in yourselves, nor do you allow those who are entering to go in' (Matthew, 23:13); hence the cardinal import of fresh spiritual inspiration as the sustaining force of tradition, which can only be activated by one's 'entering the kingdom.'

What we call Hinduism is indeed arguably more accurately referred to as a tradition than a religion. The *Sanātana Dharma*, as Hindus sometimes refer to it, is a perennial law or order of things, expressed through countless forms and ways, that is both grounded in unmovable being and running through immemorial times and many historical vicissitudes. It encompasses a wide array of beliefs, metaphysical deliberations and spiritual practices that have flown through the centuries as a manifold universe of meaning and paths of spiritual liberation. Like its art, which 'has something of the heavy motion of the sea and at the same time the exuberance of a virgin forest,'[17] what we call Hinduism appears as a rich unity and continuum within which virtually everyone and everything appear to be able to find their due. The term 'tradition' is therefore likely to be more appropriate in referring to Hinduism than is the word religion, since the latter may suggest a single vertical thread, as it were, joining—*religare*—heaven and earth, as it is in a way the case in Abrahamic religions. By contrast, the Hindu world is like a complex texture of most diverse threads. Moreover, the Hindu tradition is one in which spiritual realization, in the form of wisdom or sanctity, together with its facilitating agents, such as the *guru* or the *mantra*, play a role that is arguably more determining than that of sacred scriptures or institutions. The relationship between tradition and experience is therefore more fluid than it might be seen in, say, Abrahamic religions, in which the literal bedrock of the Book lies at the foundation of everything. Notwithstanding this, the diversity and the fluidity of the Hindu tradition are in no way exclusive of formal supports of the most constraining kinds. In fact institutional boundaries, profuse intellectual systematization and meticulous ritual formalism are indeed three major aspects of the tradition. So any spiritual odyssey and awakening occurring in the context of Hinduism must be situated in relation to the specific forms and norms of this traditional universe.

Now within this manifold tradition the teachings of Ramana Maharshi are most consonant with the school of *Advaita Vedānta*, or those interpretations of the Vedas that highlight their non-dualistic message. Taking stock of this fundamental affinity, John Grimes' *Ramana Maharshi: The Crown Jewel of Advaita* has provided invaluable insights into the Hindu traditional dimensions of Ramana Maharshi's teachings. It has convincingly shown that the Maharshi's realization is an experiential validation of *Advaita Vedānta* rather than the practical outcome of a meditation of its tenets. The young Ramana knew nothing of *Advaita* when he reached Self-realization; in fact his philosophical and religious culture was virtually inexistent.[18] His words, however, are unmistakably consonant with Shankara's *Vedānta* of non-duality. There is therefore both an intrinsic convergence and an extrinsic tension between the Maharshi and the Advaitin tradition, its presuppositions and its intellectual and methodical protocols. The fourth chapter of the book is dedicated to elucidating this apparent paradox and the various facets of the relationship between the awakening recognition and the traditional climate in which, and in a way from which, it emerged. This aims at providing a picture of tradition that, within the Maharshi's universe of meaning, is both inescapable and relative.

Religious identity and pluralism

The contemporary ethos is fundamentally pluralistic. This is so primarily as a result of globalization, which has resulted in an increasing recognition, and sometimes appreciation, of cultural and religious differences, while concurrently 'formatting' religions and uniformizing ways of living and practicing religion.[19] The modern world has certainly not invented religious pluralism, if by this term is simply meant the validation or legitimization of a *de facto* religious diversity. Such a recognition of plurality, with all the avenues of communication that it involves, has been a fact of life in parts of the world such as South Asia, for instance, where the intersections, oppositions and cross-fertilizations of the most diverse faiths have been part and parcel of the civilizational landscape for millennia. This type of pluralism, if one may call it so, was rarely oriented, however, toward the idea of a convergence of beliefs. From the point of view of the various religious communities that were involved in convivence such a religious pluralism was more *de facto* than *de jure*, and any further philosophical or spiritual statement of a common horizon of meaning and salvation was indeed an exceptional occurrence. One may mention, as one of those extraordinary instances, the case of the Moghol prince Dara Shikoh, who worked toward the recognition of a metaphysical unity between Islam and Hinduism.[20]

Today, however, it is probably fair to say that the religious revival experienced by the fastest growing religions of the world—modern forms of Christianity and Islam—has entailed a stricter exclusivism cemented by a strong sense of collective identity. It has also involved a growing ignorance, if not disdain, of the civilizational depth of meaning and production of the great religious traditions, particularly perhaps on the part of their own faithful. But independently from the limitations of the modern religious context, an intensity of faith has rarely been wedded with a plain recognition of other religious treasures. By contrast, liberal views of religion tend to gravitate around a somewhat amorphous concept of pluralism that amounts to a flattening down of the theological and spiritual content of particular religions. This type of pluralism aims at fostering a humanistic ethics of a global utopia that is not uncommonly fueled by economic interests and political ideologies. Thus, one way or another, finding a suitable situation for religious identity on the horizon of spiritual universality has been a challenge for many contemporary believers, seekers and scholars. For those who hold fast to their faith while not being blind to the treasures of other traditions one major question today might be 'how can I retain my own religion while sharing common universal principles and spiritual experiences with people of other faiths?'

Now, the Maharshi provides unique answers to this concern by taking back religious principles and beliefs to what he conceives to be their root reality: the search for the true Self. This perspective sheds light both on the ultimate meaning of a spiritual pluralism while allowing one to account for the plurality of religious paths. It provides a synthetic, direct, spiritual hermeneutics of religious expressions that may reinvigorate their message and open up new vistas to some seekers. In a way, the readers who might benefit most from this book are those who, faithful of a religious tradition, seek to make sense of the ways the Maharshi's Self-realization can be most relevant to their faith. They might also be among those who, alienated from religious traditions, are open to rediscovering the farther-reaching meaning of the latter through the prism of Self-knowledge. Delving into this wide opening and challenging conception, the focus, in the fifth chapter, is on the Maharshi's non-dualistic understanding of religion and religions.

The Maharshi and the postmodern context

The very mention of a postmodern outlook may appear deeply ill sounding in the context of the Maharshi's message of timeless Self-realization. In point of fact, the Maharshi's focus on the Self knows of no anterior and no posterior, and therefore no time, and so the very terms 'modern' or 'postmodern' must appear meaningless in the context of his 'absolutist' vision. His spiritual perspective takes the present as an absolute that, when fully grasped, transcends time; therefore, it does not envisage reality in terms of conditions or eras. Indeed its trans-historical outlook may sound as provocative or obsolete in a world in which any kind of religious experience is perforce approached by paying tribute to its presupposed cultural and historical determinations. What could, therefore, be the relevance of the Maharshi to the postmodern outlook and climate?

If by postmodernity is meant, in a deconstructive sense, a way of casting doubt on any stable meaning, and highlighting an irreducible plurality of moving perspectives that do not afford any objective point of view, then the Maharshi's teachings do provide insightful and far-reaching responses to such an ideological and cultural standpoint. They do so in a way that helps situate some of the partially cogent intuitions on which postmodernism feeds—considering that everything can ultimately teach us something about the Self and pondering that the postmodern unsettling of conventional certainties may be perceived in this light. Such are, first among many, the postmodern suspicions of conventional reality and their rejection of the deluded pretensions of rationality to reach beyond certain limits. While opening spiritual vistas onto the ways such ideological positions may play an epistemologically purifying role, any sustained meditation of Ramana Maharshi's words can only reveal, I suggest, the radical flaws of the post-modern anti-metaphysical premises.

The world as a projection of the mind

Postmodernity postulates the plurality of truths and the absence of a single unifying vision or narrative, while also highlighting, in its constructive forms, the value of interconnectedness. As a whole, it tends to emphasise the constant mobility of perspectives and the self-referentiality of meaning. It postulates the irreducibility of diversity and the elusiveness of presence— to sum up, it scoffs at universal notions of being and truth. As we will see, the Maharshi does not deny the manifold mobility of phenomena on the plane upon which the latter is undeniably at work, nor does he ignore the cognitive limitations inherent to the subject-object relationship, as the latter undermines any form of naive and one-sided realism. He actually recognizes those factors as constitutive of the very nature of the mind, and the very stuff of reality as perceived by the mind.

Taking on one of the major aspects of this consideration, a chapter of this book is devoted to elucidating the implications of the Maharshi's assertion that the world is a projection of the mind. This statement would seem to echo the postmodern questioning of objective reality, and dovetail with the relativistic bent of self-referentiality in deconstructivist culture. The recent forays of postmodernist discourses into the study of non-dualistic mysticism bear witness to such trends. An extensive critical examination, however, demonstrates that the matter is much more circumstantiated and multi-layered than it would appear at first sight; the Maharshi's statement about the mind and the world cannot be reduced, at any rate, to a literal solipsism devoid of all sense of objectivity. Even though they may be characterized by a certain 'idealist' inflection in comparison with Shankara's discriminative metaphysics, the sage's teachings must be understood against the backdrop of Advaitin metaphysics as evidenced in the specific context of his realization and spiritual presence. This is the focus of the sixth chapter, in which I argue that the Maharshi's assertions on the nature of the world can save some of the very partial intuitions of postmodernity from spiritual sterility and existential nihilism.

Who sees? The symbolism of the eye

Concomitantly, postmodernity, by contrast with modernity, is characterized by an emphasis on the elusiveness of the subject. Is not the self a vacuum, a mere construct, a myth that the old concept of the soul has for too long held in unchallenged certainty? Indeed, the Maharshi often makes the point that when one inquires into the mental self the latter vanishes, a fact that would seemingly give credence to a deconstructivist view of the subject. It must not be missed, however, that beyond this vanishing of the mind and the egotic constructs that it entails the question 'Who am I?' reaches a center of consciousness that is the essence of reality. It does not end in a vertiginous nothingness but in a blindingly evident Light. Addressing this cardinal distinction, the last chapter of the book is devoted to the Maharshi's reoccurring use of the eye as a most adequate symbol of this ultimate Consciousness that not only dislodges the illusory centrality of the individual self, but also gives each and every unit of selfhood reality and meaning within Itself.

The simplicity of the Maharshi's teachings, as epitomized by his re-occurring question 'Who am I?' may *prima facie* be considered relevant to our times when viewed as a response to the growing complexities of contemporary life. Contemplated in this light, it reaches to the core of our existential predicament in a way no theological systematization or philosophical speculation can match. This is all the more true at a time when religious intellectuality has arguably reached a low ebb. The current call for simple formulae and tangible realizations may make the Maharshi's direct question appealing to contemporary audiences, but it does not do so without a considerable measure of ambiguity that must be attended to. On the other hand, the intricate demands of the modern lifestyle, which is evermore bent on multiple stimuli and activities, make it increasingly arduous, if not seemingly impossible, to keep a single-minded focus on a sustained self-inquiry of the kind that the Maharshi advocates. The current book revolves around these paradoxes, tensions and questions. I wish to convey that, concomitant to the irresistibly glowing inspiration of the Maharshi's presence and the inviting power of the fundamental question that flows from his own exalted state of realization, the need for a serious consideration of the sage's relationship with religion(s) and tradition is imperative for an integral understanding of his perspective, so as to make it integrally and effectively applicable in most circumstances of our times. I believe this is a consideration that many contemporary readers and seekers will not find unwarranted.

1

WHOSE LIFE?

As has been mentioned from the outset, Ramana Maharshi is probably, among the main Hindu spiritual sages of the last century, the one that is most widely known outside India. The name Maharshi might be deceptive to many, however, and lead one to confuse Ramana with other contemporary Hindu figures, most likely among them Maharishi Mahesh Yogi. The latter was a *guru* who passed away in 2008, and is famous worldwide for having introduced and taught the so-called Transcendental Deep Meditation and founded the Transcendental Meditation movement, which has had a following of millions around the world. He was also responsible for the foundation of various academic, humanitarian and media organizations. Ramana Maharshi, on the other hand, never taught any psycho-physical technique nor started any public movement, and he led a very sedentary and secluded life; 'he has always been anxious to avoid publicity.'[1] His public fame and appeal was in no way the result of an effort of proselytism on his part, quite the contrary. It simply proceeded from the radiance of his spiritual personality. In fact, several biographical accounts make it clear that the Maharshi was eager to withdraw completely from the public gaze and live in utter isolation. When he and his ashram found themselves at the receiving end of a defamatory publication that worried some of his close devotees, he responded that he actually welcomed these critiques: they might give him the reputation of 'a false Swami' among some, so that people would 'no longer come to visit [...] and then [I] shall be able to have a quiet life.'[2] His public destiny was imposed upon him by circumstances, or by the 'divine decree', but its unfolding was in fact contrary to his inner disposition and his personal wishes.

As other authentic sages, the Maharshi shunned any individualistic affirmation of self and paid very little attention to his own person. He might have replied like Ulysses to the Cyclops' query: 'my name is nobody.' Like another great sage of the twentieth century, Mā Ananda Mayi, who used to refer to herself as 'this body', Ramana rarely used the pronoun 'I' to refer to himself, and once, when asked to write his name in a notebook by a visitor, responded by simply stating 'I have no name.'[3]

The name 'Maharshi', which may give rise to misidentifications, simply means 'great *rishi*', i.e., great seer, and it has therefore been widely used in India to refer to spiritual figures. As for Ramana, it is an abbreviation of the Maharshi's first name, Venkataraman. The sage is also often referred to as Bhagavān Srī Ramana Maharshi. This name was conceived and first used by Ganapati Muni, a highly respected Sanskrit scholar who was born one year before the Maharshi, in 1878, and who met him for the first time in 1907.[4] Śrī is an honorific title commonly used in India, and one of its etymological meanings entails the ability to diffuse light. The symbolism of light, as we will see in Chapter Six, is particularly central to the Maharshi's exposition of the doctrine of the Self, the latter being fittingly understood as the Light that makes everything appear in Its own. Bhagavān, finally, is a title of spiritual reverence that was bestowed upon Ramana by his devotees.[5] This title, most often used in reference to divine beings, like Hindu gods, or—in Buddhism— to the Buddha himself, can be translated as 'blessed' or rendered by its close Christian equivalent, 'Lord.'

Much of the life of the Maharshi has been told by himself, and a significant number of devotees and biographers have written extensively about it. Probably the most authoritative source in this respect is the first book of the seven-volume series *Arunachala Ramana: Eternal Ocean of Grace,* entitled *Biography.* The collection is an augmented and revised edition of a prior series, published by Ramasramam, the ashram of Ramana Maharshi, in 2018. This first volume includes many autobiographical accounts from the mouth of the Maharshi himself.

The life of Ramana spans a period of over seventy years, most of which were spent in the vicinity of the Mountain Arunachala, on the edge of the bustling town of Tiruvannamalai in Tamil Nadu. The life of Ramana can be regarded as consisting of two parts, with the decisively determining event of his spiritual awakening at the age of sixteen as the parting line between them.

In few lives does a single event change one's perception of oneself and the world to such an extent as to delimit two profoundly different distinct ways of living; hence the second intimation of the title of this chapter, 'whose life?'

The decisive existential event took place in July 1896. It has been narrated in many books on the Maharshi, but we do have his own words as a record of how this extraordinary inner experience unfolded, and what it entailed. The catalyst of the experience was a sudden and unexpected fear of death. What is extraordinary about this upsurge of fear was both its intensity and its utter lack of an obvious connection with anything that could have precipitated it. It was quite spontaneous, and at the same time irresistibly exacting. Even though the young Ramana had lost his father a few years previously, which had been the reason for his moving to Madurai from his native Tiruchuli, there was nothing in his health or in that of any member of his family that could be deemed to have been the trigger of the sudden emergence of this fear of death.

The other unusual aspect of this occurrence is that Ramana did not feel the need to go anywhere or to talk to anyone to resolve the issue, but instead held fast to a resolute determination to find an answer to the question it raised here and now. Now, of course, the theme and experience of death plays a central role in any form of spirituality, and countless mystics have spoken and written about 'inner death' as a prelude to spiritual growth or union with God. What is quite particular about the Maharshi's story, however, is that it involves a very literal experience of physical death as a door to enlightenment. Equally unique is the simplicity and directness of the way in which the crisis was resolved. First came a spontaneous inward motion whereby the mind inquired about the actual reality of death, or, in the Maharshi's words, 'What is it that is dying?'[6] Hence came a concrete and fundamental *discernment* between what dies and what does not die. One may wonder how such discernment might be possible, since that which does not die cannot, one might think, be known from within the context of life. One would seem to have to reach beyond life in order to know for sure what, if anything, survives physical death. A possible response to this difficulty is threefold. On the one hand, there was a simulation of physical death that helped precipitate the inner awakening. In other words, the young Ramana lay down with his 'limbs stretched out still, as though *rigor mortis* had set in and imitated a corpse to give greater reality to the enquiry.'[7] But although this imitation may be understood as a kind of suggestive magic by helping bring about a heightened sense of awareness of death, it does not in itself allow one to grasp

19

how it could have been able to produce some kind of certainty, had not it been complemented, or perfected, by a form of deeper, inner meditation. This was a form of meditation that dissects the components of the experience and discerns the elements that are bound to disappear at the time of physical death. This is, properly speaking, the investigation, *vichāra*, which will become the central component of the Maharshi's teachings. In a way it is a form of Advaita *viveka*, or discrimination between the Real and the illusory, or, more specifically, an existential modality of it. In Advaitin metaphysics, as taught by Shankara and his followers, the critical moment in the way of *jñāna* or knowledge is one of intellectual discrimination between the eternity of *Brahman* or *Ātman* and the temporariness of everything else. This is the distinction between *nitya* and *anitya*.[8] While fundamental discernment is referred to in temporal terms, it is also and first of all grounded ontologically, for only *Ātman* is real while all other realities have merely an appearance of being. This ontological, or rather metaphysical, discrimination is, however, in a sense only accessible *a posteriori* in Self-realization, while discernment with respect to time is more immediately accessible by the conventional mode of consciousness. This is why the suggestion by some commentators, such as Anantanand Rambachan, that the possession of *viveka* could imply that the very path would be made superfluous—since its aim appears to be precisely such a discernment—might overlook the crucial distinction to be drawn between a preliminary, rational discrimination and one that constitutes a lived and fully realized recognition. Now, with the Maharshi, this sense of preliminary time-related discernment was taken a step further in that it was 'incarnated' and anticipated in a way that made it more directly compelling. In other words, there is clearly an existential urgency in the dramatization of death that takes one beyond the confines of a purely intellectual exercise.

In itself, however, even this dramatization could not possibly result in an unshakable sense of certainty were it not for an intuitive insight that is, in itself, independent of any meditational, reflective, or for that matter physical, activity. Such an intuition does not involve thinking, or, if so, only in a very faint and indirect manner, like the shimmering edges of an intense and central light.[9] Ramana Maharshi puts it very clearly in the terms of a spiritual 'possession' by a 'mysterious power', taking away from this term any of the negative connotations that it entails. This is so true that, according to a commentator, 'in the first few weeks after his realisation he alternately thought that he had either been taken over by a spirit or afflicted by a strange but rather pleasant disease.'[10] Ramana Maharshi had not read any traditional

Advaitin literature about Self-realization, and was therefore at that time not in a position to establish correlations with such texts. This new state of consciousness that befell him could only be interpreted in terms of the elementary categories that were available to his mind. What was clear at any rate was the emergence of an identification with an 'I' which did not connote the limitations of the empirical ego.

In fact the ethical traces of this realization were obvious, since it entailed a change in the ways of acting and relating of the young Ramana. Contrasting his post-realization moral dispositions with those that preceded them, the Maharshi notes that, while he used to complain of unjust treatment, assert himself, and even respond violently to those who would poke fun at him before his inner experience, thereafter 'all that had changed. All burdens imposed, all chaffing, all fun was put up with meekly. The old personality that resented and asserted itself had disappeared.'[11] Self-realization entails ethical virtues to the extent precisely that the latter flow from one's freedom from the limitations of the ego. Spiritual ethics is not based on striving or moral debates and resolutions: '[the *jñani*] need not cultivate any excellences; they come to him automatically.'[12] This is enough to illustrate why any attempt at disconnecting Self-realization from moral considerations is misleading. While Hindu non-dualism clearly recognizes the incommensurable gap that separates morality as a human reality and the Self as a divine, universal and in a sense amoral, or trans-moral, reality, it also implies that Self-realization cannot but profoundly modify the *jīva*'s relationship with the world and others in ways for which we have probably no better word to suggest than 'morality.'

With respect to the phenomenology of spiritual experience, the Maharshi later on compared the new sense of 'I' to the *śruti* that underlies all other notes in a musical piece.[13] The term *śruti* usually refers to direct revelation, that of the Vedas, but it denotes more generally anything that is heard by someone. The *Omkara*, the sacred syllable AUM, constitutes in that sense the essence of *śruti* as divine revelation. Revelation is 'heard' by the *rishis* and there is no question that, for the Maharshi, the essence and the main content of the Vedas is the *Ātman* itself. Like the AUM that is the beginning, the end and the underlying sound of sacred chanting, the Self is the beginning, the end and the underlying reality of all modes and states of consciousness. From a certain point of view the *śruti* underlies everything else, but from another standpoint it is blended with everything else, and this is why it is not distinctly perceived by ordinary consciousness. There is always a sense of selfhood, but the real Self is not clearly identified for what it is because it is confused with limitations that feed the appearance of reality of the ego. The term 'blended' should not, therefore, lead one to think in terms of a modification, or even less a corruption, of the Self.

At any rate the spiritual event experienced by Ramana while he was alone in his uncle's house in Madurai was unarguably the central point of his life, one that divided most strikingly what followed it from what preceded it. Before that event, Ramana's life was ordinary, apparently insignificant, or only in some rare occurrences premonitory of what his vocation was to be. With respect to the ordinariness of Ramana's first sixteen years of life, little can be said, except that it stands in sharp contrast with what ensued. These are early years of life that, typically, are punctuated by the activities of a young boy, whether they pertain to family life, school studies or sports and play. It could be said that the extreme directionlessness of Ramana's early years stand in a contrast made all the sharper when compared with the extraordinary recognition and destiny that marks the later parts of his existence. It might be significant to note, therefrom, that the ordinariness of Venkataraman's early life bears witness, if only indirectly, to the transcendence of the Self. From an Advaitin point of view the *Ātman* levels down, as it were, all human differences in qualities and destinies, and there is indeed no common measure between the experiences and abilities of an individual and the universal immanence of the Self as contemplated in non-dualistic Hinduism. No amount of human gift or extraordinary world experiences can lead to Self-realization, which belongs to a totally different order of reality.

Notwithstanding the ordinariness of Venkataraman's early years, three aspects of his childhood and adolescence bear some importance when considered retrospectively in light of Ramana's later spiritual eminence. First, there is clearly a Hindu traditional context that served as the spiritual incubator of the young sage. His parents were pious, traditionally-minded Brahmins, well respected and loved in their village of Tiruchuli in Tamil Nadu. His father was a judge and his mother a homemaker, but 'one male member of the family in every generation gave up his home and all comforts to become an ascetic.'[14] Thus, Venkataraman bathed in a traditional and devotional ambience since his birth, in 1879. It is difficult to overstate the manifold and subtle ways in which his early life may have been penetrated and determined by principles and practices that used to mold the entire collective ambience of a small Hindu village of Tamil Nadu in the late nineteenth century. Even though it is related in several of his biographies that Ramana did not show any particular religious inclinations during his earliest years, several passages from various accounts should help us qualify this evaluation. It may be that the de-emphasis of the early marks of religious feelings and attitudes on the part of Venkataraman has been a result of a more or less conscious intent on the part of analysts and biographers, and especially so among Westerners, to highlight the unconditioned unicity of Self-realization, or an attempt at secularizing the latter, as it were, in order to distinguish it from religious beliefs and practices that may be subconsciously identified with Christian devotion. Be that as it may, it appears that such de-emphasis of religion in the life of the young Ramana does not represent a completely accurate reflection of the matter.

A particularly interesting testimony is, in this respect, that of his classmate Abdul Wahab, a Muslim boy who was his close friend at the American Mission School of Madurai. Abdul Wahab recounts that Ramana was in fact quite religiously inclined and used to frequent twice weekly Tirupparankundram, a temple that is one of the abodes of the god Murugan, as well as another temple of Madurai.[15] According to Abdul Wahab's testimony, this was not only a matter of conventional or sentimental piety, but it involved a deep sense of the presence of God in the universe. This sense extended to all religious ambiences and practices, on the basis of an inner consideration of religion, to such an extent that Abdul Wahab recounts that the instruction he received from the young Ramana led him 'to a better understanding of the secret (inner) approach to religion', and that 'in the company of Venkaraman [he] never felt that there was any difference between a mosque and the Subramania Swami temple.'[16] The foundations and ramifications of such spontaneous recognition of the Divine in all authentic religious manifestations will be explored in Chapter Five, but Abdul Wahab's remark already suggests the extent to which a sense of the unity of the Self permeated Ramana's sensibility even before his awakening.

Aside from his religious molding and devotional leanings the young Ramana presented, according to autobiographical and other testimonies, a rare personal predisposition that curiously anticipates a key component of his teaching. A. W. Chadwick mentions that, in his youth, he was 'an abnormally heavy sleeper.'[17] He is said to have experienced such deep sleep that, on occasion, his friends or family were unable to wake him up even when dragging his sleeping body.[18] As will be developed in Chapter Six, the state of deep sleep has been considered, in *Advaita Vedānta*, as being the closest— in a way—to Self-realization, since it is characterized by an extinction of dualistic states of consciousness, namely wake and dream. Indeed, in his commentaries on the *Brahmasūtra*, Shankara goes as far as to write that 'it is the general Vedānta doctrine that at the time of deep sleep the soul becomes one with the highest *Brahman*.'[19] This is to the extent that the egoic nexus of consciousness, based on the duality of a subject and an object, is extinct during sleep. By contrast, in both of the other states of consciousness, the presence of an object is implied, be it physical or simply psychic. In deep sleep only consciousness has no object, which means that it appears to be 'nothing' when contemplated from the point of view of the waking state. It is not nothing in reality, however, since—as the Maharshi often noted—when awaking from deep sleep one would spontaneously come to the conclusion 'I slept well.' The Maharshi sees this reflection as a piece of evidence that the 'I' is the common thread running through the various states of consciousness.

It goes without saying that deep sleep is not Self-realization, but an ability to experience the former in such an extraordinary way as Ramana did in his early days, with such unusual depth and resilience, could be interpreted as an inner predisposition to 'sleep without sleep', an expression that the Maharshi sometimes used to evoke the recognition of *Ātman*. Thus, it is significant to note that Ramana refers at times to the Self as that 'which sleeps in the body.' During a night circumambulation of Arunachala mountain Ramana and his devotees chanced to see bullock carts in which people were sleeping— all legs stretched in perfect abandonment. The sage commented upon this episode as being a perfect illustration of the 'sleep' of the Self: 'Supposing the man continues to sleep even when the cart stops on reaching its destination, is unloaded and the bullocks removed, and he continues to sleep all through. That is like the sleep of a Realized Soul. The body is for him a cart.'[20] The young Ramana's extraordinary capacity to stay asleep in spite of external disturbances of all sorts provides an unusual image, and a striking premonition, of the central teaching of the future sage.

Thirdly, one must mention the early impact of a particular devotional text, the reading of which was a catalyst in the young Ramana's spiritual development. This is the twelfth-century 'Great Epic', *Periya-purānam*, a Tamil religious classic that tells the stories of sixty-three Tamil sages and saints, the Śaivite *Nayanars* or 'hounds of Śiva', who lived in the sixth to eighth centuries in Tamil Nadu. They were also great devotional poets in the Tamil language. Here again, the discovery of this book by the young Venkataraman was not the result of a deliberate search on his part. He came across it just by chance, as his uncle had been given this book by a *swami*. It made a deep impression on Ramana, however, and awakened in him a sense of *bhakti,* and a longing for spiritual purity; in fact, following his enlightening experience, and as he spent hours in contemplation at Arunachaleshwara Temple upon his arrival in Tirunavannamalai, he would pray Īśvara to grant him as intense a devotion as the Nayanars'. However, the early impression made upon him by the Tamil saints' stories was not so long lasting as to prevent him from returning to the ordinary daily mode of consciousness of his earlier years. These were only seeds that would germinate later on. It is meaningful, however, that the first manifestations of a strong spiritual impulse in the heart of one who would become the epitome of *jñāna* in India, were of a decidedly bhaktic or devotional nature. This is already an indication that the notion of any radical severance between knowledge and love, or discrimination and devotion, in this case as much as in others, would be profoundly mistaken and dangerously misleading.

The second part of the life of the Maharshi, which spans the time from 1 September 1896, the day of his arrival in Tiruvannamalai, until his death on 14 April 1950, entirely flows from his Self-realization, and can only be understood in relation to it. One can consider it from the two points of view of space and time. With respect to space, it is characterized by the fact that these nearly fifty-four years were all spent in the proximity of Arunachala Mountain. Since the time of his arrival in the city the Maharshi never left Tiruvannamalai. This was not, however, a kind of ascetic practice on his part, one that would be analogous to a monastic rule of cenobitic sedentariness. When asked why he did not travel through India like Shankarāchārya and other peregrinating figures, including his contemporary the *bhakta* Swami Ramdas, his answer would typically be that there was no need for it, since space has no reality when it comes to the Self. Where could he go? And the fact is that many people came to him as if drawn by a motionless spiritual magnet. His sedentariness was in a way a reflection of the fact that the essence of all travels had been accomplished through *Moksha*. Moreover the young Ramana's move from Madurai to Arunachala, following his realization, was in this regard, in its unicity, the external paradigm of all travels as a motion toward the center, a truest pilgrimage.

Notwithstanding, his being grounded in Arunachala did not prevent the Maharshi from moving from place to place near and on the mountain, until he finally settled in the *ashram* that was built around him. These motions were largely accidental, however, and most often prompted by this or that physical circumstance, at least *a priori*. The important factor was the magnetism of the holy mountain, Ramana's various moves being but incidental episodes around this axis. When considering this period of this life one cannot overstate the centrality of Arunachala as an embodiment of Self-realization. The static majesty of the mountain incarnated the unmoving centrality of the Self. The exclusive sedentariness of the Maharshi cannot be understood without referring to a sense that Arunachala, being identified with the Self, is indeed the center of the world, and therefore renders it unnecessary to wander around the earth. This is the specifically jñanic point of view on the matter, since knowledge by identification lies at the core of the way of knowledge. From a more bhaktic vantage point it must also be noted that the Maharshi referred to Arunachala as his Father, a characterization the implications of which will be analyzed further in this volume.

With respect to time, one can in the main distinguish two phases. The first one is characterized by spiritual silence, *mauna*, and—although not in total synchronicity—a series of moves from dwelling place to dwelling place in the vicinity of the mountain or in some of its caves. The second one is marked by a sedentary and regulated life at the ashram, surrounded by devotees and visitors and punctuated by numerous interactions with them, in the ways of a combination of silent 'action of presence' and oral teaching. Many of his responses to questions and subsequent *upadēśa*, or spiritual instruction, as well as relations of spiritual experiences that occurred in the presence of the Maharshi, have been collected in volumes devoted to the sage, such as *Ramana Maharshi Day by Day* by Devaraja Mudaliar and *Letters from Ramasramam* by Suri Nagamma. The shift from pure, silent, inner experience in the early years of Ramana at Arunachala to the community life of a *guru* surrounded by devotees is representative of the two sides of the Maharshi's spiritual influence. The first is epitomized by purely spiritual presence, and pertains to the intrinsic reality of Self-realization, while the second is extrinsically determined by the needs of seekers while manifesting the Self-communicating and compassionate nature of the Self.

The relationship between spirituality and silence is central in the Hindu tradition, to such an extent that one of the titles ascribed to any sage considered to have attained high reaches of spiritual consciousness is *muni*, the silent one, as was the Buddha Shakya *Muni*. Self-realization lies beyond verbal expressions of any kind, because it contains within itself the very essence of consciousness and bliss. From that point of view, any sort of manifestation may appear as a kind of betrayal of the pristine perfection of the *Ātman*. The Maharshi himself taught that 'silence is eloquence unceasing.'[21] With spiritual silence, the fullness of expression does not entail any interruption, since there is no 'going out' of the plenitude of being: silence contains everything because it *is* everything.[22] There is, however, a sense in which silence could be understood in a restrictive way, as excluding manifestation in the form of meaningful sounds; but this view of things would amount to reducing silence to the inability of stones to utter a word. The Maharshi is, by contrast, quite keen on suggesting that truly spiritual silence is also a mode of meaningful blossoming that has more to do with the language of flowers than with the inert soundlessness of stones: 'To be silent like a stone without blossoming—can it be Silence true, my Lord?'[23]

However, even when considering spiritual silence as a symbol, or an evidence, of spiritual elevation, and not simply as an absence of words, it bears noting that it must not be absolutized to the point of assigning to it some sort of unqualified superiority. This is why the *Brihadāranyaka Upanishad* situates the *muni* on a scale of spiritual eminence that demonstrates the relativity of the view of *mauna*: 'So let a *Brāhman* put away learning with disgust and lead a childlike life. Let him then put away both the childlike life and learning with disgust, and [become] a silent sage (*muni*). Let him then put away both silence and its opposite with disgust, and [become a true] *Brāhman* (a man who really knows *Brahman*).'[24] While silence intrinsically and ultimately means plenitude of being and consciousness, it could also be understood as implying that the breaking of silence would amount to an alteration of this plenitude. While such cannot be the case in reality, an extreme ascetic understanding of silence could lead to a form of dualism, i.e., silence/sound, which would be utterly contrary to an integral grasp of the Self. If such an absolute contrast were warranted, then even the syllable AUM would be a breaking of silence—when in fact it is a sort of manifestation of silence, the sound of silence.[25] Accordingly, as he put it himself, the Maharshi's early silence was less a result of some sort of mystical vow than the spontaneous expression of a full satisfaction with the Self.

The sequence of silence and oral teachings, as the shift from physical retreat to life in an ashram, signals two emphases, one on the inner fruition of spiritual awakening, and the other on a spiritual imparting of blessings upon others. For the Maharshi, however, there does not seem to be the least conflict or even essential difference between the two. In fact silence is often referred to by him as the most effective way of teaching—he equated it once with eloquence, while the life of the *jīvan-mukta* in relative physical isolation does not impede in any way his subtle influence on the world and his power of attraction.[26] Notwithstanding this crucial caveat, it is not infrequent for spiritual figures, whether prophets or mystics, to go through distinct existential phases that reflect both the primacy of the inner realm of spirituality and its fundamental connection, indeed unity, with the outer field of experience.[27] Moreover, the two phenomena of silence and solitude are not absolute; indeed, they reveal patterns of interweaving. It is told that the Maharshi wrote 'Who am I?' in response to Ganapati Muni's questions while he was still keeping silence. This clearly indicates, if need be, that silence was not a way to retreat from teaching but rather a higher form of it. Conversely, while receiving visitors and listening to their questions, the Maharshi would sometimes respond by mere silence. This was probably a way to suggest the fruitlessness of concentrating on the antinomies of the mind, alluding thereby to the dangers of being hypnotized, as it were, by mental questions that are in no way essential to Self-realization. Another aspect of the Maharshi's emphasis on silence in the very context of verbal communication appears in numerous accounts of interviews and conversations. Thus, a number of Suri Nagamma's letters narrating interactions, whether in the form of story-telling or spiritual teaching, between the Maharshi and visitors end in a culminating silence. Responding to a devotee's speculative remark about the ability of Arunachala Mountain to manifest as a human being, 'Bhagavān merely nodded his head in silence.'[28] Evoking an anecdote in which Ramana was asked to repair an instrument of worship, the Maharshi acknowledged that he did so, and 'so saying, [...] became silent.'[29] Upon the mention that older women who used to visit the Maharshi found the energy to do so in their spiritual aspiration to be in the presence of the sage, the Maharshi approved and 'was silent.'[30] When told by a devotee that the cockerel who had died in his lap was fortunate to do so, the Maharshi just said 'yes, yes [...] and was again silent.'[31] The enumeration of the occurrences of such conclusions could go on and on. In each and every case such a silent *coda* brings the conversation to an end in suggesting the mystery of events and ideas that pass human understanding, or the return of all words to the silence of the Self.

Analogously, the relationship between solitude and spiritual company revealed, in Ramana's case, paradoxical contrasts. On the one hand, during his retiring years in Virupaksha Cave, his spiritual radiance would attract many young children in contemplation.[32] On the other hand, even in the company of his devotees at the ashram, he is said to have behaved not uncommonly as a distant witness. Thus Paul Brunton wrote that the Maharshi 'remains mysteriously aloof even when surrounded by his own devotees, men who have loved him and lived near him for years.'[33] This has contributed to foster the image of a 'non-human' sage indifferent to human predicaments and struggles, and as if devoid of individuality. Obviously, such a view of things is a result of a simplifying and one-sided apprehension of things. It goes without saying that the Maharshi was indeed a human person, and in a sense more truly human than most of his fellow humans, as becomes clear in many anecdotes told by his devotees or visitors. The mystery of distance in proximity, and proximity in distance, pertains in a way to the perplexing interplay of transcendence—the way the Divine lies 'above'—and immanence—the way God is 'present'—in most streams of contemplative metaphysics. Like God in mystical theology, the sage is both most intimate and most distant. He reconciles opposites in a way that is at the same time unsettling and inspiring. It is perplexing, because it involves the coincidence of two seemingly incommensurable orders of reality, with all the paradoxes and sometimes enigmas that this entails; but it is also and mostly inspiring, in that it provides a connection of the above with the below. It becomes a channel of grace without which the transcendence of God would amount to abstraction and result in indifference, while His immanence could give rise to a debasing familiarity. Thus, Ramana's unassuming approachability and charitable teaching do not take anything away from his dignified mystery.

Apart from its paradoxical implications, the relationship between silence and oral teachings can be envisaged from quite a different perspective when attention is paid to the human degrees of spiritual receptivity. Thus, Ramana recognizes that silence is not always an effective means of transmission: 'Dakshināmūrti, i.e., the great Siva himself could not express the truth of the one Reality except by silence. But that silence could not be understood except by the very advanced. The others have to be told. And yet how is one to say in words that which God himself could not express?'[34] We come, here, to the difficult question of the degrees of receptiveness and maturity on the part of the devotees. The ability to benefit from silence presupposes that the soul be ripe for letting itself be drawn toward its innermost core. A number of those who have experienced this transforming silence have borne witness to its intrinsic effectiveness. Thus, the first Western devotee of the Maharshi, F.H. Humphreys, a British police officer, tells of his first meeting with the sage in January 1911:

> When we reached the cave we sat before Him at His feet and said nothing. We sat thus a long while, and I felt lifted out of myself. [...] For half an hour I looked Him in the eyes which never changed their expression of deep

29

contemplation. I began to realise somewhat that the body is the temple of the Holy Ghost—I could only feel His body was not the man, it was the instrument of God, merely a sitting motionless corpse from which God was radiating terrifically. My own sensations were indescribable.[35]

The use of a Christian terminology, the Holy Ghost, is here all the more striking, in showing that the experience transcends all confessional boundaries. Meditating upon his second meeting with the Maharshi, Humphreys reflects on the transforming power of this hypnotic silence when writing that 'it is strange what a change it makes in one to have been in his presence.' The lasting and decisive effect of the silent presence of the Maharshi—and its radiance beyond religious forms—cannot be overemphasized, especially when considering that Humphreys, upon retiring from the service, became a Roman Catholic monk.[36]

While silence may be a difficult language to fathom for some of the devotees and arguably most human beings, verbal expression is a challenge even for the *jīvan-mukta* who attempts to put into words that which is the essence of the non-dual 'experience': 'how is one to say in words that which God himself could not express?'[37] This silence of God is an allusion to the traditional mode of teaching of Dakshināmūrti, Śiva as *guru*, which the Maharshi considered to be the epitome of all modes of spiritual silence; it highlights the fact that the matter is not as much one of divine power, or lack thereof, as it is one of metaphysical transcendence, or ontological impossibility. Since in Dakshināmūrti, Śiva is taken as teacher, he is therefore associated with the ability of the god to formulate the truth in various ways. In fact, Ramana Maharshi has been considered by some of his devotees as a manifestation of this aspect of Śiva.[38] The name Dakshināmūrti is sometimes, thereby, associated with the notion of the efficient or effulgent form of the god. The Sanskrit term itself can be understood as meaning 'facing South'— which is the orientation of the Dakshināmūrti representation in Śiva temples of Tamil Nadu, including the temple at Tiruvannamalai, in which the Maharshi remained for days in silent *samadhi*; but it can also be understood as referring to the meanings of skillful (*dakshīn*) and formless (*amūrti*).[39] It is clear that this latter meaning is exactly what the Maharshi has in mind when referring to the supreme power of Śiva as teaching in silence. Moreover, it is significant that this emphasis on silence is indeed associated with Śiva: this is because the third god of the *Trimūrti*—the supreme Hindu Divine Triad— is traditionally associated with destruction and rebirth. Silence is indeed a kind of 'decreation' of the order of discourse: it is a return to the essence of Reality, rather than a sustaining of the forms in which the latter might be expressed, which would correspond to the Vishnuite function. Śiva is the god of destruction of forms in the name, and for the sake, of That which lies beyond forms: silence is *a priori* the negation of words and *a posteriori* the most direct symbol, and indeed manifestation, of the Transcendent. In other words, the choice of silence is simply a consequence of the awareness of the incommensurability between the Divine and human orders, between the Self and the ego. The incapacity of God to articulate the Mystery of the Self does not stem from any flaw that would be incompatible with His all-powerfulness. It flows rather from the metaphysical gap between God as a relational Being and the Divine Self that both transcends and encompasses everything. This is the gap that Hindu Advaitins have in mind when they state that *Māyā* spans from the god 'Brahmā to the blade of grass.'[40] When God, *Īśvara*, is contemplated in relation to mankind and creation, or for that matter in any kind of relation, then He cannot 'fathom' the Mystery of the non-dual Selfhood as Essence. In medieval Christianity, this cardinal distinction led Meister Eckhart to assert with boldness that 'God Himself never looks in there [in the Essence] for one instant, insofar as He exists in modes and in the properties of His persons.'[41] Eckhart's assertion rings all the more strikingly analogous to Ramana's teachings on the Self when one considers that the 'there' in which God cannot look actually lies in the soul itself, and is symbolically referred to by the German mystic as a 'citadel' therein, or as a 'noble power' within. This makes it clear that the deepest reality of silence pertains to a degree that utterly escapes the subject-object relationship, and in which, therefore, the God with Whom the human self relates and to Whom it prays is as incapable of penetrating as is the soul itself, since in order to do so He would have to divest Himself of his own 'Godness', as it were.

From all this, it results that the transcendence and all-embracing nature of the Self, or *Ātman*, in Ramana's spiritual realization, demonstrates most clearly that the Selfhood at stake is of a radically different degree than the self as it is ordinarily understood. The Self-inquiry that lies at the core of the Maharshi's spirituality is, it bears stressing, not of a psychological nature: the *Ātman* that is the true Self does not amount to the complex network of experiences, perceptions and feelings with which most human beings identify, and which we refer to as the psyche or the mind. For one thing, the Self is the eternal Witness of all modes of consciousness, while the ordinary self is woven through with impermanent phenomena, whether the latter be external or internal. In fact the Maharshi taught that the mind is nothing else than its thoughts, which means that it is in no position to be a witness. Delving further into this fundamental distinction between what Hindus would refer to respectively as *Paramātman*, supreme Self, and *jivātman*, living self, is all the more necessary, as the search for Self-knowledge that lies at the core of the Maharshi's perspective is often considered to be the central motivation of spirituality in our day and age.

In the contemporary world, the term 'spirituality' has come to refer to a somewhat ineffable, if not diffuse, domain of human aspiration that virtually summarizes every value of inner authenticity, meaningfulness and fulfillment. It is therefore connected to a sense of true selfhood, beyond the appearances of cultural and social conditionings. Moreover, the multiform crisis of religions and the growing secularization of culture have contributed to make of 'spiritual self-realization' the rallying symbol of human yearnings for something akin to a religious life without religion. In this context, the phrase 'I am spiritual but not religious' resonates as a kind of manifesto for many inner aspirations.[42] Moreover, the pluralistic ethos that permeates our global culture calls for a sense of inclusiveness, one that established religions, with their differences, are often deemed to be unable to provide. There is no doubt that the Maharshi has represented for many Westerners an incarnation of this spiritual intersection of personal quest, inner integrity, distance from institutions and traditions and cross-, or trans-religious, inclusivism. Thus, the Western literature devoted to the sage has been by and large disconnected from any religious references, or has tended to minimize their significance and impact while emphasizing the supra-religious aspect of his teachings. Furthermore, the fact that Ramana's Self-realization did not appear to be bound to, or by, traditional training or ritual practices, has no doubt served as a powerfully attractive feature for most 'spiritual but not religious' seekers. Here, the Self is conceived and experienced as independent from religious conditionings and unshackled from any focus on God as a constraining and even, for some, alienating ultimate Object. All of the dogmatic and ritual system of religion is seemingly replaced by an inward motion toward the source of one's own being. From this perspective, the unmediated nature of Self-realization makes the objective components of religious identity and experience fall away as dispensable impediments. Thus, it bears reiterating that the very concept of 'self' lies at the center of all kinds of ambiguities and possible misunderstandings. It may easily lead one to understand the Maharshi's odyssey in terms of a psychological discovery, since selfhood is ordinarily understood as referring to the inner workings of the individual psyche. Indeed, the notion of self is usually not associated with transcendence and universality: the self is thought to be the very locus of personal choices, needs and preferences. It is this personal dimension that, perhaps more than any other, ties together the various threads of 'post-modern' spirituality. The gradual disappearance of traditional religious orders, the distrust of religious authority and the threat of totalitarian and authoritarian powers, have promoted a sort of widespread spiritual individualism. In this view of things, spirituality ought not to be a matter of traditional heritage, but one of active, personal, deliberation and option. The very spontaneity of Ramana's Self-realization, as well as his utter absence of reliance upon any authoritative institution or instruction, would seem to echo the modes of such a personal odyssey, untrammeled by the teachings and norms of traditional religious universes.

In order to contextualize Ramana Maharshi's seemingly unmediated Self-realization it is important, however, to understand that the traditional Hindu universe is characterized by an emphasis on the immanence of the Absolute: the Self is the Self of all.[43] This universal pervasiveness and presence is a key to grasp the ways in which the freedom of the Spirit transcends normative forms without breaking them; the Self can in principle bloom anywhere at any time, because it is the essential substratum of everything. In the non-dualistic traditions of India, freedom is from the Self and for the Self, and there is no genuine liberation outside of this recognition. The relative consciousness *qua* relative consciousness is never free, simply because to be determined means to be bound; but the Boundless is the very essence of these determinations and may therefore undo them as It pleases. Two foremost examples of the ways in which the liberating immanence of the Self breaks down, in the Hindu universe, the boundaries of relativity are the spiritual potentialities of animals and the status of the renunciate, the *samnyāsin*. In both cases the omnipresent immanence of the Self makes it possible to transcend what appear to be *prima facie* unavoidable and impassable differences.

The life of the Maharshi is replete with occurrences of spiritual contacts with animals. A publication of Ramanasramam entitled *The Friend of All Creation* provides a rich array of accounts of interactions between Ramana and animals of all kinds, from monkeys and dogs to elephants and cows.[44] Indeed his respect and love for all beings—including plants and animals— has been known in India as one of the defining features of a true *jñani*.[45:46] What interests us most here, however, is not this important characteristic of the human being who has realized the Self, and is therefore in spiritual unison with the entire universe, but the fact that the unity of the Self may also manifest in the rare ability of some animals to realize the Ultimate. One of the most striking claims of the Maharshi lies indeed with his assertion about the ability of animals to reach spiritual liberation. From the sage's focus on the Self flows a stress on the equality of all beings from the point of view of their participation in the Being, Consciousness and Felicity of the Ultimate. The Maharshi's emphasis on the equality between humans and animals can in this respect be quite astounding. In monotheistic religions it is understood that humanity does enjoy a privileged status in relation to God and to His creation. Mankind is the caretaker of the animal kingdom and holds a kind of vicegerential dominion over it, which entails a privilege and a hierarchy of creatures. By contrast, Ramana's *Advaita* contemplates the relationship between humans and animals from a non-dual and unitive point of view. Thus, responding to a devotee who had affirmed that humans and monkeys are different, Ramana responds that 'they [the monkeys] are exactly the same as people' because 'all are same in Consciousness.'[47] This bold affirmation is characteristic of a spiritual perspective entirely centered on the universal immanence of the Self. From the point of view of this immanence of *Cit*, or Divine Consciousness, it is impossible to draw any line of demarcation within the manifested universe, since the latter is none other than the Self. Even though humans and monkeys obviously differ in many ways, beginning with their unequal karmic access to spiritual liberation, the Maharshi's view, as it proceeds primarily from his non-dual and contemplative intelligence steeped in the Self, tends to de-emphasise or—as circumstantial intents may invite him to do so—to deny, any radical chasm in the unity of Consciousness. From the point of view of the latter, everything and everyone bathes in the unity of its Light. This is a point of view that has been expressed by mystics from diverse traditions, like the fourteenth-century German Dominican Meister Eckhart, for instance, when he writes of the 'place' where 'the highest angel, the fly, and the soul are equal, there where I stood and wanted what I was, and was what I wanted.'[48] The 'I' that is mentioned by Eckhart is none other than the Self, as this assertion presupposes a point of view that is precisely not that of our ordinary relative stance—where a fly is indeed not equal to an angel, and must therefore be carefully distinguished from it.

Another essential dimension of the sense of universal immanence of the Self lies in the Maharshi's contemplation of the mountain Arunachala. One cannot evoke the life of the Maharshi without delving into the central meaning of the sacred hill, not only in his biography, but with regard to his spiritual personality and ultimate teachings. The mountain itself has occupied a super-eminent position in the spiritual mythology of Hinduism. It is referred to as the *tejolingam*—the Lingam of fire—which is the formless emblem of Siva.'[49] The holy hill quite obviously belongs to the sacred topography of India, one that lends to particular places a divine status, such as Banaras, Vrindavan, Dwarka and others. These are *tīrthas*, or 'upward crossovers' where earth and heaven meet.[50] No wonder, therefore, that Arunachala was able to work as an irresistible spiritual magnet on the young *jīvan-mukta* as soon as its name flashed into his consciousness. It became the very symbol of the reorientation of Ramana's life, and the axis around which the second part of his existence revolved. He lived for over twenty years in different parts of the mountain, including Virupaksha Cave and Skandashram, and the final twenty-eight years of his life at the ashram built at the foot of the sacred hill. For Ramana, Arunachala was evidently much more than a mountain, be it a sacred one. The mountain itself was, or is, a manifestation of God; indeed it is God. In order to fathom the meaning of this extraordinary and perhaps unsettling perception, which is so foreign to a modern outlook, one must refer to the principle that the symbol and the symbolized are one. In the traditional universe the symbol does not only stand for the symbolized, it is indeed none other than what it symbolizes.[51] For a Western reader, an entry into this mystery may be provided by the Christian notion of the Eucharistic species. The faithful experiences the Divine presence of Christ through the bread and wine that are—in whichever way they may be conceptualized theologically—none other than the body and blood of the Saviour. This analogy is all the more useful in that it also denotes an inherent salvific power, which is equally at work in the Maharshi's understanding of Arunachala. The sage often referred to the spiritual principle that thinking of Arunachala is a means of reaching deliverance. This would be inconceivable, were it not for the 'sacramental' reality of the mountain, where the mountain itself is seen as a manifestation of the Self. Indeed, it is by virtue of this essential reality that the magnetic pull of the mountain was such that the henceforth Self-realized Ramana could not but come and live in the proximity of its theophanic aura. Like attracts like, which ultimately means that there is indeed only One. Thus, even a consideration of the matter in terms of a mere spiritual correspondence would not be sufficient to account for the deepest reality of Arunachala. Indeed, it has to be recognized that, for the Maharshi, Arunachala was none other than the Self: 'In the lotus-shaped Heart of all [...] there shines as Absolute

Consciousness the *Paramatman* who is the same as Arunachala-Ramana.'[52] The unity of Ramana and Arunachala in and as the Self is evidently the deepest way to contemplate the unmovable life of Ramana as rooted in Arunachala. Thus, a Hindu devotee once wrote that when seeing Ramana for the first time she was sure she was seeing Sri Arunachala.[53] It is as if at the time of his arrival at the foot of the mountain the human reality of Ramana was existentially reintegrated into its archetypical unity with Arunachala. The two distinct stages of the Maharshi's life in Tiruvannamalai, first on the mountain itself and then at its foot, may account for this mystery. The first would correspond to an extinction in the Self, the second to a permanence in It.[54] Moreover, these two stages provide meaningful resonances with the two phases of the Maharshi's life in Tiruvannamalai that have been sketched above: the radiating silence of the young sage on the one hand, and the giving and interactive presence of the full-grown liberated soul on the other. It must be added that the second modality of the Maharshi's presence was, in the most literal sense, sacrificial, in the sense of 'making sacred'—which means here Self-like—everyone and everything that came into contact with him. Moreover, the sacrificial aspect of the Maharshi's presence was also noticeable in that it involved contacts with hundreds and thousands of visitors whose concerns and questions were most often much below the level of the gist of the spiritual teaching. The motivations of many of the Hindu visitors to the ashram were not of a significantly different nature than those of the Christian faithful seeking the blessings of a saint; and not a few of the Western travelers' cares and inquiries hardly extended beyond psychological or social problems. This wide exposure to a myriad of human issues and disharmonies could not but result in the sage's taking upon himself much of the karmic burden of his visitors. It has been very plausibly claimed by some of the devotees that the intensity of this sacrificial exposure to all who came to him contributed to the physical decay and sickness that quickly accelerated, in the 1940s, his departure from this world.[55]

Although the first stage could not be deemed to be lacking anything from the vantage point of its sovereign abidance in Peace and Bliss, the second stage does convey a sense of spiritual fulfillment inasmuch as it radiates and embraces. This is the meaning of *satsanga*, or 'company of being', whereby the liberated sage, incarnation of being or *sat*, offers his presence as a central means of contemplation. This takes place through a variety of modalities, as if the infinity of the Self were reflected in a limitless diversity of the *jñani's* ways of teaching.[56] Thus, the Maharshi's life at the ashram epitomizes the way spiritual realization involves an ability to attend to reality on all of its levels of manifestation, including the humblest ones. We could not be farther, here, from the conventional and misleading vision of mysticism as a kind of evasion from worldly duties. The Maharshi embodies the point of intersection between divine transcendence, and the utter detachment, not to say aloofness, that derives from being rooted in it, and, on the other hand, the human excellence that flows from the extinction of the ego. In this regard, the Maharshi referred on several occasions to the distinction between two kinds of spiritual attainments, *kevala samadhi* and *sahaja samadhi.*[57] The first is an ecstatic immersion in the Self in which all external modalities of existence are suspended. *Kevala* means 'alone', and the word denotes a withdrawal from all ordinary multiplicity. This state of consciousness is considered to be temporary precisely to the extent that it is incompatible with one's habitual functioning on the level of daily existence. *Sahaja*, by contrast, is most often translated as 'natural', which implies that in this case *samadhi*, or the liberated consciousness, is spontaneously and harmoniously involved in all modes of consciousness and activities, in a manner that makes the extraordinary ordinary. It does not interfere, or even less conflict, with the natural flow of life, its norms and its laws. This *distinguo* points to the possible bifurcation between a mystical absorption in the *Brahman* and a Self-realization that involves both absorption in the *Brahman* and the ability to function on the relative plane of consciousness. The first is compared by the Maharshi to a 'mental bucket under the water', whereas the second is comparable to 'the river that has linked up with the ocean from which there is no return.'[58] The latter bears witness to a higher degree of Self-realization whereby unity and multiplicity are experienced in non-dual simultaneousness. The difference could also be couched in terms of mystical imbalance and spiritual balance. *Kevala* implies imbalance in the sense that it suspends the natural equilibrium of the physio-psychological complex. The term imbalance cannot be taken in an utterly negative fashion, however, but only relatively so: it expresses in this case the undeniable incommensurability between the Self and ordinary consciousness. When the Absolute Consciousness 'touches' the relative selfhood, it cannot be so without upsetting the prior, superficial, equilibrium of the latter, and sometimes suspending it altogether. This holds true even to some extent outside of the periods of *kevala samadhi*, since there is no possibility of an absolute balance between the Self and 'another' reality. This explains why it even occurs that, in the course of ordinary life, the physical body may bear the weight of the infinite power of the Self. In this connection, it has been reported that the persistent tremor of the neck that the Maharshi experienced in the later parts of his life—it is apparent on the filmed footage of the Maharshi from the 1940s—was in fact a chronic condition unrelated to any physical pathology. When asked about it, the Maharshi responded that this trembling was actually a result of the pressure of the Self upon the body.[59] Notwithstanding such disruptions of the natural course of existence, *sahaja*—by contrast with *kevala*—can be referred to as a relative state of equilibrium that coincides with full spiritual maturity, and therefore with an ability to function effectively on the relative plane of existence while being totally absorbed into the Self. This could also be approached as a mysterious ability to alternate from interiorization to exteriorization without ever losing contact with the inner pole of attraction. Such a thoughtless state of consciousness can obey the imperatives of external life out of a kind of existential and compassionate necessity, without lessening the intrinsic pull of the Self. Here is the way the Maharshi suggested this existential rhythm of the *jñāni*: 'You ask me questions and I reply and talk to you. If I do not speak or do anything, I am automatically drawn within, and where I am, I do not know.'[60] From another point of view, *sahaja samadhi* also refers to the fact that nothing can take place away from the Self, so that Self-consciousness is indeed compatible with any kind of relative involvement. Everyone and everything is taken within the fold of the Self. By definition, the essence of non-duality cannot be limited by the exclusion of any reality or experience. As he was once treated for his disease with 'rectified spirits' that inadvertently flowed onto his body, the Maharshi joked that one should always been in a 'spirit bath.' When asked to explain the meaning of this humorous statement, he added 'Fish are always in water and cannot survive on coming out of it. Similarly, we are in Spirit or Pure Consciousness and should always be in it as fish in water. One should always consciously remain in Pure Consciousness or Self.'[61] This is the essence of *sahaja samadhi*, whereby the unity of Consciousness is a matter of continuous experience. Needless to say, the contrast between *kevala* and *sahaja samadhi* does not imply any difference whatsoever from the essential point of view of full Self-realization. The distinction can only be meaningful, and indeed serviceable, from the point of view of relative consciousness.

The evidence of the pedagogical fruits of *sahaja samadhi* appears in what could be called the 'ordinary' dimension of the Maharshi's presence. Accounts of his life at the ashram actually stage two dimensions of the sage: one belongs to the sovereign radiance of the *satguru* whose *satsanga* was sought by thousands of seekers and devotees visiting Ramanasramam, while the second pertains to his everyday engagement with practical tasks, and the many spiritual lessons that ensued. At the ashram, the Maharshi routinely or occasionally participated in chores such as cutting vegetables, laying bricks or binding notebooks: 'there was no task which he deemed beneath him.'[62] In the 1930s, for instance, Ramana was very closely involved in the building of the ashram, which he supervised with a minute attention to detail. It is as if the building of the ashram were an emanation of the Maharshi's spiritual presence as manifested in the most practical aspects of its realization. A foremost devotee of the Maharshi, Annamalai Swami, told how he was charged by the sage, over a period of eight years, with the task of overseeing the building of the ashram. This project enlisted dozens of masons and needed be organized and supervised with a strict sense of organization and planning. The Maharshi provided continuous practical guidance on what to do, and when and how to do it. Annamalai Swami relates that 'in the evening, when I went to give him my daily report, he would tell me what work should be done the following day [and] if there were any difficult jobs to do he would explain how to do them.'[63] But perhaps the most instructive aspect of the Maharshi's engagement with the construction of the ashram lies in his further remark: 'I am not concerned with any of the activities here. I just witness all that happens.' Annamalai notes that while this aloof detachment was undoubtedly real from the point of the Self, still, 'from the relative standpoint I can say that no stone was ever moved in the ashram without his knowledge and consent.'[64] This is a striking piece of evidence of the ways in which the *sahaja* degree of spiritual realization involves both unmovable centering and effectiveness in peripheral activities that do not in the least affect the former's definitiveness.

Another facet of Ramana Maharshi's ability to stand spiritually above relativity while being efficaciously engaged in it appears in his ability to communicate profound spiritual truths while performing the simplest of tasks. Thus the preparation of food at the ashram was a subject of much attentiveness on his part. A female devotee remembers that the Maharshi's spiritual gifts in the kitchen were as potent as the ones flowing from lengthy ascetic practices. This held true both in terms of the sage's teachings and by way of his transforming presence. In the first respect his 'love that suffered as it laboured' manifested at times in rigorous demands to such an extent that 'his sometimes-harsh treatment would bewilder [us] and make [us] cry.'[65] He would not tolerate carelessness and waste. At the same time, 'the small tasks of daily life he would make into avenues to light and bliss.'[66] We have here an exemplary *karma-yoga*, a path of action, that finds in practical, and even menial, supports a way of reaching a state of heart-presence. Hence the provocatively evocative claim 'whoever has not experienced the ecstasy of grinding, the rapture of cooking, the joy of serving idlis to devotees [...] does not know how much bliss a human heart contains.' This is reminiscent of the Zen Buddhist emphasis on the need for mindfulness as a gateway to the realization of the Buddha nature, when 'even the most ordinary incidents of daily life "vibrate with divine meaning and creative vitality", making us live in the world "as if walking in the garden of Eden".'[67] One could not be further away from misleading conventional views of mysticism as an ethereal idealism bordering on so-called escapism. For the Maharshi, as for Zen Masters, there is nothing from which to escape, and nowhere to escape.

T.M.P. Mahadevan made the judicious remark that 'this age demands on the part of a world-teacher neither absolute silence nor much speech, neither total stasis nor constant movement. We had such a teacher in Bhagavān Srī Ramana who was both *achara* (unmoving) and *chara* (moving), who taught both through silence and speech.'[68] While spiritual silence is essentially the best of teachings and the Maharshi has repeatedly asserted its being more powerful than any outer activities, it is indeed a matter of evidence that, on the relative plane of our existence, 'absolute silence' cannot be easily comprehended by the standards and ways of this age. This is so *de facto* because silent teaching would likely be unable to pierce through the shells of superimposition and forgetfulness that define our existential condition. Silence presupposes some deeper receptivity than most of us can garner. Moreover, utter silence today is most likely to be taken to be an absence of communication—in a way the gravest of sins of our time, since the imperative of external connections— exponentially magnified by virtual means—is so intrinsically wedded with what our existence is expected to be. On the other hand, 'much speech' is likely to feed into the activist and interactive frenzy of our world. It runs the risk of being lowered to the level of just another voice among many, in the cacophony of postmodern discourse. The flattening down of the contents of expression and communication appears to be the price to pay for a universal, instantaneous, access to virtually everything communicable. By contrast, words of wisdom must have an essentiality and a simplicity that allow them to cut through the unending chatter of our contemporary life: 'Speak little, hold to your own nature', as Lao Tzu put it.[69] It may be that the ponderous question 'Who am I?' is intended to function in such a way, alluding thereby to what is arguably the very essence of all spiritual paths.

2

GRACE AND DEVOTION

The spiritual perspective of the Maharshi is most often introduced, at least in Western secondary literature, as a psycho-spiritual technique centered on a consistent, if not constant, meditation on the inquiry 'Who am I?'[1] There is no question that such was the primary teaching of Ramana Maharshi, one that comes back again and again as a leitmotif in his interviews and teachings, in his own writings, as well as in the dozens of books devoted to him. This investigative question was in fact, as we have seen, the seed and the very core of his own spiritual experience, the key to his extraordinary breakthrough. Ramana's enlightenment was not the outcome of a formal path, a *sādhanā*, which he would have followed under the guidance of a human *guru* within the traditional framework of one of the Hindu ways. Indeed, Hinduism provides seekers with countless spiritual paths adjusted to the diverse qualifications and needs of human beings. Ramana did not tread any of those *margas*; he simply actualized through ad-lib meditational inquiry a Self-realization that had been latent in him and merely waited for a catalyst: a sudden and intense fear of death. In a sense his breakthrough was akin to the Śivaite *anupāya*, the 'pathless path' that does not rely on any available spiritual means, or *upāya,* while being an immediate Self-realization of the Absolute.[2] It is sometimes taught that in very rare cases the most minimal or subtle spur may quicken Self-realization without apparent spiritual antecedent; such was the case of the question 'Who am I?' in the Maharshi's epiphany. While it is therefore undeniable that the Maharshi's overall perspective lies in the three words of his basic inquiry, the argument of this chapter is that reducing the Maharshi's teaching to this shortcut fails to do justice to his integral radiance and the full spectrum of the spiritual resources that he made available to his devotees. More specifically, the fact that no explicitly God-centered perspective or formal practice played a role in the 'event' of Self-realization itself must not lead one to draw the conclusion that the Maharshi's 'pathless path' is in no significant way related to the fundamental categories of religious experience. In fact, the focus of this chapter is to highlight the cardinal weight of grace and devotion, the divine and human sides of the religious equation, in the process of spiritual awakening and its existential concomitants.

Before delving into major aspects of this crucial question it is necessary, however, to briefly consider the problem of the modes of transmission of the Maharshi's message. When examining the ways in which the Maharshi's teachings have been made available to non-Indian audiences, it is important to take into account the background and sensibilities of those who introduced the sage to the West. The modalities of reception and transmission are, after all, partly determined by the prior experiences and conceptions of those who are charged with them. In this respect, it must be observed that many of the Western seekers who sought the presence and the guidance of the Maharshi throughout the years, including those who devoted volumes to their experience of his spiritual personality and teachings, were generally alienated, in one way or another, from their Christian or Jewish religious backgrounds.[3] It is enough to consider the way Paul Brunton entitled one of the chapters of his *Conscious Immortality—Conversations with Sri Ramana Maharshi*, i.e., 'Fallacies of Religion,' to understand that this matter is not without significance. This is especially the case when one notes that the same chapter includes unambiguously religious reflections by the Maharshi such as 'worship is a method of concentration of mind' and '*Īśvara*, a personal God or Supreme creator of the Universe, *does* exist.'[4] While it must be granted that Brunton is not necessarily representative of Western devotees of the Maharshi, there is little doubt that the British writer's perspective on the matter reflects a widespread negative *a priori* vis-à-vis the religious phenomenon. Thus, it is fair to suggest that many Western seekers' attraction to the Maharshi and his teachings, aside from being a response to the sage's irresistible spiritual magnetism, was at least extrinsically connected to a sense of liberation from the perceived limitations of their own religious heritage. Those negative strictures might have been circumstantial, resulting—as they most likely did in many cases—from a sense that Christianity and Judaism had become incapable, for a variety of historical and cultural reasons, of nourishing the deepest spiritual aspirations of Westerners endowed with contemplative dispositions. A certain flattening down of the message of those traditions, arising out of an all too frequent 'moralization' or 'socialization' of its content, left many Western spiritual seekers with little other options but to turn to the East.[5] There was also, no doubt, some more structural theological reasons in the dissatisfaction of most seekers with their own religious heritage. On the one hand, radical metaphysical non-dualism is hardly a foreground religious teaching in the West; on the other hand, the apparent reduction of the whole spiritual life to a contemplative inquiry such as 'Who am I?' appears to move one away from theological creeds and devotional practices. Thus, the simplicity and essentiality of such features of the Maharshi's perspective were probably not the least important factors that attracted Western seekers used to considering religion within the boundaries of faith and piety. Among the central elements of religious experience in the spiritual economy of the Christian tradition, grace and devotion stand, in particular, as defining components. The first refers to the omnipotence of God, His power to impart, but also, and above all, to His love and His propensity to give; while the second element epitomizes the specifically human side of religious life.

Now it bears stressing that the young Ramana's Self-realization was in fact in no way exempt from religious and devotional determinations and antecedents. Upon his spiritual realization, Ramana's way of life was not only radically changed in terms of his perception of himself and the world, but it also saw him adopting new habits. The matter was not only one of spiritual cognition, but also, and consequently, one of moral consciousness. One of the new habits of the young sage was the regular visit of the temple, which before then he had been visiting only occasionally. This indicates that the extraordinary spiritual experience that he had undergone was spontaneously translated by him into religious terms. Moreover, the seemingly formal and conventional character of his early religious practice, and its contrast with the profound spiritual concentration that marked his post-enlightenment *darshan*, or contemplation of the gods, casts even more significant light on this fact. Changing from a sporadic and routine external practice into an overwhelming mystical experience, religious devotion took on an utterly different meaning. Here is the way the Maharshi analyses this change, one that he characterizes as 'God's (Īsvara's) play with the individual spirit': 'The former hold on the body had been given up by my spirit, since it ceased to cherish the idea I-am-the-body [and] the spirit therefore longed to have a fresh hold and hence the frequent visits to the temple and the overflow of the soul in profuse tears.'[6] In other words, the shift in consciousness experienced by the young Ramana had to be accompanied by a different grounding of the individuality. This implies that the latter could not float around or hang out in the air, if such familiar expressions may be allowed here. Indeed, and quite interestingly, telling the story of the days that followed his awakening, Ramana mentioned a trace of anxiety connected to his new state of consciousness. This is paradoxical *a priori*, when considering that Self-realization is associated with a sense of definitive peace. But it becomes understandable when it is recognized that, upon Self-realization, the *jīva* does not disappear, but is, as it were, relativized by the new mode of consciousness. It needs, therefore, to find a point of anchoring in a world that has been thoroughly shaken by the new spiritual recognition. This is a matter of equilibrium for the soul in the relative realm: to the extent that the soul is not identified with the body any more, it must be fixed on a reality that is both relative, thus relatable, and absolute, i.e., not subject to the illusoriness of existence. This is precisely what God is: He is the Absolute inasmuch as the Absolute can be related to from a human point of view.[7] Thus, for the young Ramana, realizing one's true Self also meant concomitantly rooting one's soul in the Divine. The 'fresh hold' had to be the result of a shift from the relative to the Absolute, from the soul to God.

This point is significant in several ways. First of all, it indicates that the individual self, the *jīvā*, inasmuch as it can be differentiated from the Self—that is from the point of view of illusory or dualistic empirical existence—has need of a spiritual hold precisely because it is limited, and therefore relational by essence. Limitation, by contrast with the limitlessness of the Self, necessarily entails difference from other limited realities. It is the limitations of individual existence that make the latter illusorily different from the limitless Self, and therefore set it in relation to other-than-itself, starting with the Divine Other, God. Thus, as *jīvā* and only as *jīvā*, the *jīvan-mukta*, like all human beings, is actually in need of a principle of identification. In such a case this principle cannot be the limited body any more, or any bound phenomenon, since the illusion of this identification has vanished through Self-realization. It can only be, therefore, the relational God as 'objectified limitlessness.'

This situation could be conceived as a transitional phase, in another way it ought to be understood as an intrinsic, permanent, existential reality. In the first sense, the Maharshi himself conceived of this new circumstance as a form of *līlā,* the play of God with the soul, inasmuch as it involves modifications in the ways of experiencing the world. The Hindu concept of *līlā* refers to the innumerable manners in which the Divine appears in the life of the soul, and more generally on the plane of universal manifestation. The expression may seem deeply ill-sounding to Abrahamic ears, given that monotheistic religions tend to place an emphasis on the 'serious' purposefulness of God's creation.[8] In the Hindu tradition, by contrast, *līlā* has positive connotations: it suggests Divine freedom and creativeness, while also evoking thereby artistry and beauty.[9] It therefore pertains to the unexpected changes that occur in the devotee's life as expressions of Īśvara's infinite creativity. Consciousness of God entails recognition of this play in one's life, and in the entire universe. From this point of view, the human self is intrinsically prayerful, which means that it turns toward Divine grace as the principle of its own spiritual life. We must also note that what is at stake here is not, therefore, Self-knowledge but devotion, for the former transcends any play, being none other than its Witness. Now devotional depth and intensity are considered to be subject to increase through grace: '[I would] pray for the descent of his grace upon me so that my devotion might increase and become perpetual.'[10] This petition may be taken to be in contradiction to the sense of utter fulfillment and definitiveness that followed Ramana's enlightenment: 'whether the body was engaged in talking, reading or anything else, I was still centred on "I".'[11] This is not so, however, when considering that permanence is situated on different levels in each of the two cases. 'Perpetual devotion' is not to be confused with permanent 'Self-centeredness.' The 'I' who prays for increased devotion is obviously not the 'I' upon which Ramana is centered, since the latter is fulfilled in Self-recognition. What makes this passage so acutely important is precisely that it brings to the surface the complexities of the concomitants of Self-realization. The latter is simple in itself—indeed it is ultimate simplicity, but its refractions on the mirror of relative awareness are necessarily multiple, and therefore should not be confused with It on the empirical level. As some gnostics have insisted, there is, strictly speaking, no such thing as an experience of the Self, simply because any experience is perforce an experience of something distinct from the experiencer.[12] The 'devotional self' who prays cannot be equated as such with the Self, since it experiences a separation from the Lord to whom its petition is addressed. We must note, however, that the Maharshi does not stop at this consideration, as he actually recounts: 'mostly I would not pray at all, but let the deep within flow on and into the deep without.'[13] Thus, it is evident that the devotional experience is not the core reality of Self-realization, and it occurs in this case as a mere 'interlude' in the context of a mode of consciousness that is, as it were, supersaturated with non-dual bliss, *ānanda*. Even though the Maharshi's formulation still distinguishes between a within and a without, it appears that the Self-effulgence of Consciousness abolishes in the end any sense of duality. The 'deep within' is obviously none other than the 'deep without.' Even the physiological effects of this new mode of Consciousness would escape the causal categories of human emotions: 'Tears would mark this overflow of the soul and would not betoken any particular feeling of pleasure or pain.'[14] This 'gift of tears' is not without resonance with the sense of metaphysical disproportion between the soul and its God that is evoked in its Christian mystical equivalent, and which is sometimes more specifically translated in terms of an acute sense of sin deriving from the limitations of the creature *in relation to* the infinite Love of God.[15] In the Maharshi's case, however, the transcendence of prayer, if one may put it this way, indicates a non-dual stage in which the very need to turn toward another has disappeared. This is evidenced by the very absence of any sensations of pleasure and pain at the very height of what would appear to be a mystical ecstasy.

The notion of grace is sometimes considered to be foreign to the world of *Advaita*. Whether from a neo-Vedantic apologetic point of view, or from a Christian polemical vantage point, some would have us believe that Hindu non-duality is a purely human and intellectual exercise that requires no 'sense of God,' and certainly no Divine intervention. The corollary of this kind of view is that grace would be particularly, or exclusively, associated with theistic teachings, while being contrary to the tenets of any non-dual teachings centered on Self-realization. Far from being centered on grace, the latter are therefore understood to be dependent upon individual initiative, efforts and practices. This is, however, a partial, superficial and ultimately quite misleading view of what is at stake in the process of spiritual realization according to the Advaitin tradition; one that does not account, moreover, for the fullness of the Maharshi's teachings. It is worth stressing from the start that the individual self can never realize the *Ātman* since it is, by definition, a kind of veil or superimposition upon the Self. The idea that the individual self would be the agent of Self-realization is diametrically opposed to *Advaita*. Only the Self can know and 'free' Itself, as it flows from the obvious observation that the finite can in no way realize the Infinite as such. Not only does the very notion of Self-realization exclude that the individual self be the realizing agency of Liberation, but it can no more be the 'realized reality' itself. From the strict point of view of the *jīva*, Self-realization is literally unreachable.

What is realized, or liberated, is therefore not the personal self, even though the latter may, and must, draw benefits of this realization on its own level of reality and consciousness. *Prima facie* this observation may sound at odds with the Maharshi's fundamental question 'who am I?' Nevertheless, a close consideration of the actual process of inquiry recommended by the Maharshi demonstrates the crucial validity of this point.

In order to develop this assertion one may observe that David Godman distinguishes, in the teachings of Ramana Maharshi, two levels that are often mistakenly conflated.[16] The first is the human investigation into the 'I', which results—at a second stage—in its subsiding in the center of consciousness, that is the Heart. Thus, the *vichāra* or inquiry is, in its inception at least, an individual process of investigation. The mind looks for its source, which it cannot find without disappearing, for it cannot be both the subject and the object; but 'this, according to Sri Ramana, is as much as the devotee can do by himself.'[17] It is only when this freedom from thoughts and misidentifications has been achieved that the 'power of the Self pulls the "I"-thought back into the Heart-center and eventually destroys it so completely that it never rises again.'[18] Now the second of these moments is obviously akin to grace inasmuch as it remains utterly independent from human efforts or doings. *Ātma-vichāra* is therefore not a psychological exercise, and it is in this respect radically different from the various forms of self-help spirituality that have inundated the market of the 'search for meaning' in the last decades. Self-inquiry entails transcendence since the Divine Power that draws the 'I' toward its source belongs to an incommensurable order of reality. Any bypassing or belittling of this transcendent reality falls short of the real meaning of spirituality in the Maharshi's perspective. Thus, the sage underlines that the striving of the mind is in itself powerless if Divine Grace does not exercise its pull upon it: 'If God, who is in the mind, does not draw the [...] mind inwards by the might of His grace, who can attain Peace by diving into the Heart, by the [mere] power of his own mind, which is treacherous?'[19] This point about the powerlessness of the mind left to itself also echoes Shankara's claim that actions are only 'an indirect aid' to liberation, while only knowledge itself does liberate.[20] In this regard the term 'action' refers mostly to ritual actions, and therefore clearly differentiates *jñāna* from the ritual practices of the Brahmanical tradition. But it is clear that this very term can be extended to include all human doings, whether they are outer actions or inner doings in general, including contemplative practices such as the *Ātma-vichāra* itself, for this is at any rate the human side of the equation. The second moment, by contrast, which is the 'Divine moment', as it were, is clearly identifiable with knowledge because only the *Ātman* can know the *Ātman* in pure Self-knowledge, only the Self can know the Self as Self, for a Self known by other-than-the-Self would not be the real Self. In the Advaitin tradition, the only knowledge ultimately worth this name is knowledge through identification, that is, the knowledge *Ātman* has of itself; and this is, from a human point of view, pure grace, the grace of the Self. Although the spiritual practice is deemed to be preparatory, and in a way necessary, for Self-realization, the latter cannot be explained in terms of the former; and this is because the two are indeed incommensurable. To put the matter in a nutshell, it could be said that there is no grace but through and by the Self, and more fundamentally that the Self is grace. Such an expression may present some difficulty to those who have been conditioned to think of grace as something 'supernatural' and, as it were, external to the human self, since it comes from 'above.' In *Advaita*, however, there is no such thing as a severance between the natural and the supernatural, no more than between the below and the above. The grace that is at stake here is not to be equated with the gift given by one being, be it supreme, to another—although this concept of grace is not absent from the Vedāntic perspective on some level of conventional consideration, but rather contemplated as the deepest nature and influx of Reality itself.

In another passage relating the Maharshi's direct teachings, the sage makes use of the metaphor of the 'stick used for stirring the funeral pyre' in order to illustrate the process of disappearance of the ego through self-investigation.[21] In Hindu cremating grounds, a wooden stick is often used to facilitate the thorough burning of the dead body. The latter is sometimes pushed and turned so as to allow the fire to fulfill its function. The image is particularly striking in that it conveys a sense of annihilation akin to the death of the ego, but also because it highlights the way in which the instrument, that is the stick or the mind, is itself destroyed in and by the goal—complete cremation or spiritual liberation. Is this destruction to be understood as a mere annihilation? Religiously the burning of the body is, in the Hindu tradition, experienced as purification, which is why the liberated soul, and the *samnyāsin*, is not cremated. This purification is a prelude to, or a symbol of, *Moksha*, the body appearing in this case as the principle of attachment to *samsāra* and therefore the prime obstacle to liberation. This means that the annihilation of the body is therefore also, and above all, the virtual means of a spiritual reintegration into the *Ātman*.

Godman's statement that the 'I-thought' is utterly destroyed as a result of the return to the Heart-center, and is therefore never to return, raises the question of the way one must understand this 'destruction.' This would appear to contradict other seemingly less absolute statements about the surrender of the self—for how can that which is destroyed surrender? It also seems to run contrary to the commonsensical observation that any individual state of being implies the particularity of an existing 'I', be it in the case of an ordinary individual or that of a liberated soul. When T.M.P Mahadevan writes that the ego 'stripped of all its interests, its coverings, ceases to be ego', he alludes to this spiritual 'death' of the ego that must not be interpreted in the literal sense of a fall into non-existence.[22] The 'ego' that functions by virtue of existence and the causal unfolding of the present life, called *prārabdha-karma,* 'ceases to be an ego.' It results from this that the *jīvan-mukta*'s body, and by extension the embodied empirical ego, is in no way a limitation, or an impediment, with respect to his state of liberation *per se,* even though bodily death constitutes a relative fulfillment of this delivered state, inasmuch as it means the end of the karmic unwinding. This is Shankara's understanding of *karma,* which allows us to better understand why and how the ego is, and is not, destroyed.[23] The term 'ego' is, of course, potentially misleading in such a case, since it has two different meanings before and after Self-realization. Before *Moksha,* it is the very principle of obfuscation that precludes the radiating of the Self by virtue of functioning as an illusory superimposition upon It. In the wake of Self-liberation, by contrast, it simply refers to an individual empirical continuum that unfolds as a contingent refraction of the light of the Self. As the Maharshi put it on numerous occasions, this individual self, by contrast with the prior ego, is not the 'doer' of his life. One can therefore refer to the destruction of the ego as to a transformation of the ego if one wishes to emphasise the relative continuum of the mere empirical consciousness. After all, while shunning any self-affirmation and demanding to be treated like all others, the Maharshi himself made use of the personal pronoun 'I' as a subject of many of his sentences, for instance when telling stories about his past, thereby referring to his being the apparent agent of an action or a statement. One must therefore infer that the reference to a destruction of the 'I' must not be understood in the sense of a personal identity as empirically distinct from others, but to something of a deeper and subtler nature. When we read Godman's point that 'the mind and the individual self (both of which Sri Ramana equated with the "I-thought") are destroyed forever' the keyword is probably less 'I' than 'thought.' The thought of the 'I' is obviously different from the 'I' itself,

and this disjunction is nothing else than the source of what *Advaita* refers
to as superimposition, *adhyāsa*. 'Thought' implies paradoxically both a de-
doubling of consciousness and an identification of an erroneous kind; which
is why the Maharshi often mentions that spiritual perfection is absence of
thoughts.[24] This means, first of all, that the 'I-thought,' which is according
to the sage the first of all thoughts, is a mistaken bifurcation from the true
'I.' From the point of view of the spiritual path, or *sādhanā*, one has to start
from a distinction between the 'I' and that congenitally mistaken reality,
which is the thought 'I.' The misleading identification of the two, which
Shankara's *Advaita* would put in terms of a superimposition upon the *Ātman*,
is none other than ignorance, or to use the standard traditional image, the
confusion of the snake and the rope. The source of all benighted miseries is
adhyāsa, defined as 'the apparent presentation to consciousness, by way of
remembrance, of something (being) previously in some other thing.'[25] The
'I-thought' is the result of such a remembrance—for instance, that of the
body which is presented to consciousness as 'I'. Thus, that which is given to
consciousness as being the 'I' is not the 'I' itself but something that pertains or
belongs to another reality. The destruction of the 'I-thought' means, therefore,
the radical and permanent elimination of this mistaken identification. It does
not, nor cannot, mean the disappearance of all individual characters, but it
refers to a complete freedom from superimpositions onto the *Ātman*, hence
an utter transcendence of egoic concretions.

This liberation from the ego, which amounts to a destruction of the latter's
illusory sense of reality, is directly connected by Ramana to the very motion
of self-inquiry: 'The moment the ego-self tries to know itself, it changes its
character.'[26] This means that the ego is gradually removed from its grounding
in matter (*jada*) and increasingly re-absorbed into the Self, which is pure
Spirit. However, the gradual character of this process cannot be assigned to
the Self, since the latter is eternally what it is without any modifications. The
provisional notion of a progress simply means that, since the ego is nothing
but the crystallization of an error of perception, the methodical move toward
a correction of this error results in the disappearance of that which was
formerly taken to be real. It can be understood negatively as being a removal
of that which obstructs the Light of the Self: the progressive opening of a
window does not add anything to the sun, while involving an incremental
expansion of its light within the room. The human side of the spiritual
process is therefore a kind of undoing. Moreover, besides being envisaged as
a process of 'de-creation' from the created into the uncreated, to make use of

Simone Weil's expression, this path could also be described in terms of the acquisition of a greater reality and a truer life.[27] The absorption to which Ramana refers in numerous occasions entails a bestowing of a greater reality onto the individual selfhood not *qua* limitative individuality but with regard to its actual being in and by the Self. The death, or the destruction, of the ego must therefore be understood also, and above all, as a deeper life, since the *jīva*, the living soul, becomes consciously participant in That which constitutes its essence or its true reality.

While Self-inquiry can be equated to a 'gnostic work,' that is a path of *jñāna*, reducing it to the status of a psycho-spiritual technique would be a grave misinterpretation.[28] It would amount to ignoring that which is the actual ground and engine of Self-realization, and that is the Self Itself. Self-realization is a metaphysical reality, or the cognitive recognition of the latter; it is not a technical or psychological process, even though such means may remove obstacles in view of its actualization. Here metaphysics is not an abstraction, but a call to concrete realization. By definition, the mind abstracts, since it separates, for better or worse, according to the Latin meaning of the verb *abstrahere*, to draw away. This 'drawing away' may be the prelude, however, to a 'bringing together' on higher grounds, like in the Advaita *viveka*, or metaphysical discrimination, or it may proliferate indefinitely in further and further abstraction, in the direction of a nothingness that is never reached. By contrast, the Self is 'concrete' in the sense that It brings together that which has been abstracted; this is the etymological meaning of the term as it flows from the verb *concrescere*, 'to grow together.' Most significantly, this is also akin to the meaning of the word *Brahman*, which derives from the root *bṛh-*, meaning to grow or to expand.

Grace is, therefore, nothing other than the manifestation of the 'growing' wholeness of the Self. This growth does not involve any essential modification: the Self is the Self, while entailing the endless unfolding of the Divine *līlā*, which is like the extrinsic expression of the infinity of the *Brahman*. The 'development' of the Self is not a transforming evolution in the usual sense of the term, however, since everything is already included in the Self, as seeds, from the very beginning. The intellect, as a first and foremost instance, did not evolve from the Self, but 'must always have existed in the Self in order to have manifested: hence latently it was co-eternal with Self and did not come later.'[29] In that sense, everything is grace. It is on the basis of such an understanding of the nature of Reality and Knowledge that the Maharshi does not shun putting the matter in definitively 'religious' terms, when he asserts: 'the very fact that you are possessed of the quest of the Self is a manifestation of the Divine Grace.'[30] This notion of Divine grace encompasses within itself all the theological distinctions of the Christian ideas of prevenient, cooperating, and sufficient grace. This means that the Divine reality first predisposes humans to seek the Self—for only the Self can initiate the search for the Self, then accompanies the human acts of the *sādhāna* as the true Doer, finally actualizes Self-realization by virtue of its inherent nature as Being-Consciousness-Bliss, and more generally constitutes the essential and permanent substratum of all existence as signified by the prefix sub- in the adjective sufficient.[31] Thus the question 'Who am I?' and the human effort of delving into its deepest implications are themselves manifestations of antecedent grace, and more fundamentally the bursting forth of the very ground of Reality *as* grace.

Difficulties might be raised as to the way such an emphasis on grace can be articulated with the strict Hindu principle of *karma*, which appears to exclude any grace by virtue of its seemingly inexorable concatenation of actions and reactions. Similarly, in an Abrahamic context, one of the major theological dialectics is that of human works and Divine grace. Human participation in the work of salvation must be a necessary part of the soteriological equation, while grace is even more imperatively called for given the incommensurability between human limited power and Divine All-Powerfulness. The Hindu context is different in that it connects the realm of individual free will and action to both the principle of *karma* and the reality of grace, *kripa*. Here the matter is not so much the relationship between limitation and limitlessness, but rather that between onto-cosmic necessity and Divine freedom.

It must be remembered, however, that Self-realization frees the *mukta* from most, and ultimately all, forms of *karma*. This is precisely what *Moksha*, or Deliverance, means: liberation, indeed the only true liberation, from the chains of karmic necessity. Karmic existence is necessarily relative, being dependent upon specific causal conditionings, while the transcendence of the Self as Absolute Reality (*svātantrya*) in relation to them implies that It can supersede, in principle, at any moment and in any circumstance, its law. This is what the Maharshi recognizes in response to a question by Devaraja Mudaliar when he carefully evaluates the respective weights of God's order and God's freedom. Although he tended to remain significantly silent during arguments, among devotees, as to the primacy of grace or *karma*, he appears to have admitted that *karma* cannot be treated as an absolute and that Divine freedom, as manifested through exceptional occurrences, is an expression of the *Brahman's* infinite possibility.[32] In one sense God is That which cannot but be, in another sense God is All that can be. The structure of destiny and the necessity of *karma* reflect the former, whereas the unfathomable and 'miraculous' works of grace pertain to the latter. The Divine binds itself, as it were, through the order that it establishes, and which entails predestination, but it remains sovereign and free in its Essence, and can therefore overcome through grace the seemingly inexorable necessity of karmic existence. It is important to note, however, that such a rare possibility is specifically connected to faith and surrender on the part of the human being. Thus, to a devotee's conviction that 'Grace can help one even to overcome *prārabdha*', Ramana Maharshi responded by saying 'If you have such faith it will be so.'[33] In other words, the faith 'that moves mountains' amounts here to a perfect abandonment to God's will whereby the door of the *jīva* becomes wide open to the work of Īśvara. This amounts to saying that only to the extent that the ego has been completely surrendered can the course of necessity be overcome or changed.

Hence, Divine Grace should not simply be considered as the trigger of spiritual exercise, in the way of a sudden intervention and impetus descended from above; the very nature of the Self is Grace, because the Self is, to use the Maharshi's image, like a most powerful magnet that draws any awakened form of consciousness into Itself.[34] The Grace of the Self is incommensurably deeper than the human endeavor of self-investigation. The latter might be compared to moving a piece of metal close enough to the magnet that it may be drawn into it. To use another symbolic analogy, the human investigation into one's true Self is like the wavelet at the surface of a deep current that determines it from all sides. The Maharshi refers to Grace, in this latter sense, as 'the deep inner movement.'[35] Thus, ontologically, Grace is infinitely more real than human efforts; while human efforts are indeed also a manifestation of grace. Methodically, or spiritually, both are necessary for the goal to be reached: 'there is no real *Vichāra* without Grace, nor is there Grace active for him who is without *Vichāra*.'[36] The latter remark implies the distinction between a Grace that is fundamentally sufficient, inasmuch as it is ontological and therefore the condition for anything else, and one that is efficacious, in so far as its power is activated through human receptivity and spiritual work. Grace can therefore be contemplated as a dualistic concept and as a non-dual reality. From the former point of view, it is a response to human works. From the latter vantage point, it is the very nature of Reality, it is indeed the Self, which means that Grace is everything.

The question of Grace needs also be considered in relation to the specifically ascetic aspects of individual effort. Traditionally, Hindu spirituality is founded on the need for a *sādhanā*, a spiritual path. In fact there is perhaps no other tradition other than Hinduism that places more emphasis on contemplative techniques. These include elaborate physical postures, complex meditational skills, control of breathing, diet and fasting. And still it is also distinctly emphasised in Advaitin circles that actions as such do not deliver. Metaphysically this is a consequence of the incommensurability between actions and the *Brahman* or *Ātman*. In other words, there is no way of passing from the finite to the Infinite through finite means, and there is no way for a conditioned being to reach the Unconditioned through conditioned, and conditioning, actions. When devotees confess to him the sense of discouragement that befalls them as they consider the rarity of occurrences of Self-realization, the Maharshi responds by pointing to the need for the Grace of God.[37] This sense of Grace is the other side, as it were, of one's awareness of the impossibility for the human mind to free itself from itself. To understand the nature of the mind, the *manas,* or even of the individual portion of the intellect, or *Buddhi*, is to understand the necessity of something infinitely greater than it; and this is Grace.

Furthermore, the question of Grace is fundamentally connected, in *Vedānta*, to the role of the *guru* in the *sādhāna*. Advaitin texts have referred to the grace of *guru* as a *sine qua non* for Self-realization. In fact the grace of the *guru* is perhaps the most readily available form of divine transformative blessing in the world of Hindu mysticism. While it is recognized that the Grace of Īśvara, the personal God or *Saguna Brahman*, is a requisite for any spiritual realization, the grace emanating from the *guru* is more directly integral to the way of knowledge than any other of its components. Ramana Maharshi's view of the matter is no different. This is because the *guru* is indeed the very manifestation of Grace as a Self-realized being. It is very meaningful to consider that such is very strongly the case in the context of the Maharshi's presence. Countless reports from devotees and visitors of the Maharshi bear witness to the determining impact of the grace emanating from his presence, and therefore the grace emanating from the *satguru*. John Grimes recounts, for instance, a non-dual 'experience' of the Self in the 'cave of the heart': he 'noted that, in fact, it was the center of the universe, the center of everything, it was everything and yet, how is it possible, it was there in the center of my chest.'[38] The point to highlight is not, however, the nature of the experience itself, which is quite obviously aligned with the Advaitin perspective of the Maharshi, but the fact that this 'shift' in consciousness occurred as the narrator 'had been chanting a hymn in praise of the *Guru* since 6am and it was now around 7:30am [...] and the sun had just come over the horizon.'

In response to the question of knowing whether *jñāna* may be reached without the grace of the *guru*, the Maharshi responds: 'The grace of the *Guru* is absolutely necessary.'[39] It is well known in Hinduism that God appears as a human being in order to catch mankind in the net of this human form itself.[40] This is, in a way, the essence of Grace as Divine 'descent.' It could also be said that the limited cannot become limitless without the abettance of limitlessness. Accordingly, the Maharshi specifies that 'God, who is immanent, in his Grace takes pity on the loving devotee and manifests Himself as a being according to the devotee's standard.'[41] Grace is always connected to transcendence in some way since it presupposes that a Higher Reality provides humans with ways and means that their terrestrial limitations do not afford, but it must always do so, in order to be effective, in a manner that is 'comprehensible' by the faithful. The *guru* as Divine being is therefore the quintessence of grace, since he lies *apparently* at the intersection of *Ātman* and *Māyā*. This is only a semblance due to *Māyā*, following which 'the devotee thinks that he [the *guru*] is a man and expects a relationship as between bodies [...] but the *Guru*, who is God or Self incarnate, works from within [...].'[42] The relationship could be described as a ruse of the Self, whereby the externalized nature of the mind is re-orientated inwardly through the intermediary of the human *guru*. However, in his essential and effective nature, the *guru* is definitely not a human being, but the very Self which guides the disciple inwardly like an infallible compass.

Once the *guru* has been recognized by the devotee, his grace becomes efficacious on three accounts: transmission, explanation and being. The first has to do with his traditional lineage, *paramparā*, i.e. the sequence of spiritual teachers, originating with the gods and the *rishis*, to which he is attached. This aspect of the *guru* is 'divinely technical,' if this expression be allowed, in the sense that it guarantees formally the authenticity of the transmitter, and therefore also of that which is transmitted. The idea is that there is no authentic spirituality without tradition, although it is quite obvious that the Self is inherently independent from tradition, which is why there are few exceptions to the rule. The second qualification of the *guru* has to do with intellectual understanding and oral explanation of the doctrine. Given the private access to study through the printed world and the pervasive individualistic ambience of our times, modern students of *Advaita* may be led to consider that the personal meditation of scriptures and classical texts is a sufficient medium of access to Self-realization. This was never the case in classical *Advaita*, as illustrated by Shankara's following words: 'even someone who knows the scriptures should not seek the knowledge of *Brahman* independently [without a *guru*].'[43] The reason for this is not simply that the *guru*, as a qualified instructor, is able to explain what needs be elucidated, and respond to the seeker's intellectual difficulties. It pertains, more profoundly, to the modalities of oral instruction, which are both 'presential' and circumstantiated. In his *Phaedrus* Plato makes the point that written language is actually an impediment to spiritual cognition.[44] From this point of view, written language gives rise to a semblance of knowledge that may be a major pitfall and prevent one from reaching actual knowledge. The information gained through the written word may puff up those who are merely skilled at it, and are therefore prone to substitute *polymathia*, or 'the knowledge of the many', for actual *gnosis*, the knowledge of the One. The need for oral instruction is also connected, moreover, to the principle that real learning needs always be adjusted to the capacities of the learner. Traditional knowledge is conditioned by transmission, and this transmission can only happen from person to person, from soul to soul. To sit at the foot of a teacher implies that a relationship has been established which is different from any other human bond. In a way, the requirement of a lineage and a qualified human instruction reflects the pervasive influence of a third, more fundamental, imperative, which is that of spiritual presence itself. This is so inasmuch as the traditional lineage is more than a mere register of administrators; it entails the passing of a spiritual influence that transcends the individuals themselves. Similarly the ability to explain the meaning of scriptures presupposes more than a mere mental understanding of their conceptual surface. Thus, in the Advaitin tradition, the *guru's* qualifications are not limited to his traditional affiliation and his ability to comment upon scriptures, they must actually include Self-realization itself. The authentic *guru* is a *satguru*, a *guru* of being, in and through his very being, which means no less than the actualization of Being, *Sat*. It is precisely to the extent that the *guru* is a Self-realized human that he can be an efficacious catalyst of grace and indeed an embodiment of Divine Grace.

This observation is all the more meaningful when considering the case of the Maharshi. He was not a *guru* in the sense of belonging to a *parampară*. His belonged neither to a traditional lineage, nor had he been trained in scriptures, nor had he followed a formal path, nor was he endowed with the ability to transmit a traditional initiation, a *dīkshā*; however, he was considered as a *satguru* by his devotees. It follows that the distinction between the traditional and the purely spiritual meanings of the term *guru* that is implied by the Maharshi's special case has an important bearing upon the question of grace. The grace that was at work in and through the Maharshi's presence was not a matter of horizontal transmission but one of vertical gift and succor. It did not obey traditional protocols, and in that respect it corresponded more exactly to the very definition of grace, one that implies freedom from forms in its apparent gratuitousness. While the Maharshi did not provide his devotees with formal initiation, nor even with a fully fledged metaphysical doctrine, he bestowed his grace on them; which amounts to saying that the Self's grace poured over them, since there was nothing individual in this bestowing. He was primarily a spiritual dispenser or catalyst of grace by virtue of his being, by virtue of *Sat*; as an embodiment of Self-realization his presence radiated therefore in ways that were powerfully transformative, of its own accord and without any seeming individual initiative on his part.

Numerous accounts from devotees and visitors illustrate this transformative power, one that overwhelmed individual limitations and ordinary points of view. Many of these testimonies pertain to inner openings that involved a 'taste' of the Self and the extinction of the ego in pure Consciousness, according to different modalities and at various degrees. It bears stressing, however, that the spiritual gifts bestowed by the sage were so in informal ways, and did not follow the traditional conventions of blessing or ritual initiation. While the Self is intrinsically one as *Satcitānanda*, Being-Consciousness-Bliss, its grace manifests in different ways depending on the receptivity and needs of the human receptacle. It could be said to range over four degrees: first, Self-realization itself—which is not a degree *per se* since it is in no way relative; second, the reflection of the Self in the cosmic order as an all-encompassing Higher Power or Ordainer;[45] third, the circumstantial interventions of this Power in one's personal life; and fourth, more generally, all of the realities that are the natural wherewithal of the way of Self-realization, that is to say virtually everything that can serve as an occasional *guru*.[46] Needless to say, the distinction between these levels of reality is only meaningful from the point of view of the unenlightened consciousness, since the Self is pure Unity and Totality. When considered from a relative vantage point, the supreme 'grace of the Self' is none other than the modification of consciousness that is entailed by the removal of superimpositions. This is the uncovering of the Grace that has always been present, but was heretofore unknown. It is the realizing Grace in the deepest sense of the term, the one that is envisaged by Shankara and other Advaitin authorities, when they state unequivocally that actions do not liberate. Only knowledge liberates, and Self-knowledge is only of the Self.[47] Now this does not mean that the *guru* himself can make the devotee realize the Self. The Self has to bloom from within, as it were, and nobody can realize for somebody else, not even the *satguru*. Even though the *guru* serves as a spiritual catalyst, he 'does not bring about Self-realization [...] he simply removes the obstacles to it.'[48] This is in keeping with the principle that the Self is actually already realized, in the sense of being ever-immanent pure Consciousness. The Self is none other than the ever-present Grace that flows from Self-effulgence. Flowing from his reality of Being as embodiment of Self-realization, the *guru's* function, through his compassionate attention, teachings and spiritual advice, consists therefore in facilitating the elimination of everything that obstructs this fundamental recognition. This is particularly true of the predispositions that stand in the way of Self-realization, the *samskaras*, which are 'rendered ineffective by practice as prescribed by the *Guru*.'[49] This could be achieved by way of silence, oral teachings, or any other modalities that are appropriate to the seeker's needs.

Notwithstanding its ultimate meaning as Self-realization, the grace of the Self may also be experienced extrinsically as a reality that is all embracing and protective. This level of consideration corresponds to the human disposition of surrender, to which I will return further on. The human subject abandons itself to the power of the Self, in such a way that the latter is gradually revealed to be an omnipresent grace.[50] This can be referred to, moreover, as the manifestation of Unity within the world of multiplicity. Unity is not realized *per se*, but it is experienced as the mysterious and merciful ground and all-embracing matrix of relative existence. This means that the surrendered *jīva* is under the care of the Self as Presence, Love and Power. Finally, the grace that was often attributed to the Maharshi could also be connected to specific external interventions in the life of the devotees. His function could be analogous, in this respect, to that of an *ishta-devatā*, a divinity of predilection. On this level the *satguru* becomes an object of devotion, and his devotees recognize his grace as being active in the very unfolding of their lives.[51] There is little doubt that most of the Maharshi's visitors were primarily in search of such devotional consolations or succor. This type of intercessory blessing corresponds to a profound need of the human soul, and it epitomizes what the devotion to saintly figures means across traditions. However, it is plain that such a bhaktic consideration of the *guru* does not fulfill the deepest function of grace. Actually it is likely to prevent one from realizing That which the *guru* not only teaches but embodies and manifests, unless it is transcended and recognized to be a mere stage in the Divine pedagogy of the soul. When asked about such not uncommon occurrences of intercessional expectations, the Maharshi consistently shifted the matter to the level of an impersonal spiritual economy transcending personal petitions, and pertaining simply to the effluence of the grace of the Self.[52] Thus the Maharshi made it clear that the 'miraculous grace' that was experienced by the devotee derived from the Self, and was nothing else than an invitation to follow the path leading to It. When asked whether he had had the intention of saving a child who was brought to his attention he replied: 'Even the thought of saving the child is a *sankalpa* and one who has a *sankalpa* is not a *jñani*. In fact such thinking is unnecessary. The moment the *jñāni's* eye falls upon a thing, there starts a divine, automatic action which itself leads to the highest good.'[53] The notion of *sankalpa*, which refers literally to any determination of the will, is ambivalent in Hindu thought. While *sankalpa* is presupposed in the actualization of any reality, beginning with the creative act of the Divine, it does, from a gnostic point of view, also constitute a limitation and a veiling of Reality that is antithetical to non-dual knowledge. There lies the core of the hermeneutic debate over the meaning of scriptures, whether their fundamental teaching implies a dualistic perspective or is utterly non-dualistic. On the one hand, scriptural accounts of creation by Īśvara's will do presuppose an ontological distinction between the Divine Principle and universal manifestation. On the other hand, Shankara's reading of the *śruti*—the Hindu revelation— argues for its non-dualistic perspective by taking stock of statements like *Aham Brahmāsmi*[54] or *Tat Tvam Asi*.[55] This type of Advaitin teaching is considered by Shankara to be the fundamental meaning and intent of scriptures, while 'mythological' narrations of creation are nothing more than expressions of a Divine condescension toward human ignorance steeped in dualistic consciousness. Given such premises, any understanding of *sankalpa* as real and determining is therefore incompatible with the Advaitin point of view. In the *Ribhu Gītā,* one of the Maharshi's favorite spiritual sources, it is written that 'whatever is *sankalpa*, that itself is the great delusion. [...] that itself is superimposition, [...] that itself is all suffering.'[56] Therefore, a strict non-dualistic point of view excludes an intention of individual intervention in the destiny of another human being, since such an interposition would entail a superimposition upon the Self, which is excluded by *jñāna*.[57] Now, the Maharshi's 'miraculous' intercessions did not involve, according to his own account, such an interposition. They were nothing but a direct irruption of the Self, as it were, by virtue of a mere contact with its transformative grace. In other words, the non-dual reality of the Self is the impersonal principle of any positive spiritual modification. Thus, the 'magic touch' of the sage's eyes, which has been referenced by many of his visitors, is nothing else than the Self itself.

Finally, the notion of grace can be extended to encompass realities that are ordinarily considered to lie within the range of mere relativities, or even to those that are deemed to be obstacles to Self-realization. This is, for instance, quite significantly so in the way the Maharshi envisions apparent 'curses' as in reality being 'blessings.' In response to devotees who complained to him that they had not observed any improvement in their ability to master the mind and reach inner peace, the Maharshi quoted verses by the eighteenth-century Tamil *Śaiva Siddhanta* sage Thāyumānavar in which the mind is wooed so as to become an instrument of grace: 'No one is as kind to me as you are, no one. When I ponder on this, you [the mind] are equal to the grace of God.'[58] This is obviously not an address to the mental disposition inasmuch as it is a principle of superimposition, but to the mind which, 'freed from your [his] defects', undergoes an alchemical transmutation by returning to its source in the Self. Since the mind is the principle of ignorance, this transformative virtue can actually be extended to any phenomenon inasmuch as it is turned into a wherewithal of spiritual realization. Thus, for instance, one of the questions most often raised in the presence of the Maharshi was whether *grihastha,* the social status of householder, is a radical impediment on the way to *Moksha.* The response to such questions was invariably to shift from a consideration of the object, or the experience of the object, to one of subjective apprehension of the object. Work, for instance, can only be a hindrance if it reinforces the mistaken misidentification of the body with the mind. Hence, when asked whether the social status of *grihastha,* householder, is an obstacle to Self-realization, the Maharshi typically answers that it is not the case. In the normative economy of traditional Hindu life, *grihastha* corresponds to the second stage, which amounts to giving one's due to the social sphere of family and community through marriage and house-holding responsibilities. This implicitly means that *grihastha,* like other preliminary stages of life, is traditionally conceived as a condition befitting the one who is not mature enough to reach *Moksha,* the ultimate goal of life. Now, the Maharshi relativizes such normative life stages in the name of the immediacy of the Self, and an exclusive focus on the intrinsic inner ripeness of the *jīva:* 'if one is [...] fully ripe, he or she can and does go straight to the goal, without minding the stages.'[59] This amounts to saying that the obstacles to Self-realization are never truly of an outer nature, and do not pertain to outer activity as such. The real hindrance has to do with misidentifying the Self as manifested by an attachment to the idea of 'doership': 'The feeling "I work" is the hindrance. Inquire, "Who works?" Remember, "Who am I?" The work will not bind you. It will go on automatically.'[60] The recurrence of the adjective 'automatic' in the Maharshi's references to ways of acting aligned with Self-realization must remind us that the term originates from the Greek *automaton* that literally means 'self-thought,' and by extension 'self-moved.' The Maharshi envisions real action as being 'Self-moved,' by contrast with ordinary action that is intrinsically tainted with a sense of being 'mine.' The latter binds to the limitations of the ego, which it actually reinforces, hence, for instance, the delusions of 'disinterested' activism on this level. By contrast, 'Self-moved' action is liberating, both subjectively and objectively. It liberates the human agent from the strictures inherent to ego-centeredness—with all the flaws and vices that are connected to it—while opening up avenues of creative freedom within the field of action. Indeed the behavior of the Maharshi himself was a perfect illustration of the way in which the sage is the most authentically spontaneous human being, since there is for him no conventional binding limitation onto the Self.

The identification of the *jīvan-mukta* with the Self means that his is an identity that transcends all relativities and is constrained by none. Death, space, or time have no bearing upon it. Ramana recounts that, in the wake of his Self-realization, all fear of death vanished forever, since he had severed all identifications with anything that dies. On the threshold of his departure from this world, as his devotees were saddened, and apprehensive of his leaving them, he answered their concerns by saying: 'They say I am dying, but I am not going away. Where could I go? I am here.'[61] The *jīvan-mukta* is present at all times and everywhere, and his reality escapes all the categories of ordinary human relationships. In fact, how can one still speak of relationships in the usual sense when the latter entail difference, whereas Self-realization is pure non-dual identity?

This recognition, however, does not cancel out the plane of relations in so far as it is humanly irreducible, no more than it excludes *per se* the laws of physical reality as they relate to the bodily envelop of the liberated soul. And it is at the degree of this relational, albeit provisional, reality that the crucial question of religious devotion arises. To conceive of jñanic perfection as being solely characterized by a kind of impersonal aloofness would therefore be one-sided and indeed fallacious. The sage has an ego like all other human beings, the only difference is that his is 'harmless; it is merely like a skeleton of a burnt rope—though with a form, it is useless to tie up anything.'[62] Accordingly, while the equanimity and impartiality of Self-centeredness precludes individualism and passionate biases, it does not erase individuality or its relational and devotional expressions. Thus, the Maharshi's life is actually replete with occurrences of bhaktic elements.

Such manifestations relate to the Hindu reality of the *ista-devatā*, the divinity of predilection that expresses the personal nature of the worshipper. It is told by Suri Nagamma, for instance, that during the Festival of Lights, *Deepotsava*, Ramana Maharshi contemplated the procession and rituals surrounding the *giri pradakshina*, the circumambulation of Arunachala. He put holy ashes on his forehead and, while 'his voice seemed choked with emotion', he said: '*Appakku Pilai Adakkam*', 'the son is beholden to the father.'[63] In order to understand the full import of this ritual episode, one has to be aware of the fact that Ramana was regarded by some of his devotees as an incarnation of Śiva's son, Skanda. Three points may be drawn from this anecdote that have a bearing on one's understanding of *jñāna* and the *jñanin*. The first is that religious emotions are far from being excluded from the jñanic perspective embodied by the Maharshi. Numerous accounts bear witness to the Maharshi's acute religious sensibility, which manifested at times through tears. This is so inasmuch as a human being always remains human, irrespective of the level of spiritual realization. The very term *jīvan-mukta* is inclusive of the word *jīva*. This may sound like a truism, but it is perhaps not unnecessary to bring this point home given that the *jīvan-mukta* also exhibits traits that are by conventional standards 'more than human.' Indeed the very name Bhagavān denotes Divinity. This seeming ambivalence of the *mukta* may give rise to perceptions and interpretations that entail either the ignorance or the confusion of different planes of being and consciousness. This is, in principle, not an issue from a Hindu point of view, given the strong leaning of the tradition toward a sense of Divine immanence, together with a quasi-instinctive familiarity with experiencing the Divine in all things, beginning with the *guru*.

A Western point of view may lead one, however, to postulate a kind of depersonalization, or even dehumanization, of the sage, for a variety of reasons. Perhaps by virtue of a latent rejection of one's Christian heritage as involving an all too human God, to paraphrase Nietzsche, there is a potential danger of underestimating the human dimensions of the way of the sage, beginning with devotion and ethics. Now, as will be illustrated in the coming pages, such a view of the Maharshi could not be more mistaken, and could even entail, as a practical consequence, a fateful lack of awareness of the need for an integration of the human and psychic dimensions. Reversely, this sublimizing tendency may also give rise to a sort of disappointment when the human envelope of the *jīvan-mukta* leads the unprepared or undiscerning observer to misidentify the spiritual stature of the delivered soul with ordinary human aspects of his nature. In such cases, expectations of Divine sublimity come into conflict with the empirical limitations of human *qua* human existence. The Benedictine monk Henri Le Saux, who became a Christian *samnyāsin* under the name Swami Abhishiktananda, relates, in one of his works, that such was his very first impression of Ramana Maharshi, even though his meeting with the Maharshi proved to be ultimately the most determining of his spiritual encounters. Having heard about the Maharshi's extraordinary spiritual radiance, his first *satsang* with him was marked by an extreme sense of anticipation: 'This visit could not but be an event in my life. Since the moment it had been decided, I had been waiting with an avid and growing impatience the hour when it would be given to me to be in the presence of the Maharishi.'[64] Le Saux confesses that in spite, or maybe as he puts it, 'because' of these expectations, his first *satsang* was in fact a somewhat disappointing one: 'In the middle of this liturgy, these prostrations, this incense, this crowd sitting in silence and the eyes fixed on him, the man seems so natural, "so common", like a good grand-father full of fineness and serenity, which reminded me of my own grand-father. I did not understand.'[65] Later on the same day, the matter became more explicit: 'In truth and once again he appeared to me as a good grand-father. But the aura? It was useless for me to gouge my eyes out in trying to perceive it; my efforts were vain.'[66] Looking for visible signs of spirituality, in a way that was perhaps determined by his Catholic sensibility, Father Le Saux is unable to discern the presence of the Divine in a man whose humanity is all too familiar to him. It is only later on, when mental and phenomenal expectations have been abandoned and a docile and attentive receptivity substituted to them—thanks to a fever that has put the mind half to sleep, that Le Saux describes the emergence of a recognition that, preceding its grasp by the mind, allows him to perceive the intimate 'aura' of the sage, a fresh mode of consciousness that he compares to an 'all-enveloping *bass*.'[67] This is akin to the Self recognizing the Self, the deepest recognizing the deepest beyond mental and physical *koshas*. Arthur Osborne confides a similar experience during his first, much anticipated, *satsanga* with the Maharshi: 'I had expected something grander and less intimate [...] and then He entered, and, to my surprise, there was no great impression.'[68] It is only a few weeks later that Osborne receives a powerful intimation of the *satguru*'s grace. He described how the Maharshi's 'narrowed eyes pierced into me [...], penetrating, intimate, with an intensity [...] I cannot describe.'[69] Such experiences bear witness to the subjective need for a spiritual ripeness and the objective need for an adequate moment. The mind constructs an image of the sage that has nothing to do with the reality of the Self, and that clouds its message. This misapprehension is predicated on a confusion between the Self and the human envelope through which it manifests. Here is the way Swami Annamalai explains this error of perception:

> It is difficult to find out who is a real Guru because Self-realised people often look and behave like ordinary people. Those who are not spiritually mature don't recognise their spiritual greatness. If a grandfather plays with his baby grandchildren, the babies will think that the grandfather is just like them. They will only see him as he really is when they start to grow up.[70]

At any rate, the distinction between a human *appearance* and a Divine transforming reality points to the fact that there is always a gap between the human envelope and the Divine content. A major consequence of this distinction is that the human terrestrial status is always relational in regard to the Divine. As Suri Nagamma stresses it, insightfully, this signifies that the human has always a duty of reverence and love vis-à-vis the Divine, and this is epitomized by the profound devotional attitude of Ramana Maharshi in relation to Arunachala, whom he considered to be his father. It is significant that the relationship to God that is inherent to being human is expressed, or symbolized, here in terms of filiation. This leads the author to state that 'Bhagavan was teaching us that since all creatures are the children of Īśvara, even a *Jñānī* should be beholden to Īśvara.'[71] This way of referring to the human condition strikes a chord with the Christian apprehension of the relationship between God and man. In both cases, of course, Divine incarnation provides a prototype for the filiation of humans from God. Notwithstanding all the theological differences that could be enumerated to distinguish one from the other, there is an isomorphy between Christ as the son of God and Ramana as son of Śiva. Besides, in the image, and the reality, of humans as 'children of Īśvara' there lies evidently more than the mere idea that humans are creatures, since the latter does not necessarily entail the principle of a filial relationship—as exemplified by Judaism and Islam. However, it is interesting to note that, by contrast with the overall Christian spiritual ethos, which tends to be participative and 'fusional,' there is an emphasis here on that which in the love of the children for the Father implies a debt of gratitude and a duty to return what has been given to the Giver. Love is colored by respect and reverence, as immanence is tempered by transcendence. It is as if one lay midway, spiritually speaking, between the Christian sense of being children of God and the Muslim spirituality of debt and gratitude toward one's Creator.

From another point of view, it is important to keep in mind that Īśvara is none other than the *Brahman* and therefore no different than the universal *Ātman;* in light of this metaphysical identity one can infer that even though the human subject shines from the light of the Self, the later remains transcendent to the *jīva*. The subjective transcendence of *Ātman* is as if projected outwardly in the relationship of filiation between humans and God. The accent on filiation evokes immanence, while the sense of duty suggests transcendence. Finally, this interplay of transcendence and immanence allows one to form a clearer picture of the relationship between *bhakti* and *jñāna*, one that is not affected by an abusive sense of dichotomy between the two. Suri Nagamma best encapsulates this ultimate convergence of the two ways when she quotes the ancient saying 'the culmination of devotion is knowledge' (*bhakti poornathaya jnanam*, in her own transliteration). This statement implies continuity between devotional love and knowledge, by contrast with others that present the two in light of a complementarity or a contrast.

When *jñani* and *bhakti* are approached in contradistinction, what is at stake is the irreducible difference between the jñanic principle of the unity of the Self, and the bhaktic duality of God and the worshipping soul. From this vantage point there is no continuity—even by way of a culmination— from devotion to non-dual knowledge, since the former presupposes the persistence of a devotee while the latter denies it. Distinctly from the general perspective of Advaita, Rāmānuja's *Viśistādvaita* exemplifies the perspective of the irreducibility of the distinction between the human self and God.[72] By contrast, the idea that knowledge is the culmination of devotion must be understood to refer to a point where human devotion has reached such an intensity of sincerity and a depth of realization that it entails its extinction into the unity of the Divine Self, that is the very essence of non-dual knowledge. While knowledge may be envisaged as a culmination from a human point of view, the idea of a peak of devotion that would coincide with knowledge is, however, strictly incompatible with non-duality, since it would seem to imply degrees of reality within the Self.

Notwithstanding the metaphysical divide that has just been outlined, the term *bhakti* is far from being always used, in the tradition, in contradistinction with *jñāna*. This is first of all because the distinction between *bhakti* and *jñāna* is only valid on the plane of duality, which is the very terrain of *bhakti*, and it disappears in the non-dual realm beyond. Thus, when devotion is referred to as *parabhakti*, or supreme *bhakti*, it is not uncommonly equated with knowledge.[73] The reason for this might be that the latter is identified with religious sincerity, or rather its pinnacle. Thus the Maharshi received a letter in which a devotee stated that 'seeing only *Brahman* in everything and everywhere is *jñāna-uttara-bhakti*, (*jñāna* culminating in *bhakti*.)'[74] In other words, when *jñāna* is envisaged as the doctrinal crystallization of the nature of things as projected in the mind, *bhakti* may be considered as its 'existential' realization. In that sense, *bhakti* may be contemplated as the culmination, or even the perfection, of *jñāna*. However, the full reality of *jñāna* goes well beyond a mere intellectual recognition in the usual sense of the term. It is in fact synonymous with the realization of the Self, which is the only true knowledge. Understood in this way, it is *jñāna* that is the culmination of *bhakti*, inasmuch as the latter amounts to a partial recognition of reality, one characterized by a dualistic outlook. This is the reason why the Maharshi responds to the aforementioned statement as follows: 'Whether you call this stage *jñāna-uttara-bhakti* or *bhakti-uttara-jñāna*, it is only a matter of words.'[75] Everything depends therefore on the meaning that is assigned to the terms, and this meaning is itself dependent upon one's perspective. The *bhakta* understands *bhakti* as the perfection of worship. For the *bhakta*, *jñāna* can only be a starting point. In this perspective, *jñāna* refers to knowledge as 'information' or perhaps at best as study of the doctrine. *Jñāna* means theory and *bhakti* means practice. From the vantage point of *jñāna*, on the other hand, the fundamental dichotomy is not that which separates theory from practice, but the one that distinguishes between duality and non-duality, relationship and identity. Whatever might be the particular perspective from which one envisions the relationship between *jñāna* and *bhakti*, however, one must pay heed to Sri Muruganar's advice, backed by the Maharshi, that

> When scanned, *bhakti* supreme and *jñāna*
> Shine as in their essence one.
> Saying that one of them is but

A means to the other is only due
To understanding neither.[76]

As it is asserted by Ramana Maharshi in several instances, the merging of the two paths into a single spiritual reality already appears in classical Advaita. In the *Crestjewel of Discrimination* (*Vivekachudamani*), traditionally attributed to Shankarāchārya, we read—following an enumeration of the virtues that are required for Liberation—that *bhakti* is 'to seek earnestly to know one's real nature', which 'among all means of liberation, [...] is supreme.'[77] It is nothing else, therefore, than 'the search for the reality of one's own *Ātman*.' The intrinsic relationship between love and knowledge that is implied by this Shankarian definition appears in glowing light in the famous passage from the *Brihadāranyaka Upanishad* in which the sage Yājñavalka teaches his wife Maitreyi: 'Lo, verily, not for love of the husband is a husband dear, but for love of the Self (*Ātman*) a husband is dear. Not for love of the wife is a wife dear, but for love of the Self a wife is dear.'[78] The consummation of Yājñavalka's 'love of the Self' is therefore none other than Self-knowledge itself. Similarly, *bhakti* can therefore be understood as the very motion of the *jīva* toward *moksha*. It is like the *Śakti*, the realizing energy, of the sense of Unity. One understands better, in this context, how knowledge can be deemed to be the perfection of *bhakti* as *parabhakti*. In this respect, it is not without importance to note that the prefix *para-* suggests both a culmination and transcendence; it may be rendered as supreme or as absolute. Thus ParamaŚiva is undoubtedly the highest sense of Śiva, but He is also more than Śiva, in so far as Śiva is *not* Vishnu. ParamaŚiva is the very Essence of Reality, the Divine Self. Analogously, *parabhakti* is both the highest degree of *bhakti* and a mode of being and consciousness that transcends *bhakti* taken in the exclusive sense of the term, that is, as implying a duality of the worshipper and the Worshipped.

Inasmuch as it is the epitome of the search for the Self, and therefore the love for the Self, we can understand how the Maharshi's *Ātma vichāra* can be identified with *bhakti*, indeed with the perfection of *bhakti*:

Meditation on the Self
Is devotion to the Lord
Supreme, since He abides as this,
Our very Self.[79]

This allows us to understand why it is a most misleading and potentially pernicious mistake to disconnect Self-investigation from devotion. Indeed *bhakti* can be contemplated as the very life of Self-inquiry and Self-knowledge, in the way Śakti is the living exteriorization of Śiva. Thus, Alison Williams touches upon a most profound dimension of the Maharshi's spiritual presence when she writes, 'it seems that Bhagavān lived in an ever-deepening, ever expanding, experience of [...] the ongoing enjoyment of the expression of that identity with his divine father,' i.e., Arunachala, the Self.[80] Self-inquiry is therefore not a mere psycho-spiritual exercise, but its deepening and widening ambit touches upon the very essence of the human longing for the Unconditioned, hence the legitimacy of its identification with *parabhakti*.

The devotional element, and its implicit connection with Self-knowledge, appears most evidently in the life of the Maharshi when circumstances put him in contact with *Periya-purānam*, a biography of Tamil saints. Even though the reading of this hagiography was a seminal factor in the emergence of the Maharshi's spiritual vocation, it is only following his performative 'death' and Self-Awakening that it translated into a devotional attitude.[81] This is a point that is too often ignored or glossed over: the love of God, in the most devotional and personal sense of the term, was undoubtedly an integral part of his path, and at the very time when he was experiencing a profound and powerful awakening to non-duality. The most eminent aspect of the Maharshi's *bhakti* was, without doubt, his deep love and reverence for Arunachala. This devotional relationship with Śiva in the form of the sacred hill was like an innermost spiritual instinct that underlay his life like a tuning fork, and sealed its deepest spiritual identity. It might be described as the very seed of his Self-realization in the form of a spontaneous devotion, well before he had become conscious of the Self:

> In his early years he had always felt a sense of awe when the Name Arunachala was mentioned. [...] In later years he would tell people that Arunachala was his *guru*, and sometimes he would also say that it was the power of Arunachala which had brought about his realisation and had subsequently drawn him to its physical form.[82]

Actually, it appears that the main weight of Ramana's personal life and love was directed toward Arunachala in the way of an integral devotion.

Arunachala Aksharamanamalai (*The Bridal Garland of Letters for Arunachala*), which is sung every day till this day at Ramanasramam, is indeed an erotic piece of poetry; one that many would conventionally not expect from an 'impersonal' *jñanin*. It is said that while Ramana was staying at Virupaksha cave devotees asked him to compose a song they could sing while begging for their food. Although this request was first met with no response, the Maharshi was to grant his devotees their wishes at a later stage. As he was performing *giriparadakshina* one day around the mountain, the Maharshi spontaneously composed the Tamil litany that would become intimately associated with his *guru bhakti*. The tone and vocabulary of this hymn echo the long cross-religious tradition of mystical expressions of the love of God couched in the language of human erotic love. Here are some of the verses: 'O Arunachala! Destroy my clothes, and stripping me naked, give me the clothing of grace,' 'O Arunachala! If thou dost not join me, my body will melt away, my eyes shed tears profusely, and I shall be destroyed,' 'O Arunachala! Unless Thou dost touch me with Thy gracious hand and embrace me, I shall be lost. Do bestow Thy grace on me.'[83]

Other occurrences throughout his life demonstrate the extent to which *bhakti* was a major component of the Maharshi's spiritual life. Such devotional attitudes were sometimes reminiscent of Ramakrishna's ecstatic expression of the love of God, a similarity that would surprise those who might be exclusively familiar with the Maharshi's focus on *Ātma-vichāra*. S.S. Cohen recounts, for instance, how Ramana once recited a Vaishnava poem 'in which occurred the words "Fold me in thy embrace, O Lord,"' when his arms 'joined in a circle round the air before him, and his eyes shone with devotional ardour, while his voice shook with stifled sobs [...].'[84] There could not be a better illustration, given the dramatic and effusive disposition of the Maharshi in this instance, of the principle that the true *jñani* is also a genuine *bhakta,* notwithstanding the reality of the distinction between *jñāna* and *bhakti* as paths.[85] Indeed, lest one confuse *jñana* with metaphysical discourse of a merely theoretical kind, it is edifying to note that the Maharshi 'once observed that he could sit unmoved through any amount of philosophical discourse, but he could not remain unresponsive to a passage, however small, that stirred the sentiment of devotion or sorrow.'[86]

When *jñāna* and *bhakti* are differentiated as integral spiritual ways of approach to the Divine—and no more as complementary components within the life of a seeker, *jñāna,* as we have seen, is most often based on a non-dualistic perspective culminating in a contemplative divesting from everything that is superimposed upon the true Self, which is none other than the *Brahman,* whereas, by contrast, *bhakti* is inherently predicated upon the relationship between the soul and its Lord. In this path, based as it is on the unitive power of love, there is no higher Self-realization from which this relationship could be relativized; this means that the height of *bhakti* coincides with human perfection. Moreover, while *karma-yoga* is intrinsically based on actions, and on directing the intentionality of actions away from the self and onto God, *bhakti-yoga* is not necessarily connected to actions, as it tends actually to underrate ritual actions in the name of the inner pull of love. From the point of view of the *bhakta*, actions may retain something somewhat external, a character that contrasts them with love as a principle of inwardness. This kind of perspective appears quite clearly in the poems of the fifteenth-century Indian mystic Kabir, who liked to poke fun at the ritual externals behind which too many believers hide the superficiality of their religious intentions.[87]

Beside this general typology of the 'path of love' in contradistinction with other ways, there exist various traditional understandings of the meaning of *bhakti*. Thus, in the tradition of Rāmānuja, *bhakti* differences arose as to the meaning to assign to devotion in terms of its spiritual emphasis. Hence the distinction, often drawn in manuals of Hindu spirituality, between a way of devotion that is symbolically akin to the monkey, and another one that is compared to the kitten. The first emphasises the human effort as a prerequisite for grace. The young monkey has to hold on to her mother in order to be moved from one place to another.[88] In this view of things, *bhakti* is indeed a formal path that entails specific practices and human exertion in their accomplishment. Here it is the intensity of the devotion that is the fuel of the spiritual path. The second perspective, symbolically akin to the kitten's utter abandonment to her mother carrying her around, stresses *prapatti,* or trust in God and abandonment to His Will, which is none other than the existential play, His *līlā.* This path is centered on an inner disposition rather than outer practices.[89] In fact, *prapatti* is deemed by some of its proponents to make it unnecessary to follow a formal bhaktic path. This is because the latter entails the risk of a subtle self-affirmation, whereas the former is utterly dependent upon the Divine Other, and therefore free of any sense of ownership of actions. It is in this spiritual climate that we come the closest to the Maharshi's concept of surrender to God as a way of realizing the Self. As the Maharshi often repeated, there are two ways: inquiry into 'Who am I?', or surrendering. If the main goal is to uncover the reality of the Self, then it makes sense that the illusion of selfhood be cast out by turning away from it in self-abandonment to God's will. There is, however, more to the Maharshi's principle of surrender than that which its specifically bhaktic definition, or experience, entails.

The best way to unearth the depth of meaning of surrender is to connect it directly with Self-inquiry, since these two approaches are those recommended in priority by the Maharshi. It must be remembered that, in Ramana's case, the investigation into the nature of the 'I', *Ātma-vichāra,* was initially preceded by a passage through death. This occurred, first, in the mode of an intense fear of death, and proceeded, second, in the way of a concrete, attentive, anticipation and indeed simulation of physical death. It is only on this basis that the investigation 'Who am I?' moved deep into consciousness and led to Self-realization. The anticipation of death is none other, effectively or symbolically, than the door of spiritual 'poverty,' the withdrawal, or disappearance, of the ego. This approximates the concept of *vacare Deo* in monastic Christianity,[90] and the principle of spiritual poverty, or *faqr* in Sufism.[91] The ego removes itself from its desires and the images upon which it feeds, thereby 'dying,' spiritually and symbolically, in a state of abandonment to God's Will, or surrender to God's Reality. It could actually be said that the question 'Who am I?' is the positive reverse of this surrender. This is the reason why the Maharshi recommended either internal investigation or surrender, which could also be referred to as abandonment or submission, with different shades of meaning and connotations. At any rate, inquiry and surrender are, in this sense, two sides of the same reality. This has led to the suggestion that

> if Ramana Maharshi's teachings are correctly interpreted, then it will be seen that the paths of surrender and Self-enquiry merge before Realisation, and that in the higher levels of practice, if one follows the path of surrender, then one's *sādhanā* will be the same as that of someone who has chosen the path of Self-enquiry.'[92]

As indicated earlier, on an elementary level, surrender can be equated with *bhakti* inasmuch as it entails a perfection of worship. Knowing the nature of the Lord translates into giving all of one's will to Him since He alone is truly in charge.[93] Thus, the Maharshi has sometimes referred to devotion as the 'Mother of *Jñāna,*' in the sense, no doubt, that it may 'give birth' to Self-knowledge. Interestingly, even though most of the Maharshi's devotional references would be to his Divine Father, Arunachala Śiva, the sage has on occasion even referred to the Divine Power as the Mother, and thus referred implicitly to the Goddess, or the *Śakti,* when enjoining the seeker to 'lay your ego at the feet of that Mother.'[94] However, the path of surrender knows different degrees, and it cannot be perfected from one day to the next. It is the reason why it has to be mediated, through the grace of God and the *guru*. On the one hand, perfect surrender would require accepting all aspects of destiny without even praying for the resolution of misfortune and trials—since it cannot be conditional, on the other hand, until this perfection is granted, the grace of the *guru* can serve as a kind of intermediary.

As we will see, it is therefore possible to distinguish four degrees of surrender, the first being a mere appearance thereof, the second a very imperfect stage, and the third an intermediate step toward genuine surrender, which is only realized in the perfection of spiritual abandonment. Hindu life presents us with a practice of surrendering oneself to God or the *guru* through symbolic and physical postures that are thought to compensate for one's moral and spiritual shortcomings. For the Maharshi this seemingly devotional attitude cannot be counted as genuine surrender, since nothing is actually surrendered, the individual's desire being to receive without giving or renouncing. The fundamental flaw of this type of formal posture is most vividly revealed in the Maharshi's sharp criticism of the conventional practice of *Namaskāra;* it is a 'reverential salutation by prostrating with all the eight limbs of the body touching the ground.'[95] For the Maharshi, far from being akin to a mere customary formality, the true meaning of the *Namaskāra* is the 'dissolving of the mind.'[96] This is why the *jñānī* 'is deemed to be doing *Namaskāra* at all times.'[97] This is the ultimate meaning of surrender. The formal practice is nothing but a symbol intended to facilitate an inner realization. It is on the basis of this spiritual understanding of the *Namaskāra* that the Maharshi could sternly rebuke those who came and prostrated themselves before him without serious spiritual intent. For the Maharshi, such attitudes amount to nothing more than a lowly commerce whereby the act, deprived of its spirit, becomes an illusory means of trying to 'deceive' God, hiding behind a *Namaskāra* as a way to be exonerated from one's sins by paying physical homage to the human *guru*. This attitude was deemed by the sage to be hypocritical and harmful to the self, and indeed unworthy of *satsanga*.[98] Beyond this misunderstanding of *Namaskāra*, and its reduction to an empty shell, there lies another kind of disposition that, although seemingly directed toward the *guru*, does not fulfill the requirements of genuine surrender. It consists in approaching the *guru*, or God, as the holder of a power that may help fulfill one's desires or parry the objects of one's fear. It does not hold the spiritual standards of sincere surrender, since it interposes expectations of an extraordinary intervention in one's favor, one that may change the course of events according to one's wishes. By contrast, 'if you have surrendered, you must be able to abide by the will of God and not make a grievance out of what may not please you.'[99] There seems to be a contradiction, on some level, between accepting God's will without any reservation or restriction, and praying for one's own benefit or that of others. This being said, the Maharshi recognized the legitimacy of prayers intended for being liberated from some worldly misfortune. In this case, however, surrender is effective in the way of turning toward Divine Power, which implicitly presupposes an *a priori* acceptance that what one is praying for may not happen if it is not in keeping with the Divine Will. In an analogous sense, turning to the *guru* for attending to one's problem might be a manner of relinquishing one's own will by abandoning it in the *guru*'s hands. In a thorough discussion of the meaning of surrender, it has been suggested, however, that this way of proceeding is more a concession to human frailty than a full recognition of what is entailed by true surrender.[100] In other words, it would be too difficult for many to immediately drop all concerns for their own life without an intermediary stage that put these concerns at the feet of the *guru*. This is, therefore, the highest point one may reach from the point of view of individual existence. The latter is ordinarily characterized, indeed defined, by ego-centered thoughts, which are all predicated on the belief in the reality of the ego—the instinctive idea that the ego has a reality of its own. It is this very idea that has to be abandoned for surrender to be perfected. The Maharshi compares this situation to the actions of a man traveling by train. Before sitting in the compartment and letting the train lead him to his destination, he places his suitcases in the baggage net and stops worrying about them. Analogously, what is trust in God on the level of moral attitude becomes indifference to one's own thoughts on the level of inner discipline.

Going beyond the stage of the individual involves a sort of spiritual revolution that takes us into the domain of non-duality. When it comes to realizing the perfection of surrender, the crux of the matter lies in the seeming paradox that one's desire for surrender runs contrary to the very nature of surrender, since the latter entails the relinquishing of all self-centered desires. This is the conundrum encountered by many mystical paths, particularly in the context of *bhakti*. In fact the intensification of the effort to surrender through spiritual practices may have the unintended effect of reinforcing the illusion of egoity instead of dissolving it.[101] There is in individual existence a natural bent that contradicts the ideal of a perfect surrender. This contradiction accounts for the fact that there is no real continuity, no actual passage, from the ego to the Self. The Self is incommensurable by the standards of the ego, and there is no way for that which is limited to reach the Unlimited in its own terms, or within its own ambit. In bhaktic paths, the sudden shift from works to grace is an indicator of this impossibility; it is a sudden reversal that can only be apprehended as a mystery, a kind of suspension of the laws of human existence, therefore as 'supernatural' in some way.

In the Hindu tradition, the path of knowledge provides the sole way out of this quandary. It offers the only solution to this seemingly insoluble problem through the realization that the ego has no reality in the first place. It is at this point that the two ways of Self-inquiry and surrender merge, and indeed become indistinguishable. From this perspective, perfect surrender amounts to an intuition that there is nobody who surrenders, or that surrender has already taken place in reality, or metaphysically, since the ego has never been in any real sense. The Maharshi makes explicit this ultimate meaning of surrender as follows: 'The surrender of the *jīva* is the loss of individuality in the divine feet of God, through the cessation of the ego-consciousness which is that *jīva*'s form.'[102] It must be remembered, in this context, that the term surrender is itself denotative of recognition of one's 'defeat,' of one being overcome by the 'Other.' Thus, the essence of the bhaktic perfection of surrender is none other than the very core of *jñāna*: the falling away of the illusory superimposition of egoity. This fundamental point enlightens the meaning of the Maharshi's re-occurring and seemingly puzzling statement that the main obstacle to realization is the conviction that something has to be realized, whereas in reality the Self is already, and has always been, the Self. This mystery is set out in a somewhat ironic manner in the following declaration: 'When I am shining in your Heart as "I-I", your own real nature, your attempt to "attain" me is indeed a great marvel!'[103] The real object of wonder is not the Realization, but the very search for it.

The 'static' character of Self-recognition may be deemed to be in sharp contrast with the 'dynamic' connotations we may attach to the word 'surrender.' Is not surrendering an action that requires initiative and perseverance on our part? This initiative is, however, an appearance since it flows, pre-consciously as it were, from the emergence of Reality within one. The abandonment of all cares to the Lord could not even be considered independently from the latter, and is therefore to be assigned the Lord as its real source. This discovery of the Self through surrendering to the Other echoes the Buddhist principle of *tariki*, the 'Power of the Other', as primarily illustrated in Japanese Pure Land Buddhism. This way consists in turning toward the saving power of the

Bodhisattva instead of relying on one's own spiritual efforts.[104] Some scholars of Pure Land Buddhism have suggested that this concept might actually find its roots in the classical Buddhist concept of co-dependent arising.[105] This connection does afford a rich parallel with the Maharshi's spiritual 'logic.' Co-dependent origination (*pratītya-samutpāda*) is another term for emptiness (*śūnya*), which refers to the lack of substance of phenomena, whether inner or outer. The Maharshi's analysis of the 'I' consciousness, which leads to the latter's disappearance into its source, is in its own way an undoing of the belief in the substantiality of the mind, a form of 'no-self' or *anatta*.[106] The polarity between the 'active' inquiry of the *Ātma-vichāra* and the 'passive' connotations of surrender is therefore resolved in the 'letting go' of individual shells and egoic misidentifications that is common to both.

In another spiritual universe, the world of Sufism offers other far-reaching analogies with the two paths of Self-inquiry and surrender in terms of their distinctions, their complementarity and their underlying unity. Most Sufi masters have placed a methodical emphasis, throughout the centuries, on the practice of *dhikr*, which is the 'remembrance' or 'mention' of the Names of God, as the best way to reach proximity or union with the Divine. This is, as it were, the active dimension of Sufism, the one that has to do with striving in the path of God. On the other hand, from the early centuries of Islam, saintly figures and spiritual masters have highlighted the centrality of the principle of spiritual poverty (*faqr* in Arabic). This emphasis was scripturally founded on the Qur'ān's verse: 'You are poor (*fuqarā*) in relation to God, He is the Rich (*al-Ghanī*), the Praiseworthy' (Qur'ān 35:15). In fact, Sufis have been called, or have called themselves, *darvish* or *fuqarā*, two words that, in Persian and Arabic, refer to poverty. *Faqr* was conceived as a form of detachment from the world and the ego, but its perfection is akin to the non-dualistic summit of gnosis. To be truly poor is not only to be detached from worldly concerns, but also to realize the purely metaphorical reality of the ego, *nafs*, and the phenomena with which it is enmeshed: 'Everything that one seeks in adoration other than God is an "associated," that is to say an unreal (*ma'dūm*) and hidden (*mastūr*) thing, a simple name which does correspond to any "named".'[107] As in the Maharshi's perspective, the one who realizes the nothingness of the mind and the world outside of the Self 'will know Who is the sole Agent', the only Doer.[108]

There is a deep and enlightening analogy between the Sufi *dhikr* and *faqr* on the one hand, and Self-enquiry and surrender on the other hand. Despite their difference in terms of direction and object—*dhikr* being directed *a priori* toward the transcendent God and *vichāra* oriented inward toward the immanent Self, *dhikr* and Self-investigation are active practices that have a human and a Divine side, so to speak. This means that the Sufi invocation requires initiative and perseverance on the part of the practitioner, as does Self-inquiry. Their ultimate reality is Divine, however. While *Ātmā-vichāra*, as we have seen, is ultimately none other than the knowledge of the Self by the Self, the perfection of *dhikr* is taken to be the disappearance of the ego and God's invoking Himself within the human soul, as it were.[109] In both cases, what is human effort *a priori* is actually revealed to be Grace and Divine Reality *a posteriori*. There will be more to say about this conjunction, from the Maharshi's perspective, in Chapter Three, on prayer and *japa*. By contrast, surrender and *faqr* are purely human realities, although they open the door to the emergence of the Divine Self. *Faqr* means that the soul does not seek anything, does not superimpose or appropriate anything. The soul must give itself totally to God, to His Name, without any return upon itself, without expectation of any kind. *Faqr* is but another word for a profound and consistent way of utter surrender to God. It is the realization that the ego is nothing and that the Divine Self is everything.

In Sufism, *dhikr* requires *faqr* as Divine fullness demands human emptiness. It is taught that without *faqr*, or virtues akin to it, the methodical invocation of Names of God could all too easily give rise to illusions or even, when misunderstood, to spiritual ambition and pride. It could be said that the same is true, *a fortiori*, for *Ātma-vichāra*, as implied by the Maharshi when he stated that Self-inquiry requires a deep karmic maturity. When asked whether it is possible 'for all people to hold on to that path of self-enquiry', the Maharshi makes it clear that 'it is true that it is only possible for mature minds, not for immature minds.'[110] When bereft of karmic preparation, seekers can easily confuse the Self with hidden folds of the human ego.[111] The need for spiritual ripeness is also described in terms of purity, for, 'unless one has an extremely pure sattvic mind, it will be impossible to have *darshan* in the Heart of the reality that is *jñāna*.'[112] This is all the more likely as intensive meditation may often suggest to the practitioner an ill-advised self-satisfaction that undermines the very foundations of the spiritual search.[113] It is at this point where the Maharshi's emphasis on surrender may be deemed to complement Self-inquiry in a most vital manner, notwithstanding the unity of their ultimate meaning. The deep sense of transcendence, whether outer or inner, entailed by spiritual surrender, may provide a corrective to, or a guardrail against, the possible delusions and pitfalls of the notion of subjective Divine immanence.[114]

Assuming that the previous conclusions hold true and that Self-enquiry and surrender are either complementary or essentially one, the question may be raised: why did the Maharshi, in most accounts, consider surrender rather as a substitute than as an essential complement to the question 'Who am I?'[115] He sometimes mentions the two in the same breath as equally valid and effective options, but he most often highlights the first as being more direct than the second; he sometimes affirms, moreover, that surrender is most conducive to realization for those who are incapable of Self-inquiry. It can be argued, first of all, that Self-inquiry, as *dhikr* in Sufism, holds in principle a privilege of self-sufficiency, since it summarizes the whole spiritual reality. It is affirmative and divine in its ultimate goal and content. As *dhikr* 'contains' virtually the Divine Reality, *vichāra* includes virtually the Divine Self. This is no doubt the main reason why Ramana Maharshi directed his visitors toward Self-inquiry as a matter of priority. In response to criticism concerning the likely inappropriateness of this primacy with regard to unprepared devotees, the Maharshi simply stated: 'When people ask me about meditation I always give them the best advice [...] that is I tell them to do self-enquiry.'[116] In essence, this simply means that his advice was based on the ultimate reality of the Self as such, rather than being adjusted to individual needs. The fact that the Maharshi never claimed to be a *guru* accords with this principle, since it implies that he would normally not function as a guide in the traditional sense of the term. His perspective was subjective, centered on realization, and universal, founded on the deepest and all-encompassing spiritual reality. As a qualification to this observation, however, it must be reiterated that the Maharshi has also stated, on some occasions, that *Ātma-vichāra* is, in actuality, only suitable for souls that have rare karmic possibilities.[117] Even though Self-inquiry and surrender may be deemed to be two sides of the same spiritual reality, the first one presupposes a disposition toward attentive introspection and objectivity vis-à-vis oneself that is not so widely available, especially in a world as troubled and disjointed as ours. Furthermore, in regard to his Hindu devotees, the Maharshi is likely to have assumed that the inner leanings of surrender were already to some degree instilled in their souls through participation in the spiritual climate of the tradition. As for most seekers hailing from a more secular background, by contrast, it is not unreasonable to hypothetise that the Maharshi spoke above all in terms of his own realization, without necessarily being aware of the specific intricacies and obstacles entailed by a Western background. In other words, irrespective of the actual capacity of devotees, the sage wished above all to give a taste of Self-realization through the direct simplicity of the 'Who am I?'—as a suggestive expression of the grace of his presence.

Devotion and grace are, as I suggested in the beginning, like the human and divine elements of the spiritual equation. The *guru* stands at the crossroad of the two, as object of devotion and subject of grace. This double reality appears in the seeming tension, not to say contradiction, between the non-dual view of the *guru* and the need to keep contemplating him as *guru*. In *Guru Ramana Vachana Mala*, we read that 'the idea of Non-duality is fit to be cherished in respect to all things whatsoever, but not with respect to the *guru*.'[118] So there is a plane on which the distinction is fully effective, and is indeed the fuel of spiritual motion. On the other hand, however, the reduction of the *guru* to the status of a man while he is actually 'unlimited Pure Consciousness' is deemed, in the same text, to be the fact of a 'most sinful person with a foul mind.'[119] Indeed confusing the *guru* with his human form is nothing but the projection of one's own limitations upon the *guru*: it is 'the reflection of the individuality of those who love individuality', and ultimately an incapacity to grasp that 'the Sage [...] is within himself' and that 'all Sages [...] are [...] one and the same.'[120]

3

JAPA, PRAYER AND SELF-KNOWLEDGE

Although Ramana Maharshi laid emphasis on the practice of Self-inquiry, hence delving into the question 'Who am I?', the latter was actually not deemed to be practically suitable for all. In fact, it bears stressing that, although this point is often only implicit in both his writings and interviews, Self-inquiry was conceived by the Maharshi as involving stringent pre-requisites. When asked by a devotee, in 1917, what qualifications were demanded for one to engage oneself in Self-inquiry, the Maharshi responded by enumerating several attributes of the mind ripe for *Ātma-vichāra*. These predispositions include a spontaneous detachment from sensory objects, the limitations and ephemeralness of which must be strongly felt. In a way, the intense experience of death undergone by the young Ramana was like a dramatic crystallization of these predispositions, at least inasmuch as it entailed an acute and most concrete sense of the precariousness of the ego and terrestrial existence. Moreover, the sage of Tiruvannamalai suggested that these spiritual predispositions are the fruits of a purification of the mind that results either from one's *prārabdha karma* or from regular *upāsanā*, i.e., from attending to the devotion of a divinity. From a Hindu point of view, everything in spiritual life is a matter of karmic maturity, and the acquisition of merits is not simply to be understood as an accumulation of spiritual capital, but also and above all as a readying of the soul for transcending itself into Self-realization. Grace itself participates, in a way, in this karmic economy, to the extent that it presupposes a propitious terrain for its manifestation. It is plain, therefore, that devotional practices have an important role to play as a preparation for Self-inquiry. Although moral discipline and religious practices are in principle not intrinsically necessary for Self-inquiry, since the Self is unconditioned, they are in fact needed in order to cultivate the psychic ground in which this inquiry can bear fruit. In this context, the imperative of purifying the mind pertains primarily to the negative task of shunning the various distractions that are as many obstacles to a focus on the single root of consciousness.

Truth must be told that, in response to the questions or consultations of his devotees, the Maharshi excluded none of the traditional ways and practices. For him, all spiritual paths had in common their ability to facilitate a process of concentration on the Ultimate Reality. Once it is recognized that such is the main and indeed only meaning of contemplative ways, the relativity, and therefore plurality, of their forms and emphases becomes quite apparent. In a way, the seeming paradox is that a single-minded and relentless focus on the Self as universal substratum of all selves cannot but lead to a wide pluralism when it comes to actual methods of reaching it. Among these methods, one way is often mentioned by the Maharshi as an efficacious means of spiritual realization: *japa-yoga*, the path of invocatory prayer. The fairly frequent reference to this spiritual support may be accounted for on several grounds. First of all, *japa-yoga* is an extremely common practice in India, one that has been advised by all *gurus* and systematically practiced by such spiritual luminaries as Swami Ramdas and Mohandas Gandhi. Secondly, it is often considered, within the Hindu tradition, as particularly adapted to the needs of our age, which most Hindus tend to associate with the *Kali Yuga*, the final age of spiritual obscuration. Thirdly, *japa-yoga* may be practiced and understood on different levels, and it can fulfill an important function within diverse spiritual perspectives.

Ramana Maharshi is hardly portrayed as a man of prayer in the literature that has been devoted to him. In fact, direct references to prayer as such are relatively rare in his teachings. A close examination of his teachings, as well as consideration of his life, however, reveals that the matter is more complex. This is, first of all, on account of the fact that the sage of Arunachala fully recognized the diversity of human needs. While bringing everything back to the ultimate question of the nature of the true 'I', he was also keenly aware, as a *satguru*, that there are countless roads leading to this ultimate goal, and that the karmic dispositions and qualifications of individuals must therefore be taken into account. As a biographical illustration of the importance of prayer in the Maharshi's spiritual development, it has already been mentioned that upon his arrival in Tiruvannamalai, he was as if magnetized by the Arunachalesvara Temple. He spent hours there in front of the statues of gods and goddesses. It is in this sacred setting that he sometimes prayed 'for the descent of his [Iśvara's] grace upon me so that my devotion might increase and become perpetual.' As mentioned earlier, this mode of prayer is connected to the reality of an individual consciousness that needs be fixed on a Divine object of devotion. In that sense, the prayer for 'perpetual devotion' is but a reflection on the individual plane of the definitive permanence of the Self. It is a way for the individual *jīva* to participate as *jīva* in the streams of grace of non-duality, which is its essence in any case. The perpetuity of prayer can therefore be conceived as a reflection, on the plane of the personal soul, of the permanence and eternity of the Self. This is the essence of the practice of *japa*. In the Hindu tradition, the devotional reality of prayer is commonly synthetized in this form of orison that is not strictly, nor primarily, petitional. While prayer is ordinarily understood as a way of asking for some divine gift, favor, or assistance, *japa* is a frequent or continuous call, which may be vocal or silent. *Japa* consists in the invocatory repetition of the name of a god or a *mantra*. In the Hindu world, *japa-yoga* is actually a spiritual practice that has been pervasive to this day across schools and perspectives. Equivalent forms of this practice, with different inflections, modalities and objectives, are to be found in all religious traditions, from the Orthodox Christian 'Jesus prayer' to the *Nembutsu* of the Buddhist *Jōdo-Shinshū*.

The Maharshi's teachings are rarely associated with this kind of path, since they are primarily stressing the investigative search for the Self. It is this very search, and its interiorizing modalities, that not a few of the Maharshi's visitors found to be too 'abstract.' This 'abstraction' probably pertained, in their minds, to the absence of formal supports. The *Ātma-vichāra* is a way of delving beyond forms in order to reach the very source from which they flow, or the infinite space in which they appear. By contrast, the way of *japa* may be considered 'concrete' in so far as it rests upon the verbal substance of names and formulas. When presented with this sort of difficulty, the Maharshi would respond in two ways, either in one most appropriate to the needs of the inquirer, or to the circumstantial intent of the sage. The first type of response would equate Self-inquiry to a form of *japa*. In response to concerns of abstraction, the Maharshi would go so far as to state that "Who am I?" is the best *japa*.[1] This was a way to situate the sense of the concrete in a totally different context, i.e., that of Reality as it is. Thus, the question 'what could be more concrete than the Self?' suggests that the Self is more intimately and truly present than anything else—keeping in mind that there is indeed nothing else.[2] Conversely, everything that is experienced outside of the Self is necessarily 'abstract,' precisely inasmuch as it is illusorily abstracted from the Self. Moreover, this response is also a way to redirect the attention of the seeker to the ultimate meaning and function of *japa,* which is Self-realization, and away from a one-sided conception of the invocation as directed toward an external Reality. The question 'Who am I?' is a *japa* to the extent that it is a way of 'remembering' the Self, of focusing on it, which is the function of chanting and repetition.

However, the Maharshi would sometimes respond to questions about the benefits of *japa* on more methodical and propaedeutic grounds. In such cases he would recommend *japa* as a way to keep the mind away from distractions. This is especially the case in circumstances when the practitioners are alone and need to keep their mental faculty from wandering.[3] The fact that the Maharshi could refer to chanting and *japa* as the 'best aids' suggests that, in such cases, *japa* was conceived by him as an adjuvant rather than as a central practice, which is hardly surprising when one considers the way he prioritized Self-investigation. In other words *japa* can provide spiritual support to the way of centering that does culminate in Self-inquiry. Another way of contemplating the primarily adjuvant character of *japa* is to take into account the Maharshi's reflections on the ill-fittedness of trying to impose non-dual consciousness upon the workings of daily life: '*Advaita* should not be practiced in ordinary activities. It is sufficient if there is no differentiation in the mind. If one keeps cartloads of discriminating thoughts within, one should not pretend that all is one on the outside.'[4] This is an instance of what could be termed the Maharshi's 'spiritual realism': conventional reality cannot be addressed in the terms of the Ultimate, although the latter must indeed provide the background and the essential reference for it. There is a pseudo-*Advaita* that 'pretends' that things are not different from each other on the level upon which they are indeed quite distinct, and where these differences must be attended to; and such discernment is directly relevant to the respective fields of *japa* and *Ātma-vichāra.* On the one hand, ordinary life presupposes an ability to differentiate; on the other hand, relative existence and daily functionality must be connected to spiritual reality. Whether internal or vocal, *japa* involves a non-mental spiritual practice that can easily provide the unifying background for one's activities in the world while not preventing one's practical engagement with differentiations.[5] *Japa* is therefore a very effective aid in connecting the realm of outer differentiation and the domain of inner non-differentiation.

The choice of a particular name or *mantra* can traditionally be a matter of inner predisposition, or it may be connected to the bestowing of initiation by a *guru*. Scriptures are also depositories of formulas, such as the *Mahāvākyāni*, that are sometimes used in *mantra-yoga*.⁶ Thus, one of the scriptures most favored by Ramana Maharshi, the *Ribhu Gītā*, states that the repetition of *Aham Brahmāsmi* as a *mantra* is the only form of *japa-yoga* leading to Liberation.⁷ Even though this point of view does not reflect the Maharshi's position, as we will see, what is remarkable about the *Ribhu Gītā's* assertion is that it is explicitly developed in contrast with a repudiation of other forms of *mantra-japa*. In this view of things, the limitations of other forms of *japa* do not only result from the particularity of the god who is called upon during its practice, but also, and above all, from the spiritual intentions that preside over it.⁸ On the one hand, the gods represent different aspects of Reality, not the integrality of the *Brahman*. They therefore presuppose, and in a way foster, limited points of view on *Satcitānanda*. On the other hand, by 'mundane objectives' and 'worldly enjoyments' is meant any goal that comes short of the one Selfhood. Only the *Ātman* lies beyond all aspects and vantage points. The latter presuppose a limitation and fragmentation of Being and Consciousness. The *Ātman-Brahman* alone corresponds to Reality as such, while transcending any distinction and polarities. There is a sense, therefore, in which the *Ribhu Gītā's* statement, beyond an exclusiveness that does not resonate with the Maharshi's spiritual 'pluralism,' strikes a chord with the sage's emphasis on *vichāra*. While he does not call into question the spiritual effectiveness of various forms of *japa*, and their appropriateness for given devotees, the Maharshi clearly subordinates them in principle to *vichāra*. Now, the reason why the *Ribhu Gītā* gives precedence to a particular *mahāvākya*, a statement of Non-duality excerpted from Vedic scriptures, is most likely connected to the fact that it is the only one, among major 'great sayings,' to include the first person pronoun *aham*, 'I.' Thus, it is interesting to note that the Maharshi has occasionally advised a kind of *japa* that appears to lie at the intersection of the way of *vichāra* and *mantra-yoga*. Although he rejected the idea of a use of the question 'Who Am I?' as a *mantra*, he indicated that it is possible and fruitful, in some cases, to make use of the word 'I' itself as a *mantra*. This unusual possibility is founded on the fact that 'I' is the 'the first name of God': 'It is the first and greatest of all *mantras*. Even OM is second to it.'⁹ As we have seen, *Aham* is also scripturally based, and the Maharshi reminds his listeners that the *Brihadāranyaka Upanishad* teaches that *Aham* is the first name of God as confirmed by the fact that 'the first letter in Sanskrit is A and the last letter Ha "h" and "Aha" thus includes everything from beginning to end.'[10] Elsewhere, Ramana Maharshi teaches most explicitly that the 'accurate name of God is "I"' and 'the awareness "I am" is the original and primordial *mantra*.'[11]

Besides its function as an instrument of spiritual centering, one of the most important principles in the practice of *japa* is that of the transformative power inherent therein. The virtue of the Divine Name, or Divine Statement, that is repeated by the practitioner, lies in its being one with the Divine Reality itself.[12] Such an idea may sound 'magical' to a skeptical modern mind, for which the idea that a finite verbal form and the Infinite Principle of the universe could be one may sound incomprehensible and imaginary. However, from a traditional point of view the theurgic power of the *mantra* derives either from its scriptural origin—and therefore its Divine source, or its being bestowed by the grace of the *guru*—as God's manifestation—through an initiation, or else by both. At any rate, both perspectives are rooted in the principle of a kind of Divine 'substantiality' of the *mantra*, or the name. The Maharshi was not a *guru* in the technical sense, meaning that he would not bestow any initiation nor transmit any *mantra*, although several of his assertions suggest that he considered Arunachala as the most powerful Name of God; but other instances show that this was by no means an absolute statement, as when he strongly denies that the Arunachala *mantra* might be superior to *Rāma-japa*.[13] Although he would never ask any seeker to change the form of his *japa*, he would occasionally sanction the practice of the repetition or chanting of some of his own poems on Arunachala as a most powerful form of *japa-yoga*.[14] In such instances, it appears that the fruits of the practice were considered by him to be independent from any actual mental understanding of the content of the *mantra*, or poem. At other times, though, he would provide explanations as to the symbolic linguistic meaning of a given form of *japa*, as when he assigned to both Names Rāma and Arunachala the literal meaning of 'That Thou Art.'[15] Such a theurgic comprehension of the practice is utterly foreign to any mentality that sees mental intelligibility as a prime mover of the effectiveness of spiritual practices. In other words, the 'verbal texture' of the *mantra* carries a blessing, or a spiritual 'charge' as it were, which is quite independent from its analytical meanings.[16] This sub-mental character of the *mantra* may also allow it to function as a seed that will grow when the proper inner conditions are ripe for it.

The aforementioned distinction between the 'sacramental' and 'meditational' aspects of the *mantra* should not be overemphasised, however, since the Maharshi can also allude, at times, to the identity of all practices in terms of their substantial intent and underlying power. It is therefore not so surprising that, when asked about the difference between invocation—*japa*, and meditation—*dhyāna*, the Maharshi goes sometimes so far as to deny that there is any: 'When the *japa* becomes continuous, all other thoughts cease and one is in one's real nature, which is *japa* or *dhyana*.'[17] Both *dhyāna* and *japa* can therefore be understood, in the deepest sense, as referring to the Self. *Japa* cannot be reduced to the status of a mere means, although it can function as such in many cases, and probably most; it actually coincides in its ground with Reality itself. When considering the Maharshi's statement it is important, moreover, to consider the context of his assertion. It bears stressing, first of all, that the *japa* that is referred to is brought out as a response to a question about *manasa japa*. This is literally 'mental *japa*' and not any kind of *japa;* it is therefore to be distinguished from *japa* as it is customarily understood, that is, as a vocal invocation of God or a god, in conformity with the etymological meaning of uttering or muttering. The truth is that the Hindu tradition distinguishes between a variety of *japa* practices that range from the most externalized forms, like *vachika japa* and *likhita japa*—the repetition with the voice and the repetition in writing— to the most internal, *manasa japa*—mental *japa*—and *ajapa japa*—*japa* without *japa*.[18] The latter denotes a form of invocation that is going on inwardly in a continuous way without efforts on the part of the practitioner.[19] This type of invocation lies at the point of convergence between *japa* and *dhyana*, where inner continuity of spiritual consciousness is reached.[20] In this regard it could even be said that *dhyana* is like unarticulated *japa* inasmuch as it is a mode of concentration that does not involve any utterance, while *ajapa-japa* is akin to a form of sub-conscious *dhyana* in so far as it espouses the natural rhythm of breathing. From another point of view, if *dhyana* is generally understood as an 'application of the mind', then *japa* can obviously be contemplated as a formal, verbal modality of such application. Moreover, while *japa* is generally understood and practiced as an externalized invocation, its focused interiorization opens onto *dhyana*. Sound and thought are distinct in the ways of their exteriorization, but their inmost interiorization entails their coincidence. The continuous *japa* envisaged by the Maharshi is a single stream of centered consciousness. The sage compared it at times with 'Vishnu's discus' ever spinning like an invincible weapon.[21] This *japa* is therefore to be distinguished from forms or degrees of *japa* that entail discontinuousness. Neither chanting nor writing can, for instance, realize perfect continuity; only a *japa* that is innermost to the extent that it becomes 'second nature' can be such.[22]

This important distinction is elucidated in the Sanskrit version of *Upadēśa Sāram* (The Essence of Spiritual Instruction). There, Maharshi suggests a differentiation between what could be referred to as 'bhaktic *japa*' and 'jñanic *japa*,' although such expressions are not explicitly used. The text describes a kind of gradual spiritual ascension, which is also a deeper interiorization, from religious worship to *japa* to meditation. These stages correspond to the three realities of body, speech and mind. In this view of things, worship is conceived as bodily *pūjā* before the physical representation of a divinity, *mūrti*. *Pūjā* is a highly complex ceremonial activity that involves an extremely wide array of physical actions, such as pouring milk on the deity and prostrating, and sensory components such as bell ringing and incense burning. *Japa* refers to the second type of religious practice that engages the voice, *vāc*, in the form of chanting. This is evidently a more internal type of practice inasmuch as the voice is a vibratory intermediary between the spiritual and the physical realms. In fact, this is the deepest sense of *Vāc* as primordial creative sound.[23] The third, highest, form of spiritual practice pertains to the mind, *manas*. The terms referring to it in *Upadēśa Sāram*, that is *dhyāna, cintana* and *bhāvanā,* can all be translated by meditation with slightly different inflections of meaning, the first connoting contemplation, the second consciousness, and the third the aspect of production. Now *japa* can be characterized either as external chanting or as a form of meditational activity, with a number of intermediary modes in between. The most significant point for our current purpose is the fact that the Maharshi implies a distinction between two kinds of meditation and two kinds of *japa*. In each case, what distinguishes the two forms appears to be a matter of perspective, the first being dualistic, and the second non-dualistic. Needless to say, the *Upadēśa Sāram* favors meditation that 'admits of no such difference' (*bhāvana abhedā*) over 'meditation admitting difference' (*bheda bhāvanā*). Similarly, in verse six, we read that '*japa* meditation' (*japa dhyāna*) is preferable to '*japa* done aloud' or 'in low tone.' The former only is characterized as a mode of consciousness 'which proceeds uninterruptedly like a stream of ghee or the flow of a river [that] is better than an interrupted one.'[24] Interruption is the mark, and in a way the symbol, of duality. It is therefore only when it becomes ceaseless that *japa* reaches its non-dual perfection. At this stage all differences between *dhyāna* and *japa* lose their import and meaning.

From a more relative point of view, however, the Maharshi's emphasis on the non-difference between *japa* and *dhyāna* cannot be taken too literally when considering the formal specifics of the respective spiritual practices. *A priori* at least, *japa* as a practice differs, in its modalities, from meditation, since it does not in itself involve any kind of mind activity. Other ways of understanding the Maharshi's statement, therefore, consist either in considering it as a matter of a subjective spiritual point of view or—and the two are not exclusive of one another—as a matter of guiding intent. In many cases, the Maharshi contemplates human predicaments, thoughts and practices from the vantage point of his own realization; which amounts to saying that he perceives them from the non-dual point of view of the Self, with which he is intrinsically identified. While the questions put to him by devotees most often presuppose a diversity of issues, ways and circumstances, his answers almost invariably involve a reference to the non-dual ultimacy of the Self that resolves these distinctions or oppositions. If we content ourselves with this most plausible interpretation, however, it could be argued that such abrupt reductions to the Self may not always be the most effective way to respond to the devotees' predicaments. Thus, it may appear that most interlocutors are not in a position to reach at once this highest level of consideration, not only practically— that is, from the standpoint of their actual spiritual realization—but even theoretically, for lack of information or personal resonance with non-dualistic teachings. So this must lead one to assume that there is indeed a spiritual intent behind the recurrent, consistent reduction of every question to its non-dual background. One likely interpretation would consist in considering that in doing so, the Maharshi exercised a presence of merciful comforting. Even though many interlocutors might not be able to make direct concrete use of the Maharshi's reduction of each and every problem to the Self, his doing so provides his interlocutors with a sense of relief inasmuch as the words used are in a sense nothing but the formal punctuation of an action of presence that underlies them, and is actually the main *modus operandi* of the teachings. A second type of understanding might be provided by a consideration of the function of *kōan* in Zen Buddhism. This is a way, on the part of a spiritual master, to convey the spiritual reality of his own state by means of an unsettling riddle.[25] 'Who am I?' functions as a *kōan* in the sense that it shakes up, undermines and undoes the daily, conventional, ground upon which our misperception of reality is illusorily set. Whether the devotee is ripe or not to make of this question his *viaticum,* the very raising of the question has the virtue of reorienting the search in a more central, inward, essential direction.

A most intriguing and suggestive aspect of the relationship between the *mantra* and the Self lies in a document written by the nineteenth-century British poet Alfred, Lord Tennyson. The Maharshi asked once that it be read before his devotees, and made the comment that it actually describes an experience of 'immersion in the Self.' The document is a letter Tennyson wrote to B.P. Blood, in which he describes the following experience:

> I have never had any revelations through anæsthetics, but a kind of waking trance—this for lack of a better word—I have frequently had, quite up from boyhood, when I have been all alone. This has come upon me through repeating my own name to myself silently, till all at once, as it were out of the intensity of the consciousness of individuality, individuality itself seemed to dissolve and fade away into boundless being, and this not a confused state but the clearest, the surest of the surest, utterly beyond words—where death was an almost laughable impossibility—the loss of personality (if so it were) seeming no extinction, but the only true life. I am ashamed of my feeble description. Have I not said the state is utterly beyond words?[26]

On the one hand, the experience that is here described corresponds quite accurately to the two moments of the phenomenology of spiritual recognition as envisaged by the Maharshi. These are the concentration of the sense of 'I', and then the dissolution of the 'I' in a reality that is infinitely greater than it. The other aspects of the experience that perfectly align with the Maharshi's teachings are the clarity and sense of certainty of the insight, its ineffability, and the definite sense of immortality that it entails. The clarity relates to the absence of any psychic interferences and delusions: this is not a psychological state the vagueness and inconsistency of which would betray themselves by doubts and fuzziness. It runs contrary to what is conventionally considered to be a mystical state, one in which the subjective and emotional character of the experience is highlighted. Also, it defies verbal crystallizations, precisely because it transcends any formal apprehensions. Finally, it is synonymous with immortality, not out of a sense of unending perpetuity of the experience, but by reason of the perception being grounded in a reality that lies beyond time, and that time can in no way affect. The main relevance of this testimony to our current reflections, however, pertains to the way in which the repetition of a name, akin to a *mantra*, functions. First of all, it is quite surprising, *prima facie*, to consider that an individual human name may operate in a way that is analogous to divine Names. It appears, here, that the purpose, or at least the end point, of the practice is not a way of identifying with the Ultimate, but rather an attempt at crystallizing and seizing, as it were, the reality of the 'I.' In that sense Tennyson's practice sounds analogous to the imitation of the *rigor mortis* staged by the Maharshi before his Self-realization. In both cases, the matter is to grasp the very source and substance of the personal identity, either by concentrating on its association with a given name, or by identifying that which is bound to die at the time of physical death. In both cases, as well, the result of this crystallization is actually a sort of dissolution that opens *ipso facto* on a new dimension, or rather degree, of subjectivity. In terms of a phenomenology of *japa*, Tennyson's experience is quite in keeping with the Maharshi's teachings on the way the repetition of a name or formula may help the mind focus on its inmost layer. This is quite different from, although not contrary to, those spiritual ways that see the *mantra* or *japa* as vehicles of transcendent presence, or divine grace. In other words, a form of verbal repetition, be it silent or vocal, may be only technical and instrumental, with a view to reach a higher concentration, or—and one is not necessarily exclusive of the other—the sacred means of an actualization of Reality. In Tennyson's case, it appears that the former function is at the same time connected to an insight into the non-reality of formal, verbal identifications. The name of a person is a purely conventional marker of the identity of that person, with which it has learnt to identify along the years. In that sense, it is a central locus, and in a way the symbol, of a false identification, or a limitation of consciousness. Repeating one's name while focusing on its relationship with the sense of 'I-ness' may therefore give rise to a dispelling of this misleading or limiting identification. It could be referred to as a kind of *japa* of radical undoing by contrast with the most frequent forms of *japa* which function as means of transformation by calling onto a higher or greater Reality.

There is no doubt that, for the Maharshi, the most profound and furthest reaching aspect of *japa* resides in its leading to Self-realization, indeed in its being none other than the Self. Even though it is often considered as driven by individual striving, if not as formal and quantitative in its outlook, *japa* is ultimately, or in its essence, independent from any human effort, since it is indeed the 'true nature' of the practitioner.[27] As a synthesis of the spiritual dimensions of the practice, Ramana Maharshi connects the various steps of *japa-yoga* in a way that elucidates most powerfully how a seemingly external practice opens up onto the innermost reality of the Self: 'The object of mantra *japa* is to realize that the same *japa* is already going on in oneself even without effort. The oral *japa* becomes mental and the mental *japa* finally reveals itself as being eternal. That *mantra* is the person's real nature; it is also the state of realization.'[28] *Japa* is an intermediary reality, a spiritual in-between that makes the transition from devotional duality to non-dualistic Self-realization or, from another perspective, which actualizes the supra-formal and non-dual Self 'from within' the formal Name. Thus, the deepest reality of *japa* has nothing to do with the individual effort to articulate the invocation, whether vocally or mentally. The Self, which is *a priori* the object of the invocation in the objectified form of the Lord, is ultimately realized to be the very subject of the utterance. This is the hidden secret of the invocation, and the true nature of the Self.

4

SELF-REALIZATION AND TRADITION

One of Ramana Maharshi's apparent paradoxes—'apparent' because ultimately resolved in the unity of the Self—is the conjunction of his unmistakably Hindu background and sensibility and the non-traditional, or rather supra-traditional, mode of his spiritual realization and teachings. Most volumes devoted to the Maharshi outside of India have tended to emphasise the latter; and it is no doubt the most fascinating aspect of his spiritual destiny and personality, and that which makes him a universal sage in the fullest sense of the term. His awakening comes the closest to what some have referred to as a 'pure consciousness event', seemingly independent as it is from any external conditionings.[1] Understood this way Ramana Maharshi is probably the least Hindu of all Hindu sages, although this may make him also, from another point of view, the most Hindu, to the extent precisely that Hinduism is contemplated as pointing toward that what lies beyond its formal definitions.[2] The inward orientation of the Hindu tradition, particularly in the Vedāntic teachings on the Self, runs parallel to a motion toward universality that sometimes ends up transcending the confines of the formal tradition. Although this paradox is also at work in other religious traditions, by virtue of the very logic of transcendence, it is arguably nowhere as pregnant as in Hinduism. There is little doubt that Ramana Maharshi embodies one of the most representative modes of this paradox.

Thomas Forsthoefel has suggested that the Maharshi is representative of the 'internalist' thrust of mysticism, while not being utterly independent, at least extrinsically, from the 'externalist' logic of the formal determinants of culture and religion. On the one hand, the Maharshi's experience of recognition of the Self was, at least *prima facie*, a purely internal process. On the other hand, it can be argued that external constituents contributed significantly to shaping the formulation, conveyance, and assimilation by others, of his Self-realization.[3] Without espousing the constructionist interpretation of those who see mysticism as informed through and through by the external and cultural categories that are available to the mystic, Forsthoefel acknowledges that 'although in a given epistemological framework internalism may be dominant, it is in the end insufficient in itself. [...] No matter how relativized the external mechanisms may be, internalism cannot function without them.'[4] Thus, for Forsthoefel, even though the Maharshi clearly 'privileged' internalism, he also 'appropriated,' 'defined,' 'relativized' and 'did accord provisional value' to external phenomena and processes of which he availed himself, drawing from various strands of the tradition. In this regard, one first point to highlight—it has already been touched upon in Chapter One, the biographical chapter—is the Brahmanical background of Venkataraman. This family context lent the young Ramana a degree of familiarity with beliefs and practices that could not but provide him with religious categories of experience together with a conceptual language. From a Hindu point of view, one must also assume that, irrespective of his immersion in a traditional ambience, the Self-realization of the Maharshi was the result of individual and collective karmic determinations.[5] In this regard, two sets of considerations must be developed. The first one is that the experience of Self-realization was, in the case of Ramana, as close as can be to not being determined, in its inner actualization, from any external religious influences. According to the Maharshi's own testimony, at no time and in no way were the fear of death and the Self-inquiry that ensued experienced in any traditional terms or couched in religious forms. If there were external elements involved, it was only in the ways of an 'identification' of the experience, and its interpretation in the terms made available by the tradition.[6] As for the traditional context that provided the ambience in which the experience unfolded, it was, as Forsthoefer judiciously notes, both 'relativized' and granted provisional and pedagogical worth and effectiveness. One must therefore distinguish between the intrinsic dimension of the realization and its extrinsic modes of expression on the one hand, and, on the other hand, between the relativization of traditional norms and ways from the point of view of the ultimate inner Reality and their integration from the vantage point of spiritual opportuneness. These various angles of approach must neither be confused nor disconnected from each other.

The Hindu tradition presents us with an articulation of the spiritual goal of *moksha*, or spiritual liberation from all conditionings, and a normative social order that is conceived as providing the collective and individual means most conducive to reaching this liberation. These means include the system of the four *varnas* and the four *āshramas,* as well as a host of other institutions and practices. The *āshramas,* or 'goals of life', provide a normative pattern that regulates the existence in a four-fold manner: *kama* or pleasure; *artha* or good; *dharma* or duty; and *moksha* or liberation. Each of these *āshramas* is normatively devoted to one of the primary aspects of human life, such as study, the foundation of a family, and gradual or radical withdrawal from domestic, professional and social duties. The conventional understanding of the four stages of life, *brahmacharya*, or celibacy and study; *grihastha*, or family life; *vānaprastha*, retired life; and *samnyāsa*, renunciation, can lead to consider them as imperative discharges of social duties that may be incompatible with the requirements of the search for the Self. In fact, the ordinary consideration of the four *āshramas* as constituting a necessary sequence invites one to see the two final stages, and particularly *samnyāsa*, as specifically related to *moksha*. Contemplated from a traditional point of view, that is to say in view of the preservation of structures and ways of life that condition the very existence and permanence of society, there is a need to preserve an equilibrium between the thisworldly and otherworldly dimensions of existence. One way this is achieved is by situating the full development of the spiritual vocation as the final phase of one's terrestrial career.

When asked once by a lawyer which was his among the four *āshramas*, Ramana Maharshi responded: 'I am in the *ativarnāsrama* [...] This transcends the other *āshramas*.' Among the latter, the two last stages, *vānaprastha*, a time of transitional spiritual retirement from the world (symbolically equated with periods of dwelling in the forest and gradual relinquishment of family and social responsibilities to others), and *samnyāsa*, the final 'status of non-status' of the renunciate, are characterized by an increasing existential focus on *moksha*. Beyond these *āshramas*, the *ativarna*, the one 'without color', is identified with the pristine condition of the *Satya Yuga*, the first age of the cycle during which humans were spontaneously in a state of blissful union with the *Brahman*. What characterizes this state is the absence of religion as a code of behavior. Religious prescriptions presuppose a loss of the metaphysical unity of the origin since they are commanded in view of facilitating a reintegration therein. According to the Maharshi, 'the *ativarnāsrama* is without any rules.'[7] This means that *ativarna* is both the centre and goal of the religious universe, while being at the same time situated outside of it. This is the function of the fifth element beyond the four states. Even the fourth stage, *samnyāsa*, still participates in the traditional formal system, since it is defined in relation to the three earlier stages. It has no meaning except relative to them: to be a renunciate means to renounce all social status. The *samnyāsin* is, in that sense, the last component of a normative, ideal, sequence. By contrast, the *ativarna* does not belong to a series; he actually precedes or transcends, depending on the point of view, all socio-religious position. To speak of the Maharshi as a *samnyāsin* is therefore symbolically meaningful while being traditionally meaningless. From the first point of view, the young Ramana did indeed renounce the world in the sense that he shunned any status in it. However, his path did not conform to the pattern of socio-spiritual development that is typical of traditional Hinduism. The young Ramana did not renounce the world out of a desire of his own, or in search of a spiritual realization that would be dependent upon *samnyāsa*. The duties and values of the world dropped down of their own, as it were, as a consequence of Self-realization. As a result, the Maharshi's spiritual destiny is no more intelligible chronologically than it is so traditionally. On the other hand, his Self-realization is metaphysically comprehensible, since the universal immanence of the Self makes it evidently possible that it be consciously actualized, at least in principle, at any point of the samsāric circumference.

These extraordinary circumstances present us with a number of questions as to the relationship between the Hindu tradition and the Maharshi's realization and presence. As a starting point, it is quite plausible to consider Ramana Maharshi as a Hindu mystic, and it is even factually obvious, while being potentially misleading. Technically and culturally Ramana did uncontestably belong to the Hindu world, and the scriptural and spiritual references by which he shed light on his spiritual realization were for the most part issued from the traditional treasury of Hindu wisdom. He spent his whole life mostly surrounded by Hindu practitioners and seekers with whom he shared religious symbols and traditional values. It is, however, all too clearly evident that the Self-realization that he reached and taught transcended infinitely any formal system of thought or belief. In that sense, it could be said that Hinduism provided him with a contemplative ambience, and *Advaita Vedānta* with a conceptual lexicon. His relationship with the former was multilayered and circumstantiated. His position in regard to the latter was both deeply consonant and pedagogically flexible. As was indicated in the introduction of this book, Ramana Maharshi's perspective is akin to the school of *Advaita Vedānta*, but this correlation is only *a posteriori*, since the Maharshi made use of Advaitin sources to describe his Self-realization; he made their tenets explicit without having adhered to them prior to his spiritual breakthrough.[8] Thus, his repeated references to the *Ribhu Gītā*, a song that is part of the *Śiva Rahasya Purāṇa*, was instrumental, but only *a posteriori*, in the Maharshi's presentation of the tenets of Self-realization.[9] This Śivaite text, which consists in a dialogue between two sages, Ribhu and Nidagha, must have particularly appealed to the Maharshi on account of its being centered on *sahaja samadhi*, the state of Self-realized maturity in which the unity of consciousness does not interfere with, but indeed integrates, the manifold of daily experience.[10] Interestingly, the Maharshi considered that the very recitation of this song could lead to Self-realization, thereby privileging the sacramental and transformative power of the text over its conceptual contents.[11] With regard to the latter, the language of Advaita was made available to the Maharshi through contact with scholars such as Ganapati Muni and Kapali Shastri. We have to assume, therefore, that the adequation between the experience—or rather the new mode of consciousness—and the metaphysical vocabulary of *Advaita* was spontaneously recognized by Ramana as effective, if only pedagogically or from the instrumental point of view of transmission. The verification of such an adequation is of course impossible from the outside, since it would presuppose that one be able to grasp the inner correlation of the traditional language itself with the experience to which it points, while being capable to claim an insight into the inner reality of the Maharshi himself. It may suffice to say that the civilizational availability, in India, of a language deemed appropriate by the Maharshi to translate his mode of consciousnesss is in itself a remarkable fact. Had the same spiritual realization taken place in another religious context, it would have been instructive to consider the ways in which other languages might, or might not, have been able to provide a satisfactory metaphysical idiom for it. At any rate, the fact that the Maharshi made use, occasionally, of religious vocabularies other than that of *Advaita*—as has already been mentioned—demonstrates the contingent dimension of terminology from his point of view. This implies that the use of words to convey inner realities must be informed by a particular semantic intent, and no doubt also by a mode of spiritual presence that allows these words to vibrate spiritually, as it were. Short of this intent, and short of the realizational perspective that animates it, the same words or sentences may evoke representations and realities of an altogether different nature. Moreover, this observation raises the question of the plurivocity of words even within a single system such as *Advaita*. The word *Māyā*, for instance, can accrue a wide spectrum of meanings in various schools and authors, and sometimes within the same text.[12] Be that as it may, the extreme diversity and fluidity of the lexical range called upon by the Maharshi is a clear indication of the allusive and symbolic character of his verbal teachings, as well as a further evidence of the supereminence of silence in his eyes.

Another unusual aspect of the Maharshi's vocation was his pathless inner realization. In a traditional Hindu context, Self-realization is taught to be the end of a *sādhanā,* or spiritual way, walked under the spiritual guidance of a *guru.* The Maharshi made it clear that he never followed any *sādhanā*, and did not even know what a *sādhanā* was.[13] When asked who was his *guru*, he replied: 'There is neither *guru* nor disciple to me.' And pressed to recognize that no spiritual realization can be achieved without *guru* and being asked the same question again, he simply answered: 'For me the Self itself is the *Guru*.'[14] His realization was totally independent from any path, as well as from any particular lineage. One finds examples of such unmediated realization in some other spiritual traditions. In Sufism there is a distinction, in particular, that closely echoes the difference between a *sādhaka* and one who is completely independent from any *sādhanā*. This is the distinction between the *sālik*, or traveler, who follows the specific injunctions of a spiritual way under the guidance of a *shaykh*, and the *majdhūb*, the 'one attracted' by God, whose spiritual progress is purely the result of Divine grace. The first modality is gradual and proceeds through a variety of spiritual stages that are seen as connected, although not conditioned, by the efforts of the spiritual traveler, whereas the second is sudden and completely independent from human efforts. Because he has not trodden a spiritual path, and is therefore inexperienced in its various stages and pitfalls, the *majdhūb* is normally unqualified to provide spiritual guidance to others.[15] Now the case of the Maharshi is analogous in this respect, in that his awakening was characterized by its suddenness and its lack of connection with any spiritual transmission or prior spiritual exercise.

While the central character of the Maharshi's teaching is to emphasise Self-investigation and the abiding in the Self, it is also the most synthetic way to express the relationship between the Maharshi's perspective and the Hindu tradition. This point of view is not new in the context of Hinduism, which tends toward synthesis, interiorization and universalization. It is to be found, for instance, in the *Ribhu Gītā*, the aforementioned two-thousand-verse text that forms the sixth part of the *Śiva Rahasya Purāna*, which Ramana used to consider one of the most fruitful readings for spiritual seekers, and to which he refers in his *Talks*.[16] In it the essence of all religious practices is ultimately identified with Self-realization:

> The rock-firm conviction of 'I am the Self' is the sure mark of firm abidance in the Self. Abidance in that conviction under all conditions is true divine worship, meditation on God, incantation of *mantras*, practice of right conduct in life, contemplation, integral yoga, wisdom of the Self and *moksha* as well.[17]

This supremely synthetic perspective summarizes the Maharshi's point of view and constitutes the primary evidence of what in his traditional spiritual outlook is decidedly trans-traditional.

While often referring to the intellectual traditions of Hinduism in order to respond to questions or illustrate his teachings, the Maharshi emphasised that theoretical elaborations run the risk of obfuscating that which they are expected to elucidate. Although he himself delved into doctrinal matters and demonstrated a magisterial command of the Hindu traditional teachings that he discovered only in the wake of his realization, he clearly favored synthesis and simplicity. The Self is simple, and It is the Essence of everything to Which everything returns. The Maharshi recognizes that, by contrast with this evident simplicity of the Self, the non-Self is indeed a principle of complexity.[18] This situates him, paradoxically, in the tradition of *Advaita*, since the latter recognizes that it is not *Ātman* that is difficult to comprehend, but rather *Māyā; Māyā* which, according to Shankara, is incomprehensible, by contrast with the blinding evidence of *Ātman*.

Aside from enlightening concepts of *Advaita* or being illustrated by them, the synthetic perspective of the realized Self allows Ramana Maharshi to tackle foundational problems of theology with an inimitable freshness of insight. This appears, for instance, in his response to a question on the perennial issue of the tension between free will and predestination. Typically, the Maharshi's answer does not enter the conceptual complexity of the issue, but transcends it operatively: 'Self-knowledge is beyond Will and Fate.'[19] The Self lies beyond any individual understanding of the chain of phenomena and beyond any power of the will. It is identified with pure Will, Divine All-Possibility, and pure Fate, pure Necessity; in it, therefore, the sense of being the 'doer' disappears, and so do the constraints of any 'external' reality. Fate presupposes a necessity that weighs extrinsically upon the will, but the Self is none other than the Infinite Will, and nothing can determine That which alone is. There is, therefore, no duality between fate and will, since the point of view from which the latter arises vanishes in the Self. This example illustrates the way in which the Maharshi's focus on Self-knowledge tends to undercut the philosophical and theological elaborations of the tradition.

At times, however, the sage consents to delve analytically into distinctions that may have some pedagogical or provisional value for given devotees. In response to a question about the specific location of the will, the Maharshi refers to the *vijñana-māyā-kosha* 'where the conscious individual wills and determines.'[20] This 'wisdom sheath' is sometimes identified with *buddhi*, or the intellect; it is the fourth of the five *koshas* that envelop the *Ātman*. In the case of the *jīvan-mukta*, this intellective layer of consciousness is not tainted with any sense of illusory autonomy. It is conscious of itself within the immanent Self, as it were, and does not 'think of itself' as the ultimate agency of volitions and actions. There exists, therefore, an individual stratum of the will, but it is free from any sense of being the 'doer,' and exempt of any consideration of expected fruits and fixed plans.[21] So the negation of the will's autonomy does not amount to negating the individual layer of consciousness, which must perforce function relatively, outside of 'non-qualified enstatic absorption in the Self', *nirvikalpa-samadhi*. It is a situation that is analogous to abandoning oneself to the flow of a current. This self-abandonment does not presuppose a total absence of individual consciousness and volition, but it involves unity with the deeper layer of reality and consciousness that underlies all human thoughts and endeavors. Thus, such conceptual distinctions on the part of the Maharshi, while remaining connected to the ultimate reality of Self-knowledge, do draw from the intellectual treasury of the Advaitin tradition in order to address the needs of causality of specific seekers.

By and large, however, there is in Ramana Maharshi's teachings a clear relativization, or even at times dismissal—as the case may be, in response to a perceived mental hypertrophy on the part of particular seekers—of the doctrinal universe of discourse, whether traditional or not. The essence of realization is *mauna,* inner silence, and this realization can be best communicated through the quality of speechless presence flowing from it. Accordingly, when considering a program of lectures on the occasion of the Golden Jubilee celebrations of 1 September 1946, the Maharshi could not but express dissatisfaction at the mental and verbal excesses it involved: 'Oh, what a crowded programme! [...] It is stated that all these big people will deliver lectures! What about? What is there to speak about? That which is, is *mouna* [silence]. How can *mouna* be explained in words?'[22] For the Maharshi, it was therefore quite clear that tradition could be reduced to silence. Such silence, however, does not amount to a mere absence of words, but conveys, rather, the underlying, essential, content of all words. It is unspoken language pregnant with meaning—ultimate and universal meaning. Hence, the ultimate goal and realization of the entire tradition is designated by the term *muni,* the spiritually perfected human being akin to the *jīvan-mukta,* the delivered soul, with the term *muni* being akin to *mauna,* silence. [23]

This emphasis on the inarticulated core of the spiritual meaning is, on some level, one of the reasons for the measure of tension that characterizes the relationship between the Maharshi's teachings and the intellectual and spiritual edifice of the Hindu tradition. Hinduism, like any other tradition, has to take into account the extreme diversity of means and points of reference, not to mention the fact that it has to undergo the organic growth of its intellectual and spiritual possibilities. Moreover, its implications are not strictly spiritual, but they include a wide array of civilizational concerns. In keeping with these imperatives and conditionings, the tradition cannot but involve a rich, almost dizzying, array of analytical developments. By contrast, Ramana Maharshi's outlook is characterized by extreme simplicity and relentless single-mindedness, as it is entirely centered on Self-recognition. This spiritual 'pragmatism' tends to shun everything that does not directly relate to the latter; and there is little doubt that this characteristic of the Maharshi's personality and teachings resonates with the historical and cultural context of the present time; one that is characterized by the collapse of traditional structures and the demise of the intellectual framework of most religious traditions.

In this regard, Ramana Maharshi's stand vis-à-vis the tradition is to some extent reminiscent of the Buddha's ways. In both cases, the subjective and methodical focus of the perspective cuts short the metaphysical and cosmological elaborations of the tradition.[24] One must recall, in this connection, that the Buddha refused to answer fourteen metaphysical and eschatological questions, which he deemed irrelevant to the realization of *Nirvāna.* These questions relate to the nature of the world in time and space, the relationship between body and selfhood, and the *post mortem* destiny of the one who has reached *Nirvāna.* The Buddha's silence particularly applies to eschatological questions, which are considered to be misleading with respect to the actual goal of life, whether or not they are considered to actually have an answer.[25] We find the same pedagogical pattern in the Maharshi's teachings. The sage repeatedly calls into question the legitimacy and urgency of many of the questions that are put to him. For him, too, eschatological concerns were something he often deemed detracting to seekers from Self-realization here and now. A focus on one's future destiny is for him a way to escape the present reality of the Self.

Although his relationship with the world of Hinduism could obviously not be equated with the Buddha's, since it involved neither metaphysical controversies nor any attempt at initiating a new spiritual way, Ramana Maharshi's perspective has not been without eliciting some critiques from Hindu traditionalists and reformists alike. From the point of view of the traditional path of *Advaita Vedānta*, the Maharshi's perspective is deemed to involve some substantial flaws. The emphasis he places on Self-inquiry as the primary means of realization is not actually recognized by orthodox Advaitins as being a traditional path of access to *Ātman*. According to traditional *Vedānta*, Self-inquiry in and of itself cannot be a sufficient methodical means of dispelling ignorance concerning the Self. The traditional seeker is not considered as an independent human being who could discover the Self by introspection through his or her own means. Self-realization presupposes all the qualifications and pre-requisites that are enumerated by Vedāntic sages such as Shankara and Sureśvara. The audition of scriptures, the practice of moral and yogic virtues and the sitting at the feet of an enlightenment *guru* are all outer and inner preconditions for which no effort of spiritual inquiry can substitute. This is not to say that Ramana Maharshi dismisses these mediations, however, but he does not make them explicit pre-requisites to Self-inquiry. One major qualification to this observation lies in his intermittent references to implicit moral and spiritual predispositions for the path of Self-knowledge. The latter are characteristic of the person 'whose mind has been purified through *upasana* and other means or by merit acquired in past lives, who perceives the imperfections of the body and sense-objects, and feels utter distaste whenever his mind has to function among sense-objects and who realises that the body is impermanent.'[26] Such important mentions provide a functional equivalent to the Advaitin enumeration of the six moral qualities, *shatsampat*, that serve as the foundations for Self-realization, namely *sama* or equanimity; *dama* or temperance; *uparati* or dispassion; *titiksā* or endurance; *śraddhā* or faith; and *samādhāna* or concentration. A second qualification lies in the fact that the Maharshi retains the grace of the *guru* as an imperative, while putting emphasis on the fact that the *guru* is first of all an inner reality. On this question, the difficulty lies, as I have suggested earlier, in the distinction between the traditional and technical definition of the *guru*, and its purely spiritual acceptation. Ramana Maharshi was considered as a *satguru* by his devotees, but he did not function as a *guru* in the Hindu technical sense of the term. He did not belong to a lineage, nor did he transmit formal initiation, or *diksha,* or any mantra.[27] With respect to the function of *guru,* he seemed to have held a vision that was traditional in its references and religious context but supra-traditional in its spirit. His advice was not to 'cling to the form of the *Guru,* for this will perish', not to 'cling to his feet for his attendants will stop you.'[28] The human, formal and institutional supports of the tradition are needed, and they transmit values that are irreplaceable, but contemplating their integral spiritual meaning requires that one not be attached to them in a way that would obstruct the path or distract one from its destination. Thus, the human form of the *guru* must not be confused with the 'true Bhagavān' who 'resides in your Heart as your own Self.'[29] As for the reference to the 'attendants', it subtly alludes to the fact, which is universally recognized, that the radiation of a spiritual luminary is necessarily surrounded by a collective human ambience and context that can all too often function as a veil or a barrier. This is also a more general metaphor of the human dimension of tradition, with its complexities, ambiguities and pitfalls.

Arthur Osborne was particularly intent on elucidating the nature of the *guru,* as he came to the Maharshi with a background informed by the works of René Guénon. The French metaphysician had written extensively on the nature of initiation and the need for a spiritual master, and had unequivocally made those imperative preconditions for spiritual realization. The fact that the Maharshi ostensibly never claimed the status of a *guru* and appeared to deny he had disciples presents us, therefore, with an interrogation. Now Osborne sees the Maharshi's apparent denegation as a kind of filtering that allowed him to keep at bay the mass of devotees that would have otherwise flocked to him in search of an initiation. Osborne argues that 'when asked whether he gave initiation Sri Bhagavan always avoided a direct answer,' which can be interpreted as a way of answering the question on a higher level, one which transcends the formal domain of tradition.[30] The main point in Osborne's argument is that Ramana Maharshi was indeed a *guru*; a *guru* who transmitted initiation and guiding instruction, *upadeśa,* but that he was so in a purely supra-formal way. *Advaita* highlights that one of the qualifications of the *guru* is that he must have realized *Ātman.* Although this is ultimately the most intrinsic characteristic of the *guru*, it is not the only one, as has been mentioned in a previous chapter. We are confronted, therefore, with two understandings of the *guru*. While the traditional view is, in a way, analytic and pedagogical—in the highest sense of the term—the second understanding bypasses institutional requirements and contextual needs to focus exclusively on the synthetic quality of being, *sat*, that is the essence of the *guru*, being the very nature of the Self. There remain, therefore, the questions of the initiation and that of the method. Here also the meaning of these terms can be taken differently. Osborne is adamant that the Maharshi did initiate some of his devotees, but that he did so according to informal modalities, whether through gazing into their eyes, or simply through silence, or else in a dream.[31] This was especially the case in relation to those of his devotees whom he considered most mature spiritually, and inclined toward *vichāra*. Several accounts, including Osborne's itself, have been provided to illustrate this point.[32] In fact, this supraformal mode of passing on a spiritual influence would correspond to the Maharshi's explicitly claimed status of *ativarnāśramī*, that is beyond castes, referring thereby also to the pristine perfection of the *Satya Yuga*, the 'Age of Being', in which no forms were needed.

As for the teaching, or *upadēśa*, it must be noted that the Maharshi actually wrote an essential text of instruction entitled *Upadēśa Sāram*, the 'essence of all instructions.' This work is probably the most important among all of the sage's writings, in terms of enlightening the relationship between his teachings and the ways of traditional Hinduism. The *Upadēśa Sāram* was originally written in Tamil under the title *Upadēśa Undiyār* and was first intended to be part of a longer work by Sri Muruganar. This work consists in a narration from the *Śiva Purāna* in which a group of sages, upon failing to reach Self-realization and following a war against Śiva, finally realized the identity of the god and begged him to provide teachings that would convey the synthetic essence of all spiritual methods. Muruganar wrote seventy verses and asked Ramana Maharshi to write the last thirty verses, which constitute *Upadēśa Sāram*. Subsequently Ramana Maharshi wrote Sanskrit, Telugu and Malayalam versions of the texts, with slight variations in relation to the original, particularly in the Malayalam form.[33] The essential and synthetic character of the text, and its direct connection with Śiva, the god who burns forms, is already indicative of the dual status of the teachings in relation to traditional ways. It demonstrates the latter's effectiveness by reference to their ultimate goal and destination, while transcending them, precisely, through its quintessential character. By contrast with other texts such as *Who am I?*,

Upadēśa Sāram situates Self-inquiry in a sequence of traditional practices that leads to abiding in the Self. Therein, the way of *karma-yoga* and *bhakti-yoga* appear as paving the ground for the ultimate, jñanic, dimension of the path. It is remarkable that the text opens on a consideration of action and *karma* and the ordainment of God, which means that it takes as starting point the realm of lesser reality that is the initial and immediate experience of human beings in their state of ignorance. It is from this elementary level that the mind must be first purified through the practice of God-centered and egoless actions. Religious duties form a second stage that leads the worshipper to a deeper and deeper consciousness of the source of being, which is the essence of *karma, bhakti,* and *jñāna.* This graduated vision of spiritual awakening can lead us to conclude that the Maharshi's perspective was not without integrating the domain of tradition as a preparatory stage for Self-knowledge. This has led David Frawley to caution that 'today, too many people, particularly those following recent instant enlightenment approaches, have portrayed Ramana as rejecting tradition.' Furthermore, Frawley considers that 'they may present Ramana as teaching that anyone can gain realization directly without any stages, purification practices, or any *sādhanā* at all, which they portray as not only useless but also misleading diversions,' while concluding that 'such people assume that by merely thinking they are the Self, without actually giving up the ego or removing their sense of bodily attachment, they can truly realize the Self, or even teach it to others.'[34] In this regard, the atypical status of the Maharshi has given rise, after his death, to the emergence of neo-Advaitin figures and movements claiming the sage's spiritual heritage. The Maharshi never affirmed being the originator of an initiatory lineage; quite to the contrary, as has already been mentioned, he himself denied being a link in any chain of spiritual transmission. However, such claims have come from neo-Advaitin figures who consider the Maharshi as their teacher and prime reference through the intermediary of one of the most influential devotees of Ramana, Sri Poonja, also known as Papaji. Papaji was a Punjabi sage who lived from 1910 to 1997 and reported having had determining spiritual experiences in the presence of Ramana Maharshi. Although he seemed to have had initially the dispositions of a *bhakta*, Sri Poonja ultimately realized, upon the intent gaze of the Maharshi, 'that this man who had spoken to me (the Maharshi) was, in reality, what I already was, what I had always been.'[35] The apparent simplicity and directness of the Maharshi's approach has led some to become identified, or to identify themselves, most often in the wake of Papaji's teachings, as Ramana's spiritual continuators. Taking stock of the sage's emphasis on the supra-formal dimension of Self-realization, such self-styled gurus have tended to disassociate spiritual liberation from any traditional, intellectual and spiritual mediations.[36] In this regard, one of the major aspects of most if not all Neo-Advaitin teachers lies in their claim that the Self is already realized, an elliptical statement that may correspond to reality from an ultimate point of view but, if taken at face value, begs the question of the need and nature of spiritual seeking. Hence, Arthur Versluis' felicitous reference to Neo-Advaita as a form of 'immediatism'.[37] The whole Neo-Advaitin method consists in rejecting, independently from any context or practices, the erroneous notion that one is. Thus, neo-Advaitin Jean Klein opines that 'fundamentally, you are nothing, but you are not aware of this and project energy in seeking what you are'. He goes on writing that 'when, by self-inquiry, you find out that the meditator does not exist, all activity becomes pointless and you come to a state of non-attaining, an openness to the unknowable.'[38] Although the literality of such a statement could very well parallel some of the Maharshi's own teachings, it must be emphasized that the latter are always provided as provisional pointers that draw most if not all of their effectiveness from the place of presence and realization from which they proceed. In other words, the context and the spiritual presence of the sage is herein everything, or almost everything.

By contrast with these 'immediatist' shortcuts ostensibly exclusive of any 'practices', the relationship between the three traditional paths of *karma*, *bhakti* and *jñāna* that is envisaged by the Maharshi is integrative in the highest sense; it is both inclusive and centered on the highest meaning of *jñāna* as Self-realization. In his selection and brief commentary of some verses on the *Bhagavad Gītā*, as in *Upadeśa Sāram*, Ramana Maharshi exposes the relationship between the three ways in demonstrating their unity from the point of view of *Ātmanishtha*, or abiding in the Self.[39] First of all, the synthetic identity of *jñāna* and *bhakti* is based on the principle that 'God is verily the Self.'[40] This means, on the one hand, that *jñāna* is none other than *bhakti*, and, on the other hand, that the fundamental impulse and realization of *bhakti* leads to perfect *jñāna*. The first principle appears in the statement that 'attunement to the Self [...] is but devotion to the Lord.'[41] Since the Self is God, or *Ātman* is *Brahman*, it follows that the dedication to the Self is inherently a dedication to God, and it cannot but entail, therefore, the grace of the 'constant and unfailing protection of the Lord.'[42] In this way of considering matters, *jñāna* is an implicit, perhaps even unarticulated, *bhakti*. The subsequent idea that 'the Lord (...) loves the *jñānī* as dearly as the *jñānī* loves Him' has indeed something ill-sounding when considered from a purely bhaktic perspective.[43] This is inasmuch as the latter would hardly express the relationship between God and the human being in a way that would indicate equality, as in 'as dearly as.' The *bhakta* considers himself as a lover or as a servant, and in either case, with different emphasis, the Lord must retain a position of eminence without which the bhaktic impulse would lack its fuel, as it were. By contrast, the *bhakti* of the *jñāna*, if one may say so, leads to the recognition of Unity that entails in some sense *equality*. Obviously, the term equality is somewhat ill fitting here since it presupposes two terms, whereas the jñanic perspective is radically non-dual. When the Maharshi states that, in *jñāna*, the quality and intensity of the love of man for God is equal to that of the love of God for man, he clearly suggests that this love is the same current of *ānanda* or bliss that characterizes the non-dual *Ātman*. This idea is based on verse VII:17 of the *Bhagavad Gītā,* which has, interestingly, a less 'equalizing' view of *bhakti* than one may be led to believe when reading the Maharshi's commentary: 'The man of wisdom (*jñāni*), eternally steadfast, devoted to the One alone, is preeminent. I am indeed exceedingly fond (*atyartham, priyas*) of the man of wisdom, and he is fond of Me.'[44] Ramana Maharshi identifies the *jñāni* with the Self, which means in a sense that the Lord as Self loves the sage as much as the sage as Self loves the Lord. This is 'a sage who, taking refuge in the Lord's omnipresence, sees the oneness of transcendantal Being within himself and in all existence without.'[45]

As for *karma*, to abide in *Ātman* cancels out the very dichotomy between acting and non-acting, work and non-work. This is because what matters is not the phenomenon of action, or the lack thereof, but rather the sense of identity of the 'doer.' When the sense of the ego as being the doer has vanished through jñanic discernment, there is literally no other doer, or *karta*, than the Self. This is the reason why *karma* is never in itself an obstacle to the path of *jñāna,* and this is also why the Maharshi, by contrast with traditional *Advaita*, does not prescribe, or even prioritize, an outer retreat from the world. From the point of view of the Self nothing can come in the way of the Self, while from the standpoint of the action *per se* its performance is simply perceived as being a necessity resulting from the past, accumulated, *karma*, or *prārabdha*. This process is akin to a mechanical exhaustion that does not involve the egoic agency as its principle.[46]

Even though *jñāna* constitutes the essential synthesis of other paths, which it therefore contains, it also remains fundamentally distinct from *bhakti* and *karma* in the sense of being exclusive, in its substance, of will and action.

The realization of *jñāna* is incompatible with a spiritual life that would be centered on any kind of individual desire or striving.[47] It is according to this point of view that *Upadēśa Sāram* explicitly teaches that the scrutiny of the mind that results in the latter's disappearance into the true Self is 'the direct means to experience true self-knowledge.'[48] This path is, in principle, open to all (in the Tamil text *ārkkum* means 'for all'), even though it has been asserted by the sage that it is, in fact, only accessible to those who have already reached a sufficient spiritual maturity. The non-traditional point of view adopted by virtue of the direct path, and its transcendence vis-à-vis all forms and means, corresponds both to the actual experience of Ramana, independently of any *sādhanā*, and to the metaphysical status of the Self as the ever present and effulgent Reality.

Although traditionalist critiques of Ramana Maharshi's teachings from an Advaitin point of view are hardly found in print, and do not seem to call into question the authenticity of his Self-realization, they do highlight the ways Ramana Maharshi tended to extract or isolate the core content of spiritual liberation from its traditional prerequisites and concomitants. In doing so, he also parallels some aspects of the Buddha's teachings, to the extent that the latter severed the core spiritual awakening that is the essence and goal of Hindu *sādhanās* from the concepts and forms in which Hinduism had enshrined them. The experiential and 'subjective' point of view is privileged in both cases. Thus, Arvind Sharma defines the Maharshi's approach as 'experiential *Advaita*', to distinguish it from Shankaran *Advaita*, which is scriptural and intellectual in its foundations.[49] From a traditional point of view the expression 'experiential *Advaita*' is problematic, however, in the sense that it implies a possible distinction, or even disconnection, within the tradition between theory and practice. Such a disconnection does not only open the door to a dismissal of theory in the name of realization, but it also misses the point that Advaitin theory is not theoretical in the usual sense of the term since it is predicated on a metaphysical *reality* of being.

In terms of the Maharshi's standing in relation to traditional institutions, S.S. Cohen recalls how Ramana Maharshi presided over the traditional rites of consecration of the temple of Mathrubhuteswara, which was erected over the remains of Ramana's mother, Alagammal. It took place in March 1949 and was attended by the Shankarāchārya of Puri, one of the successors of Ādi Shankarāchārya. On this occasion the Shankarāchārya sat on the floor on the left of Ramana Maharshi, who was sitting on an armchair.[50] This fact bears witness to the recognition of the spiritual authority of the Maharshi on the part of one belonging to the traditional lineage of the most orthodox Advaitin tradition. Moreover, the respective physical situation of the Maharshi and the Shankarāchārya can be read as symbolic of a subordination of traditional authority to realized knowledge, at least from a certain vantage point. Finally, the rite of consecration culminated when the Maharshi himself was led to the innermost temple and asked to place his hand on the Śiva lingam.[51]

Now the Maharshi's emphasis on the 'directness' of Self-inquiry by contrast with all other paths, which he deemed to be indirect, flows from the observation that other *sādhanās* presuppose the ego that the *Ātmā-vichāra* aims at dissolving.[52] In other words, the reason why the Maharshi holds Self-inquiry as direct is that it addresses in priority the very source of error and misery. From this point of view all other paths function as mere 'ruses' with the ego by leading indirectly and gradually to its final demise. Although the Maharshi is keen on affirming that all paths ultimately lead to the Self, what matters for him above all is to convey the highest, most complete, view of Reality and Consciousness, irrespective of the actual karmic abilities of those who receive the teaching. His was the intent to devotees that they must not 'waste time' and need to center or re-center their path on the Self.[53] This view might also be predicated on the assumption that those, presumably the majority, who are not qualified for Self-inquiry will not resolve to engage in it anyway. They will choose a path that is more consonant with their capacity and tendencies. This is especially true in a Hindu context, in which the multiplicity of paths of predilection and qualifying predispositions are integral parts of the economy of the tradition. The same is far from being as likely, however, in Western contexts, in which all kinds of predeterminations may lead seekers to turn to Self-inquiry out of a misguided disdain for other paths, or even out a subtle individualistic presumption. Be that as it may, it can be envisioned that in cases where the recipient is not ripe for Self-inquiry, its prioritization might at any rate plant the seed for future karmic cultivation. All things considered, the Maharshi's function could be characterized as that of a universal *satguru* whose light shines on all, rather than as a traditional *guru* whose teachings are aligned with the specific needs of disciples.

While traditional reservations vis-à-vis the Maharshi's perspective gravitate around the modalities of his way to Self-realization, representatives of modern trends in Hinduism have tended to direct their criticism, for their part, at the uncompromisingly inward-looking focus of the Maharshi. It is quite ironic, in this regard, that the height of the Maharshi's spiritual influence in India and the world coincided with the decades during which Indians were most actively concerned with their political fight against British colonial rule and the establishment of an independent state. Ramana Maharshi's utter lack of engagement in political discourse and action could not stand in sharper contrast with Gandhi's spiritualization of politics, if one may call it so. Gandhi's function lay at the intersection of the spiritual quest and public action since, for him, political action could only be the exteriorization of a deeper spiritual concern with the truth, by virtue of *satyāgraha*.[54] Although Gandhi never met with the Maharshi, he is said to have had a great reverence toward him, and he would consistently recommend to those who had a chance to do so to seek the *darshan* of the sage of Tiruvannamalai. In the 1930s, Gandhi actually traveled through Tiruvannamalai to make a political speech, and was about to stop at the ashram. He was prevented from doing so by a combination of circumstances and human intervention. It is told that, referring to the Maharshi with disdain,

> Rajagopalachari [the last Governor-General of India], who was also present, turned to Nehru, the future Prime Minister, and said, 'What is the point in sitting in a cave in a *kaupina* [loincloth] when the country has so many problems and Gandhi is being put in jail for struggling for independence?' Gandhi turned to him and put his finger to his lips to indicate that he should not criticise in this way.[55]

Regardless, it appears that Rajagopalachari was able to prevent the visit by instructing the driver not to stop. When told about the incident, the Maharshi commented that this was a way for the political activist to prevent a meeting which he foresaw could have precipitated a change of direction in the Mahatma's life. Here is the way the Maharshi commented upon this turn of events: 'Gandhi would like to come here but Rajagopalachari was worried about the consequences. Because he knows that Gandhi is an advanced soul, he fears that he might go into *samadhi* here and forget all about politics. That is why he gestured to the driver to drive on.'[56] At any rate, Rajagopalachari's hostility was representative of the negative assessment of contemplative spirituality that was to be found during these decades among Westernized and activist intellectuals, not only in India but in other parts of the colonized world as well. The political fever associated with the fight against colonial power, and to a large extent the emulation of its values and priorities, could not but lead many intellectuals to see in the Maharshi's utter disengagement a flagrant instance of backward passivity, if not egoism and escapism. All the same, it appears that for his part the Maharshi saw in Gandhi an exemplar of true *karma-yoga* and one through whom the Self was working. However, he never encouraged devotees to engage in political action, quite the contrary. Ramana Maharshi's indifference to political action and social reform stemmed from his assessment that the only real reform that is truly revolutionary in the deepest sense is of an inner kind. As Annamalai Swami puts it, 'Baghavan taught that one should reform oneself rather than find fault with others.'[57] Similarly, one cannot change the world without first changing oneself, while changing oneself is already changing the world in a way. With respect to the first statement, an amusing anecdote crystallizes the problematic foundations of ill-founded 'charitable' activism:

> A socially minded visitor told Bhagavan, 'What I would like to do is go around the world and set things right. I came to ask you for the strength and the power to do this work.' 'You are like a starving beggar offering a feast to all corners,' answered Bhagavan. 'How can a man who cannot help himself help anybody. First set yourself right and then only set out to improve others.'[58]

This type of remark was typical of the Maharshi's uncompromising intent not to let devotees be caught in a deceiving sense of responsibility vis-à-vis a world built on the ignorance of the Self, and therefore doomed to fall short of its goals and expectations. In regard to the second statement, one may mention the Maharshi's response to a visitor surprised that the sage was not preaching in the world:

> You have already decided that I do not preach. Do you know who I am and what preaching is? How do you know that I'm not doing it? Does preaching consist of mounting a platform and haranguing people? Preaching is simply the communication of knowledge. It may also be done in silence.[59]

The principle presiding over this point of view lies in that 'reforming oneself is reforming the whole world', and that the successful outcome of this endeavor is in and of itself an invisible guiding principle in the world, independently of any formal channels of outer expression.[60] In fact, the Maharshi conceives of 'self-reform' as being inherently productive of social reform: 'Self-reform automatically brings about social reform. Confine yourself to self-reform. Social reform will take care of itself.'[61] Needless to say, any recognition of the pertinence of this perspective presupposes a metaphysical vision in which the deeper layers of being and consciousness are more real and therefore ultimately powerful than any intent or action applied to the phenomenal periphery of existence. It is therefore extremely difficult, not to say impossible, to concede the validity of such insights within a context that is spiritually 'extraverted' and focused on changing the texture of reality before understanding its nature. Still, for the Maharshi, the picture of the 'starving beggar offering a feast to all corners' is an apt allegory of worldly and activist endeavors and the unavoidable failure of their outcome in the absence of spiritual awareness. Indeed, ignorance of the Self cannot but result in disorder and evil, and must therefore contribute to social and cosmic disturbance, be it even against the grain of praiseworthy intentions. There is a contagion of ignorance that can only be curbed by addressing its root cause.

On the other hand, as illustrated by his positive assessment of Gandhi's action, the Maharshi was keenly aware of the legitimacy of vocational differences. To those who expressed surprise or disappointment at his not entering the political fray, and his not attempting to weigh in upon events by dint of his spiritual influence, the sage would sometimes respond in terms of *dharma*:

> Our business is to keep quiet. If we enter into all these [political activities], people will naturally ask, and justifiably, 'Why is he interfering in all these instead of keeping quiet?' Similarly if Mahatma Gandhi keeps quiet leaving aside all his activities, they will ask, 'Why is he keeping quiet instead of engaging in all these activities?' He must do what he has come for. We must do what we have come for.[62]

The sage's recognition of the demands of *dharma* participates in a wider 'spiritual realism', the manifestations of which may appear contradictory on the surface while being indeed deeply in tune with Self-centeredness and an ability to situate everything in relation to it.

This important characteristic of the Maharshi's wisdom appears in full light in the ways in which he handled and negotiated the occasional tensions between the unconditioned freedom of the Self and the demands of formal orthodoxy. Annamalai Swami remarked that Ramana Maharshi's attitude in relation to Hindu orthodoxy was both reverent and free of formalism:

> He went to a lot of trouble to avoid offending the sentiments of orthodox brahmins, mainly by permitting only brahmins to cook the ashram's food, but he was not so strict that he was not willing to bend the rules once in a while if it was in a good cause. His attitude was governed by a desire to avoid complaints and dissension rather than privileging the letter of caste *dharma*.[63]

This general observation stemmed from the far from unique anecdotal evidence that, on one occasion, the Maharshi let Annamalai Swami, a non-

Brahmin, prepare food, which is normally the prerogative of Brahmins on account of the need for the preservation of ritual purity. In fact the Maharshi asked Annamalai Swami not to reveal to anybody that he had cooked the food on this occasion, because 'the brahmins will not eat it if they find out that you (Annamalai Swami) cooked their food.'[64] We know, on the other hand, that all were welcome to approach him for *darshan* without any distinction of castes, gender or religion. This undifferentiation was actually extended to domains that are normally under the regimen of strict dharmic exclusions. Thus everyone was mingling during meals in the presence of the Maharshi at the ashram, and Vedic chanting, far from being restricted to Brahmins, was given access by all. The religious 'realism' of Ramana Maharshi appears in this instance in the way he recognizes the social and psychological need of traditional rules while 'bending' them on occasion for the sake of a higher benefit, or from the point of view of a higher truth. The primary focus is to preserve order and tranquility: any outright rejection or disdain of orthodox regulations and practices cannot but result in troubles and loss of equilibrium, whether individually or collectively.

All in all the question of the relationship between traditional *dharma* rules and the ultimate goal of Self-knowledge cannot have an absolute answer, since it very much depends upon the vantage point of the practitioner. That which is conceived normatively as a facilitating factor or protection in view of Self-knowledge may also become an impediment in some contexts. On the one hand, the Maharshi recognizes that for 'competent beginners with waning attachments all these aids [ceremonial baths, morning and evening prayers, repetition of mantras, oblations poured into the fire, chanting Vedas, worship of gods, *bhajans*, pilgrimages, sacrifice, giving in charity, and observance of special spiritual practices] will make the mind increasingly pure.'[65] However, at a higher stage, they may also become dispersing and hamper one's focus on the essential core of Self-knowledge.[66] Thus, the spiritual perspective is bound to be confronted with tradition in the form of ritual practices. These ritual practices, such as sacrifice, the prime component of Vedic religion, can be referred back to spiritual realities that enlighten their meaning and make them viable supports of meditation in view of Self-realization. This is, by and large, the way the Maharshi integrates them into his teachings, and understands them with regards to their full assimilation by devotees. However, religious forms may also clash with some concomitances of spiritual realization. Such a tension appears in an anecdote relative to sacrificial rites offered to the goddess Kali at the time of the Maharshi's life in Tiruvannamalai. A disciple of the Maharshi's, Suri Nagamma, was deeply disturbed by the tantric sacrifice of goats that was taking place on a daily basis at a Kali temple situated not far from the ashram. She referred to these as a 'barbarous practice in the name of religion.'[67] Knowing the Maharshi's love for animals and his respect for all beings as the countless faces of the Self, she went to him for advice as to how to put an end to the rituals. After a pause for reflection, his response was not to enlist ashram devotees and city authorities to try to stop the sacrifices, but rather to go directly to the devotees of Kali in order to convince them. Suri Nagamma took the advice by writing verses in praise of Kali before paying a visit to the temple priests. In these verses Kali is implored as a mother; the goddess is asked to take on her purest form, her sattvic form, rather than her cruel and bloody form, her rajasic and tamasic form.[68] This prayer was effective, since the temple priests accepted to discontinue their sacrificial rites. What is interesting from our current point of view is that the Maharshi saw it fit to address the issue directly from the point of view of the tantric practitioners. Taking on this inspiration, the Maharshi's devotee addressed the issue in a language that would be amenable to them. The reality of Kali was envisaged on different levels of her reality. It is quite clear, here, that there lie within the polymorphic reality of Hinduism tensions between perspectives that address relatively inferior needs and others, such as the Maharshi's, that relate to the ultimate finality of the tradition. The Maharshi addresses the issue not by opposing the lower manifestations of the sacred, to which he does not object *absolutely* as it were, but by engaging their representatives with a view to having them bow, metaphorically, before the Ultimate that their perspective envisions without fathoming it.

A balanced attitude also appears in the way the Maharshi articulates the relationship between traditional duties, as enjoined by the scriptures, the *shāstra*, and the primacy of *jñāna*. First of all, he considers *jñāna* to presuppose a spiritual maturity that is normatively entailed by the accomplishment of prior dharmic duties in this life, or in a previous life. In other words, one cannot aspire to, and even less reach, Self-knowledge without having been profoundly prepared for it. A molding of the soul has to be achieved, and this is normally a result of one's abiding by *dharma*. So it is quite clear that the Maharshi does not dispense with the prescriptions and the proscriptions of the tradition at large. He sees them in a kind of continuum with their ultimate entelechy. Even when the path of Self-knowledge has been trodden, due to the readiness of the soul, the *jñāni* does not normally and deliberately transgress traditional laws.[69] It is so first because there is normally no desire in him to transgress them—unless it be for a specific pedagogical purpose—and secondly because he upholds the standards of society and has no intention to subvert them. The attitude of the *jñāni* will not lead him, however, to concern himself with his prior fulfillment of the *dharma* or *karma*, for this would mean falling back into a perspective that is determined by conditioned existence, and thereby forgetting that actions do not liberate. It would also consolidate the illusion of the 'I-thought.' In this context, it is important to reassert that Ramana Maharshi's point of view is exclusively centered on Self-realization. What matters for him is to convey the imperative of focusing on one's deepest identity, which is none other than the universal Self. All other matters are, at best, contingent upon this goal, which explains why some traditional and social contingencies can, depending on outer circumstances or inner intents, be either upheld as facilitating means, or bypassed as formal limitations and distractions.

Thus, the idea that Ramana Maharshi helped redefined Hinduism outside or beyond its own traditional limits is plausible in some respects, but it is also quite questionable when considering his fundamental intent and the diversity, not to say seeming contradictions, of his concrete stances. First of all, it bears stressing that at no time were the Maharshi's concerns focused on Hinduism as such. There is indeed no trace of confessional considerations in his teachings: the matter is the Self and only the Self. Like Shankara and other Advaitin sages before him, Ramana Maharshi fully recognized that no formal reality, be it traditional, has ultimately any bearing upon the Self. Two most symbolically significant instances of this transcendence of the Self—and the relativization of any other 'reality' that it entails—are actually provided in a beautifully suggestive way in the life of Shankarāchārya. In *Hastamalaka-Stotra*, we are told how a seven-year-old young brahmin boy who acted as though he was a simpleton—unable as he was to learn the alphabet, and even incapable of playing with boys his age—was revealed by his encounter with Shankara to be a *jñāni* of the highest order.[70] When asked by Shankara, to whom the boy had been presented by his father in the hope the sage's blessing might cure him from his idiocy, the question 'who are you?', he answered in pure Advaitin terms:

I am the *Ātman* [Self] which is of the nature of eternal Consciousness and which is the cause of the functioning of the mind, eye and all other organs, in the same way as the sun is the cause of the activities of all beings on this earth. But when not associated with the limiting adjuncts [in the form of the body, mind and sense-organs], I, [Self] am like space.[71]

113

Hastamalaka was later to become one of the foremost disciples of Shankara. The name given to him by Shankara is intended to evoke the *amala* fruit, or myrobalan, that fits within the hand as naturally as the unfolding of his Self-realization. This narrative illustrates most powerfully the way in which Self-knowledge is in itself totally independent from forms and ways: it is simply in the nature of things, as testified by the unassuming Self-realization of a seemingly retarded lad.

The second traditional account illustrating the utter relativity of human and traditional forms is the celebrated encounter of Shankara and the *chandala*. In the *Manīśā-Pañcakam*, Shankarāchārya enjoins a sweeper, a *chandala*, to move away from him as he passes by. This is of course on account of the strict caste rule that prevents an orthodox Brahmin from casting his eye on an untouchable. The sweeper responds as follows: 'Oh! The best among the twice born, by saying "move away-move away", do you wish to move matter from matter, or you mean to separate Spirit from the Spirit?'[72] This most insightful question leads Shankara to recognize that 'the one Consciousness which is the very life spark in all forms from the Creator down to the ant, He alone is my Guru, be he a sweeper, be he a *brāhmana*.'[73] Even though some commentators like to point out that the *chandala* was actually a manifestation of Śiva or a *sadhu* having entered the child's body out of compassion, it remains nevertheless true that one of the explicit lessons of the text lies in its emphatic affirmation of the utter independence of the Self vis-à-vis any form whatsoever, including those that are traditionally conceived as preparatory, in one way or another, to Self-realization. In both cases, therefore, traditional, religious, social, and institutional forms are revealed to be unessential, in such a way as to illustrate the principle that any traditional system founded on the primacy of ultimate non-duality is bound to undo itself from within when fathomed till the depth of its intent.

A paradox such as this is often taken today as an evidence of the disjunction between the spiritual essence of Self-realization and the orthodox structures of the Brahmanical tradition. Even though there may be some merits in this interpretation, as evidenced by the freedom and suppleness of Ramana's handling of traditional norms, it is far from being evident that his particular stance may be aligned with the reformist outlook of a Gandhi, for instance. It is sensible to consider that the Maharshi's perspective is best characterized as transcending the formal order in a way that does not imply any specific position with respect to the conservation, modification, or removal of any existing outer structures. In fact the most constant reoccurring feature of the sage's response to questions pertaining to this level of consideration is a relentless return to the fundamental question of the Self. As a general tendency, the Maharshi refuses to address political or social questions on their own level. This is quite illuminating, for instance, with reference to the question of the independence of India. The Maharshi certainly welcomed India's political emancipation, but he interpreted *swarāj*, by referring to its literal meaning of self-rule, as a first step toward Self-realization through a kind of gradual enlarging of one's perspective on the meaning of the 'self', and always as conditioned on an utter surrender to the Higher Rule of the Divine Self.[74] Questions of national or ethnic identity were perceived as misleading and obstructive in this respect, inasmuch as they rest upon obsessive limitations upon the Self: 'D.: Is it not our duty to be patriots? B.: It is your duty to BE and not to be this or that, "I am that I am" sums up the whole of the Truth.'[75] Moreover, there is no hint whatsoever, in any of the sage's reported teachings, to a need to abolish particular structures deemed to be an impediment to Self-realization or even to moral and social values and benefits. For the Maharshi it is plain that the only way to dispense with the strictures and abuses of external conditions is through turning inward to the Self. Any other way is a postponement of the real question and a hydra-like illusion. On the positive side of karmic engagement, the Maharshi's way consisted in tracing back the deepest meaning of traditional and social practices. This was achieved by linking every ritual and moral form to the Self, and pertains to Maharshi's realistic consideration of needs and qualifications as they relate to means of realization. The key to the Maharshi's 'dharmic traditionalism' lies in the capacity of external traditional realities to serve as symbols and supports of meditation in view of Self-knowledge. The sage's consistent contemplation of normative ways of acting unveils the spiritual intent that lies below the formal surface; hence this most revealing advice: 'Observe the disciplines of external conduct [*achara*], knowing in your heart their real object by properly reflecting on their inner meaning.'[76] Touching the guru's feet with one's hand and bringing the latter to one's eyes is not only an outer sign of reverence, it manifests above all one's 'joining the eye of reflected consciousness [...] to those holy feet, which are the real consciousness.'[77] Similarly, the true meaning of *prasād*, or sharing the food of the sage, is not only the outer blessing that ensues, but it means 'to be blessed [...] with the experience of the Self.'[78] Abiding by external norms of traditional and religious behavior must invite one to deepen and refine one's awareness of them as avenues of realization of the Self. On the one hand, *dharma* culminates in the metaphysical summit of all *dharmas*, and it is therefore to be revered: 'The Self-abidance that flourishes when one realises one's true nature is the supreme *dharma* of *sat-achara*.'[79] On the other hand, the end of *dharma* transcends all forms, so that being is finally substituted to doing: 'The aim of all practices is to give up all practices.'[80]

5

RELIGION AND RELIGIONS

Ramana Maharshi's understanding of religion, and religions, is obviously not severable from the realization of the Self, or *Ātman*. As we have seen, Ramana Maharshi considered all religions to lead to Self-realization. If one were to refer to Frithjof Schuon's concept of the 'transcendent unity of religions', then it could be said that, for the Maharshi, the principle of this unity is none other than the Self.[1] As in the case of most contemporary Hindu figures such as Ma Ananda Mayi and Swami Ramdas, this unity is postulated spiritually, but is rarely made explicit through specific metaphysical or theological comparisons or explanations.[2] At any rate, religion must therefore be considered from the point of view of its main intent, which, according to the Maharshi, is to 'help people give up regarding the unreal as real.'[3] This is the 'perennialist' dimension of the Maharshi teachings, as it were, since it brings back every religious form to a universal and eternal principle of discernment. In a way this is not specific to the Maharshi himself, as indicated by any consideration of similar points made by contemporary Hindu sages such as those who were mentioned above. It is in that sense that Forsthoefel may refer to a 'perennial appeal' of the Maharshi. One of the ways this appeal may be understood is through reference to a 'core mystical experience at the heart of all religions,' which is explicitly considered by the Maharshi as underlying all profound religious engagements.[4] Coomaraswamy and Schuon's perennialism may, among others', find confirmation in the Maharshi's statements to that effect. This does not imply, needless to say, that the Maharshi himself was part of

117

the so-called 'perennialist school,' since his function and destiny was not to elaborate on the ways in which the unity of the Self is modulated in world religions.[5] While this is not the place for a discussion of perennialism and its perspective, it is interesting to note that the Maharshi's outlook on religious diversity provides an argument in support of its claim of a transcendent unity of religions. Like Perennialists, the Maharshi understood unity as pertaining to the goal of religion, and religious diversity as relative to the paths giving access to that goal. Today, some of the claims of perennialism find vague echoes in Western popular discourse with the diffuse sense that 'we all worship the same God and seek the same good', while it is also true, conversely, that academic discourse, given its scholarly and analytic focus, tends to highlight differences, as do also, from a very different point of view, religious individuals and communities that uphold various degrees of exclusivism on account of the singularity of their faith. Be that as it may, it must be clear that the Maharshi's outlook was never confessional or religious as such, no more than it was comparative, academic, or even intellectual in the usual sense of the term. As we will see, he was content to focus on a few central formulae and principles that he took as *mahāvākyāni*, so to speak, in order to enlighten the meaning of Self-knowledge on the basis of the scriptural symbolism of given religious traditions.

In making discernment the essence of religion, the Maharshi was actually situating himself in the tradition of Advaitin's *viveka*, the key to the Shankarian tradition. For Shankara, discrimination is actually the methodical bedrock of the path of Advaita. Indeed, revelation, the *śruti*, as the foundation of religious life, is the first source and means of *viveka*. Thus, Shankara explains how the discriminative knowledge issuing from a steady and penetrating meditation of scriptures results in Self-realization:

> the discriminative knowledge, effected by *śruti*, on the part of the individual soul which previously is non-discriminated as it were from its limiting adjuncts, is [...] the soul's rising from the body, and the fruit of that discriminative knowledge is its accomplishment in its true nature, i.e. the comprehension that its nature is the pure Self.[6]

It is worth stressing, however, that, while revelation is the foundation of religion, at least in those traditions like Hinduism that refer to foundational scriptures, this does not mean that religion in all of its diverse manifestations is in direct agreement with their essential content. In fact, one of the most striking features of Shankara's understanding of scriptures dwells in his distinction between two levels of understanding, and in a way also two levels of scriptural expression. Although the terms 'exoteric' and 'esoteric' may not be the most appropriate here—given that its binary function does not easily fit the polymorphic diversity of Hinduism—it remains nevertheless true that Shankara distinguishes between a primary and a secondary meaning, and therefore interpretation, of the *śruti*. For him, only the primary meaning, which is *de facto* esoteric since it refers to the inner Selfhood, corresponds to the true intent: that of teaching the reality of the Self and its being the ultimate goal of the Vedic tradition. As for the secondary meaning of scriptures, which appears to concede a separate reality other than the Self—for example in regard to the distinction between the Creator and the universe—it is nothing but a concession to ignorance as a first step toward knowledge. This distinction is not without profound analogy with the Buddhist differentiation between *samvriti* and *paramārtha satya,* the conventional and ultimate truths taught by the Buddha. The first is provisional, methodical and pedagogical, the second both epistemological and ontological, having to do with 'things as they are.'

In such a general view of the matter, religion as a whole, and in all of its particularities, aims at providing means of letting go of the attachment to the reality of the world. The means to that end may certainly appeal more often to the will than to the intelligence, but even so the ultimate goal is to break the spell of the human 'worship' of the finite and the ephemeral. Accordingly, Ramana Maharshi's view of religions tends to be methodical, or even instrumental, which, however, does not imply any dismissiveness on his part—quite the contrary. The sage does not generally comment upon the origins or guarantees of religions, but his repeated references to the validity of their means presupposes, if only implicitly, that religious practices have the power to operate a transformation of consciousness. Indeed, the Maharshi does not hesitate to define religious worship as a way leading to Reality 'for perception of the Truth, worship of the Supreme in name and form is means indeed.'[7] There is, however, a clear delineation between the means and the goal. It could be argued that such a demarcation is not functionally different from the one entailed by any religious outlook, which also perceives dogmas and practices as means to the end of salvation. The gap that is involved by the Maharshi's understanding of religion is of quite a different order however. It is none other than the differentiation between the supra-formal Truth, *Nirguna Brahman*, and the formal manifestations of the same Absolute, *Saguna Brahman*. The ordinary concept of religion may well distinguish the means from the end, but it still involves a continuum between the two, in the sense that both belong to the formal and individual order. This is why, even though, in principle, religion may be envisaged by believers as a mere instrument, it is in fact rarely so because it is practically impossible, from a strictly religious point of view, to separate the destination from the way. Such a virtual impossibility stems from a *de facto* 'absolutization' of both the individual and religion. In contrast with Ramakrishna, whose bhaktic sensibility led him to place the worship of God with form and God without form practically on the same footing, Ramana Maharshi emphasises that religious worship is to be clearly distinguished from 'the state of being that in natural poise of Self [...] alone is perception true.'[8] Ramakrishna's point that 'God with form is just as true as God without form' pertains to the point of view of devotion and subjective effectiveness through religious faith.[9] In this perspective what matters is the recognition of the plurality of paths, and therefore the acknowledgment of their respective spiritual fruitfulness. The Maharshi's point of view, on the other hand, stresses that only the 'perception of the Truth [...] is perception true.'[10] Now this perception is not a formal one, and it even transcends the specific sphere of interests of the individual self as such. From this vantage point, religious worship can only be a formal mediation toward That which lies beyond all mediations and all forms.

The intrinsically instrumental association—and incommensurable chasm—between religious *dharma* and the realization of *Ātman* is explicitly encapsulated in a passage of the Maharshi's *Forty Verses*:

> All religions postulate the three fundamentals: the world, the soul and God, but it is only the One Reality that manifests as the three. It is only as long as the ego endures that one says 'the three are really three'. Therefore the perfect state is inherence in one's own Being, where the ego is dead.[11]

Religion presupposes a triad inasmuch as it involves a double relationship: one between the soul and the world, and one between the soul and God. Religion, being relational, entails by definition an alternative: the choice of the world or that of God. In its 'unredeemed' state—that is in the absence of the grace inherent to religion—the soul is necessarily determined by the world, i.e., the world conceived and experienced independently from God. Contemplated from the point of view of non-dual Self-knowledge, the function of religions is therefore primarily negative and, as it were, purgative. Thus, the Maharshi teaches that 'it is only to help people give up regarding the unreal as real that all the religions and practices taught by them have come into being.'[12] If religion appears to be otherworldly, then it is precisely because it strives to eradicate the illusion that the world is fully real. Should mankind be able to perceive the unreal as unreal, thereby asserting the Reality by which standards this unreality is perceived, there would be no need for religion. Religion is relative to a natural state of metaphysical confusion. It is therefore not absolute, even though it is practically and subjectively treated as such by believers. It is this sense of absoluteness conferred upon religion that, by informing a constant confrontation with God in worship and surrender, transmutes the individual into the Divine Self. The denial of the individual 'I' (which Christianity would refer to as the bearing of one's cross) 'leaves a residuum of God in which the "I" is lost.'[13] What this means is that the very idea of God within the believer, or that which in the believer asserts God, is none other than the very Self. Both the 'I' and 'God' have been refined, as it were, in the process of spiritual realization. The worldly 'I' has been changed into a God-centered 'I.' As for 'God', it is not anymore a notion in one's mind, but a living and transformative presence within. Both the sense of 'I' and the sense of God have been purified and the unity of the two has been realized. To become oneself more deeply is to become God and to know God more truly is to realize Him within.

However, for *Advaita*, the reality of religion is contingent upon the reality of the soul, or rather the reality of the ego, the latter presupposing a belief in the full reality of the former. For the Maharshi, there is no religion without ego; that is to say without a belief in the reality of the human soul. Religion takes this existence as a starting point, while changing the orientation of the individual selfhood from the world to God. This corresponds most accurately to the religious process of 'conversion,' which is a turning away from the world *qua* world to God. The triad that lies at the core of religion is clearly 'relative', since each of the three terms is in some way needed for the two others to be 'real.' From a human point of view, the relativity of the triad soul–world–God is, therefore, contingent upon the reality of the ego. What this means is that the human soul has no power over the reality of the world and God, but it has the power of awakening, through spiritual realization, to the unreality of the ego. 'It is only as long as the ego endures that one says "the three are really three"': once the ego has disappeared, religion has fulfilled its function and it can 'withdraw', inasmuch at least as the triad that lies at its very foundation is re-absorbed, as it were, in the unity of pure Being. Recognizing the exclusive reality of the Self means a death or a 'destruction' of the ego. Now, it is important to understand that the ego refers to an illusory center of consciousness that has no reality in itself. The 'death' or the 'destruction' of the ego cannot possibly mean the total disappearance of an individual locus of consciousness that is extrinsically limited and determined by contingencies of time and space. This would mean the total cosmic disappearance of a given individual, which experience disproves, since the Maharshi himself was recognized by his devotees as exemplifying, besides his state of Self-realization, accidental traits that differentiated him from other human beings. This clearly indicates that what is at stake in the so-called 'death of the ego' is not the 'provisional' experience of an individual mode of awareness—an experience that is irreducible on its own level of phenomenal existence—but rather the ultimate reality of this mode of consciousness, since such a reality can only be illusory when considered independently from the one Self. In other words, the 'destruction of the ego' is the undoing of the illusory view of the self or *jivātman* as essentially distinct from the Self or *Ātman*. Moreover it is this very distinction that lies at the basis of any religious reality. While religion is all about the relationship between God and the individual soul, Self-realization refers to the transcendence of all relationships and dualities, including this paradigmatically religious relationship.

The formal aspect of religion is, moreover, a direct consequence of the very nature of the individual *jīva*. This is so to the extent that the *jīva* necessarily partakes in forms. Thus the religious perspective could be defined, in a way, as proceeding from forms to the Formless. All religions are defined, or at least characterized, by credal, ritual and ethico-legal forms, while their ultimate goal is a state of proximity or union with the Divinity lying beyond forms. In response to a question by Muslim visitors who wondered whether God has a form, the Maharshi immediately changed the focus of the inquirer away from the Divine Object and onto the human subject.[14] This is because the way the question must be answered depends on the nature of the one raising the question. As long as the question is raised by the ego who partakes in forms, then the answer must keep to the formal realm. Thus the Maharshi alludes to two aspects of religion, the means and the goal, which belong to two levels of reality that are incommensurate. The first pertains to body-consciousness, which is ordinary consciousness, while the second participates in spiritual formlessness, that is to say the Divine Self. In this, Hinduism and Islam are both strikingly similar and profoundly divergent. They converge in affirming that the Divine Absolute transcends all forms: the non-qualified *Nirguna Brahman* and the One God to Whom nobody is associated. However, religiously speaking, it could be said that Hinduism focuses on the human starting point, which is formal and therefore in need of Divine forms—hence the plethora of gods and goddesses, whereas Islam is centered on the Divine Goal, which is supra-formal and therefore transcends all forms. Another major difference, of course, is that Islam as a religion does not explicitly and directly understand God as the Self. The *Qur'ān* does so in its own implicit way, however, in passages such as 'Verily I am God; there is no god but I' (20:14) or 'We are closer to him [the human being] than [his] jugular vein' (50:16). Sufism, the mystical path of Islam, sometimes reaches Advaitin positions on such a Quranic basis, especially in the school of *wahdat al-wujūd*, but when it does so it is in a way that involves an inner, esoteric, reading of the creed. Now the question of form may have a different connotation in Islamic and Hindu contexts. In the former, form evokes negatively physical presentation and representation of the Divine, incarnation and idols, whereas in the latter forms are positive and necessary and also include concepts of the Divine.

In the Maharshi's perspective, religions are both real and unreal—since they are tied up with forms leading to the Formless; they are both necessary on the plane of egoic consciousness and incomplete in their ordinary scope. In contrast with a number of neo-Vedantists, Ramana Maharshi asserts the full reality of God as the Absolute Reality *qua* distinct from the egoic soul.[15] Based on this fundamental distinction that lies at the foundation of the human sense of separateness, 'all creeds are but preliminaries for the masses, leading up to the real truth of the Self.'[16] For the sage of Arunachala, religions are real and effective inasmuch as they relate and lead to Self-Realization, directly or indirectly. An important implication of this consideration of religions is the fact that 'religions are not necessarily the highest expression or the highest wisdom of their founders.'[17] There is, in other words, a possible—perhaps necessary—gap between the highest spiritual 'content' of religious realities as recognized or realized by their originators and the actual, formal, message and language of the revelation or teaching. On the one hand, the degrees and modes of spiritual consciousness of sages and prophets may remain non-manifest and pertain to a domain that does not appear in full light to most, or all, of the faithful. This is a consequence of the transcendence, and therefore unfathomability, of Self-consciousness as perceived or transmitted within the domain of ordinary consciousness. On the other hand, Ramana Maharshi suggests that the founders of religions 'had to consider the times in which they lived and the mental capacities of the people.'[18] There is in the human nature a need for exclusiveness and complexity, or indirection, in the religious realm. In other words, the dispensation of the Truth must obey all kinds of limitations, filtering and concealments which are alluded to in Christ's often quoted admonition: 'Give not that which is holy unto the dogs, neither cast ye your pearls before swine, lest they trample them under their feet, and turn again and rend you' (Matthew 7:6). Therefore, there appears a distinction, in the world of religion as a collective phenomenon, between layers of meaning and understanding. This differentiation manifests, for instance, in some Prophetic traditions of Islam in which two kinds or levels of knowledge are distinguished, one being decisively more interior than the other to the point of being dangerous when it is shared indiscriminately.[19] The Gospel also clearly refers to two modalities and levels of expression of the Truth in Jesus' teachings.[20] Thus, the context of Abrahamic monotheistic traditions, which entails a strong theistic emphasis by virtue of their scriptures, religious injunctions and theological teachings, is not conducive to placing non-dual realization at the forefront or at the center stage. In such contexts non-dual teachings on the Self can only function as hidden or incidental components.

The innermost meaning that often remains a hidden secret in religion is brought to the fore by the Maharshi's occasional exegesis of scriptural statements borrowed from outside of the Hindu world. The foremost occurrence of such non-dual interpretations of religious statements is no doubt the reoccurring reference to the Biblical 'I am That I am' (Exodus 3:13-15). This foundational statement of Biblical monotheism is generally understood as referring to the unfathomable nature of God, His dwelling beyond 'Names' and—which amounts in a way to the same—His identity with pure Being, which is the interpretation favored by the Maharshi.[21] In fact, the Maharshi considered this statement as the most direct and satisfactory reference to the Reality of the Self:

> Of all the definitions of God, none is indeed so well put as the Biblical statement I AM THAT I AM in Exodus (Chap. 3). There are other statements, such as *Brahmaivaham*, *Aham Brahmasmi* and *Soham*. But none is so direct as the name JEHOVAH = I AM. The Absolute Being is what is. It is the Self. It is God. Knowing the Self, God is known. In fact God is none other than the Self.[22]

'I am That (or Who) I Am' is the traditional rendering, but there exist several possible interpretations and translations of the Hebrew phrase *'ehyeh 'ăšer 'ehyeh'*. *'Ehyeh* is the first person singular of the verb 'to be' (*hāyā*), which may be translated as a past, a present or a future. There is no better way to suggest how Being transcends time as such while 'being' the essence of all times. It must be noted, moreover, that the Hebrew verbal form *'ehyeh* is not accompanied by a personal pronoun that would be analogous to 'I' or *Aham*. This could be read, symbolically at least, as implying that Consciousness is included in Being. Such a perspective is aligned with the Abrahamic *a priori* apprehension of God as Supreme Being rather than universal 'I', whereas, by contrast, the Maharshi would generally take Consciousness to involve Being, since his starting point is the ultimate 'I'. As for the translation of *'ašer,* which is a connecting pronoun, it can be either personal, 'Who', or impersonal, 'That.' In a non-dualistic outlook like Ramana Maharshi's, the latter is evidently more relevant: The Self is not a Person in the relational sense of the term, although it embraces in a way the perfection of Personhood inasmuch as the core of the latter is Consciousness. To say that the Self is not relational simply means that it transcends, and annuls, all sense of otherness. Thus, to the question whether 'my Realization help others', Ramana Maharshi's answer is that 'it is the best possible help' since 'really there are no others to help, for a Realized Being sees only the Self just as a goldsmith estimating the gold in various jewels sees only the gold.'[23] It results from the previous considerations that the monotheistic concept of 'the One without another' is like the theological version, or in another sense the propaedeutic formula, of the metaphysics of the Self without a second.[24] Accordingly, the standard English translation 'I am That I am' lends itself to an Advaitin interpretation inasmuch as it echoes the *Tat Tvam Asi.* The pronouns That and *Tat* are in fact Indo-European cognates. At any rate, the Biblical 'Name of God' is of particular interest to the Maharshi inasmuch as it is akin, both in its Divine origin and in the mode of its formulation, to a Jewish, and therefore Christian, *mahāvākya.*

The young Ramana attended the American Mission High School in Madurai from 1892 to 1896, and his familiarity with the Bible led him, retrospectively, to elucidate Christian tenets in light of Self-realization. This was especially the case for the Crucifixion and the Resurrection, central mysteries of the Christian perspective. Needless to say, the Maharshi read the two key events of sacred history as direct symbols of Self-knowledge: 'The body is the cross. Jesus, the son of man, is the ego or I-am-the-body idea. When the son of man is crucified on the cross, the ego perishes, and what survives is the Absolute Being. It is the resurrection of the Glorious Self, of the Christ the Son of God.'[25] Although this interpretation of the Crucifixion is unlikely to convince most Christians, it is undoubtedly in keeping with the meaning of self-sacrifice, or self-abnegation, that lies at the heart of the Christic way, as well as with major implications of the meaning of 'the New Man,' the soul born again through the grace of Christ's resurrection. In another context, the Maharshi does not hesitate to apply the principles of Self-realization to the theological mystery of the Trinity. The triad God–mankind–world as unfolding of the one Self is taken by him as an analogue of the three Persons of the Trinity in their consubstantial unity. Thus, 'in the Trinity, the son of God is the Guru or God manifest who explains to a devotee that the Holy Spirit is immanent everywhere.'[26] The 'son of God' is therefore identified with the perfection of mankind in the *guru,* while the Holy Spirit is none other than the Self *qua* all-inclusive fullness. In this metaphysical Tri-Unity the Self is Father as Transcendent Being-Consciousness, Son as manifest perfection of Consciousness in the *guru,* and Holy Spirit as immanent Bliss.

Although the Maharshi does not appear to have ever commented directly on the Quranic *shahādah,* it is more than likely that, had he done so, he would have also considered the first Islamic testimony, 'no god but God' (*lā ilāha ill'Allāh*), as an equivalent of non-dual *mahāvākyāni.* Some forms of Sufi hermeneutics actually understand the first *shahādah* as a statement of non-dualistic metaphysics, 'there is no god but God' being contemplated as 'there is no reality but the only Reality', the Divine Essence or Selfhood, *adh-Dhāt.*[27] A Hindu *pandit* once commented informally on the first *shahādah* as being a metaphysical statement in the form of a creed. While Hindu *mahāvākyāni* are strictly metaphysical and cannot be understood theologically or confessionally, such is not the case with the *shahādah,* which is *a priori* a profession of faith, and only *a posteriori* a metaphysical pronouncement. Furthermore, when asked about the Quranic principle that 'God is immanent in all', the Maharshi responds, in typical *ajātivāda* fashion, that 'there is no 'all', apart from God, for Him to pervade. He alone is.'[28] This is, indeed, a point of view that very few Muslims would embrace. We find, however, perspectives analogous to *ajātivāda* in the teachings of Sufi like Ibn 'Arabī, which sometimes express in the most uncompromising way the exclusive reality of the Divine Essence: 'Naught is except the Essence.'[29]

While 'I am That I am' is, for the Maharshi, the doctrinal core of Judeo-Christian teachings, its *ajātivāda*[30] perspective *mutatis mutandis,* the sentence 'Be still and know that I am God' is deemed by him to be its methodical complement: '"I am That I am" sums up the whole truth. The method is summed up in "Be Still".'[31] Interestingly, the Maharshi considers this stillness to be none other than a 'destruction' of the ego, inasmuch as the latter is characterized by a chronic agitation flowing from its illusory sense of being real. The sage of Arunachala echoes thereby Christ's admonition to his followers: 'If anyone would come after me, let him deny himself and take up his cross and follow me' (Mark 8:34). Although the denial of the self enjoined by Christ is most often understood as a moral abnegation in accepting one's trials, it has been sometimes taken by Christian mystics in an ontological sense. Such is the way, for instance, the seventeenth-century mystic Jeanne Guyon put the matter in most direct terms: 'There are but these two truths, the ALL and the NOTHING; everything else is falsehood. We can pay due honor to the ALL of God, only in our own ANNIHILATION; which is no sooner accomplished, than He, who never suffers a void in nature, instantly fills us with Himself.'[32] One of the spiritual ways in which this realization of the 'All of God' is actualized, in Christianity and elsewhere, is through a focus on the Name of God as direct instantiation of Divine Presence and Reality. Quoting the first verse of the Gospel of John, the Maharshi takes it as a statement of the oneness of God and His Name.[33] The Word is the utterance of God which, although distinguishable from Him *ad extra*, is in fact none other than Him *ab intra*. It is by virtue of this essential identity that the Name is spiritually transformative.

These considerations must lead one to contemplate the ways in which the Maharshi conceives of religions as facilitating Self-knowledge, but also the type of challenges that are likely to arise in this regard. We have already considered, in previous chapters, the role of devotion and prayer, as well as the function of tradition, but the relationship between Self-knowledge and the actual practice of religion raises further questions as to the ways the two dimensions coalesce while remaining distinct. In this regard, it is important to stress, at the outset, that Ramana Maharshi never invited anybody to adopt a religion or to change their own. For him all religions do potentially culminate in Self-realization. His teachings were not intended to be substituted to religious and spiritual practices but to enlighten the latter from within.[34] Hence, his was obviously not a perspective of comparative religion, and he therefore did not enter theological distinctions, nor assess the relative orthodoxy or effectiveness of any given tradition. Irrespective of these matters it is quite clear that, for him, Self-realization can be achieved within the fold of the practice of any religion. This is the case both for intrinsic and extrinsic reasons. Intrinsically the Self is the essence of all forms of worship. It is what could be called non-dualistic worship, if such a paradoxical and seemingly self-contradictory expression were to be be allowed. The essence of all worship is, explicitly or implicitly, the affirmation of the non-dual Divine ground of reality. It is the recognition of this essence that constitutes the guiding principle of the *jñānī*'s religious life. There is therefore no contradiction, nor any hypocrisy, for the *jñānī* in participating in the rituals of the general religion. Quite obviously, the understanding of the *jñānī* greatly differs from that of ordinary believers, but it is in no way disconnected from it, since it refers to the same Object—which it understands and realizes, however, as immanent Subject. Extrinsically, the *jñānī* abides by religious practices in order to set a good example, that is to say for the good of the community, and for the benefit of each and every faithful who comes in contact with him.[35] In fact the religious practice of the *jñānī* is, according to the Maharshi, more perfect and sincere than that of other believers, since he only truly knows the meaning and end of religion. If there is an apparent duplicity in the *jñānī*, then it lies in his being aware that the literal truth of the creed is far from the last word of the religion, and that only this last word is the Ultimate Truth. True sincerity can only be reached beyond duality, and thus beyond religion as it is commonly understood. On the one hand, the sage fathoms the depth of religious teachings in ways that undercuts their ordinary meaning. On the other hand, he is not unfaithful in doing so, quite to the contrary, since only his realizing the 'whole truth' puts him in a position to convey and foster the 'conventional truth'—even though he is also aware, from another point of view, that the latter is in a way an 'error.' Conversely the apparent sincerity of the ordinary believer, mostly based on sentiments, is never immune from a measure of hypocrisy. This is so inasmuch as the dualistic perspective never reaches a perfect identification with its object. In monotheistic traditions, this is recognized even by those who embody the highest expressions of the truth. Jesus obviously speaks from a dualistic point of view when he answers the Rich Young Ruler with the words 'Why do you call Me good? No one *is* good but One, *that is,* God' (Luke 18:19). At any rate, the religious teachings and practices of the *jñānī* are more effective and compelling than those of other practitioners because they find their principle in that which lies beyond duality, and therefore beyond doubt.

From a different vantage point, the distinction between the *jñānī's* way of religion and the usual religious perspective allows one better to understand the Maharshi's reservations vis-à-vis religion at large. It could be said that the very existence of religions stems from the need to attract the *jīva* so as to reorient it toward Self-knowledge. There is a kind of luring of the soul that is the specific purview of religion. Why is it so, why this need? The Maharshi answers this question, at times, by referring to a particular inclination of mankind toward 'mystery' as opposed to the 'truth.'[36] In his own words, religions 'cater' to the human love of 'mystery', understood here not in its positive sense of unfathomable depth but under its aspect of alluring fascination. Such an understanding of the role, and limitations, of religious universes is reminiscent of Franklin Merrell-Wolff's apprehension of the matter in his poetical meditation entitled 'The Well of Ignorance':

> I dip into the well of Ignorance and pull forth toads, slugs, and blind fish. I offer them Light, and quickly they slither back into the slimy darkness. [...] Finally, one here and one there ventures out of the pool into the Brilliance. It is a long and slow labor, but in the end I will win.[37]

The 'I' that is the subject of the opining sentences of this text is evidently the *Ātman* itself, or rather the Self inasmuch as it aspires to be known and realized. It dives into 'the Well of Ignorance' in order to save the benighted beings symbolically identified as 'toads, slugs and blind fish.' These creatures cannot stand the light of day, and putting them into the full Light would mean inflicting the intolerable upon them. Hence the spiritual 'catering' that ensues in the form of pouring 'acid' and holding 'tempting baits.' This is akin to the threats of punishment, the trials, the miseries, on the one hand, and the expectations of happiness and the blissful thereafter, on the other hand. Religion is essentially characterized by these two aspects: it pronounces prohibitions while warning of chastisement and it enunciates injunctions and promises of salvation. Thus, the path is basically one of gradual exposition to, and identification with, the Light. The self is led to a greater and greater light, one that is proportionate to its ability to receive and bear with. Although the ultimate goal is the unity of the Self, reaching this end is a very long process that requires many detours and ruses. The latter involve states and phenomena that reflect the Light of the Self while falling short of it, and often distracting one from its Reality. This explains why many questions put to the Maharshi revolve around 'occult' and eschatological matters such as *siddhis*, or mystical powers, or transmigration and the destiny of the individual *post mortem*. The Maharshi systematically eludes these questions as being distractions from the only question that matters: 'Who am I?'

How can we understand this human fascination for 'mystery', and is not the truth itself a mystery? It is likely that, in the Maharshi's perspective, the love of mystery corresponds to an element of diverting curiosity that is inherent to the human mind. The mind's unceasing mobility, which an oft-quoted famous Indian image compares with a monkey jumping from branch to branch, is constantly fed by the indefinite diversity of phenomenal reality, and particularly its 'extraordinary' dimensions. The Maharshi teaches in multiple occasions that the mind has no reality whatsoever outside of the constant shifts from thoughts to thoughts, images to images. The nature of the mind is purely relative in that sense; it is empty in the way of the Buddhist *pratītya-samutpāda*. In actuality every question raised by the mind is already a question, and in a way also an answer, about its own reality. Any question presupposes a sense of self that is needed for the very raising of the question. Every question about the becoming of the self, including its *post mortem* destiny, should therefore lead to a search for the Self.

The aforementioned limitations and reservations can in no way amount to a dismissal of the validity of the religious worlds and the various experiences that they afford. Ramana Maharshi does not in the least deny the reality of survival after death, nor does he cast doubt on the manifold forms that spiritual and religious experiences may take. The primacy of the Self does not invalidate the 'dream-world' that constitutes cosmic existence, including *post mortem* states and visionary experiences. However, the latter are only real on their own plane of reality, while they vanish before the exclusive and all-encompassing reality of the Self.

Thus, as it clearly appears that the realization of the Self, which is the key-message of the Maharshi's teachings, pertains to a supra-religious realm, it remains to further understand the ways in which religion can function as an instrument of realization of the Self. This is a crucial question since ordinary religious consciousness is precisely predicated on a sense of individual self as relating to God. What is there in this religious relationship that can predispose to, or pave the ground for, the 'experience' of Self-realization? This investigation is all the more important in that it is not rare to come across contemporary interpretations of the Maharshi in particular, and *Advaita Vedānta* in general, that deny the religious nature, or even reject the religious implications, of the search for the Self.

We have seen that Ramana Maharshi enlightens and justifies religious beliefs and practices by connecting them to their ultimate horizon and *raison d'être*, i.e., the realization of the Self. In response to spiritual questions he encourages religious practitioners to persevere in their own respective ways, and he highlights that no effort is ever in vain, since it must eventually bear karmic fruits in the process of one's gradual awakening to one's own nature. On the other hand, however, he makes it plain that religious disciplines of all kinds can also be a subtle way to bypass the ultimate goal of spiritual life, either by ignorance or by incapacity.[38] He even goes as far as emphasizing the utter relativity of all ascetic practices and disciplines and the fact that specific and systematic rules are not necessary when the focus on the Self is the central element of one's spiritual vocation. One example of this appears in the treatment of restorative sleep. While recognizing the legitimacy and utility of traditional injunctions to control the amount of sleep, the Maharshi also considers the merits of a pragmatic, non-ascetic perspective. When physical fatigue and sleepiness comes, it is simply more effective to rest and sleep, and to pick up the search anew, refreshed and rested, when one awakens.[39]

While the diversity of religious doctrines and practices is for most people a source of confusion, and even either a reason or a pretext to discard religion as a whole, Ramana Maharshi's perspective on the matter is primarily pragmatic and tolerant. For him, one cannot reproach religious teachers and scholars for contradicting each other, since the real issue is that of the diversity of qualification, background, vocation and degree of understanding.[40] The diversity of religious paths and spiritual disciplines stems from the extreme multiplicity of human outlooks. It is actually one of the best pieces of evidence of the effectiveness of religion in adjusting to the diversity of human needs, thereby achieving a transformation of the soul that a uniform and universal ideological system, be it religiously inspired, would not be able to realize. This is also one of the reasons why the Maharshi actually never prescribed any particular faith or method. Even the *Ātma-vichāra*, which he taught as being the most direct approach and the essence of religion, was never advised or dictated to anybody. As Kunju Swami put it, 'he could have ordered the practice of self-inquiry, and all the devotees would have blindly and willingly followed,' but the fact is that he never did.[41] On the contrary, examples abound in which the Maharshi, when approached for spiritual advice, 'used to ask him [the seeker] what he was already practicing' and urge them to continue doing so without any change. To one who had no *sādhanā*, 'Sri Bhagavan would often ask which of the gods or goddesses he liked best', and when answered by the devotee he 'would ask him to think of that god or goddess constantly.' As the highest testimony to his 'pluralistic' outlook, Kunju Swami also relates that the Maharshi 'never discouraged anyone or decried the beliefs and practices of others.'[42]

The full recognition of the diversity of paths that the Maharshi expressed, and indeed fostered, does not contradict the recognition that *Advaita Vedānta* is the most suitable doctrinal language to convey his teachings. Moreover, John Grimes has quite plausibly made the point that *Advaita*, in any of its forms, is the only 'religious' language and view that is totally satisfactory from an epistemological point of view. Any other religious idiom and experience, inasmuch as it is not non-dualistic, presupposes a gap that can never be utterly bridged.[43] 'Otherness', be it residual or otherwise, cannot but prevent immediate knowledge, and any mediation entails a zone of obscurity. Religious faith does not escape these limitations, at least from a human point of view, even though Divine grace is not limited by them and may erupt at any time as a unifying overcompensation. At any rate, the immediacy of Self-knowledge is what makes *Advaita* most attractive to those who consider it to be their path in the West; but it is also what makes it for them appear to be 'non-religious', since religion tends to be associated with devotion toward an Other, with the 'merit' of faith and the need for proofs. Of course, it all depends on how one chooses to define religion. Religion may also be considered to culminate in union with the Transcendent, in which case the Advaitin perspective of non-duality might be considered to be the consummate perfection of religion.

From another point of view, however, Ramana's Self-realization, as it is narrated by the Maharshi himself, appears to be devoid of any religious references. It reads as a purely spontaneous psycho-spiritual odyssey that entails no metaphysical framework and no ritual supports. It is no doubt the exclusive focus on consciousness and its ground that makes Ramana's Self-awakening so fascinating and powerfully inspiring. Moreover, as I have indicated in the introduction, the immediacy and seeming simplicity of this approach, and its apparent independence from any religious forms and traditional imperatives, has no doubt contributed to attract Western seekers to the Maharshi's personality and perspective. Here is, for instance, a typical line of reasoning that accounts for the Maharshi's power of attraction in non-religious contexts: 'His purely rationalistic arguments and the lack of sentiment in his teachings had a great appeal. He never preached or laid down the law, but always concentrated on turning the seeker back on himself and pointing out to him that it was entirely up to him.'[44] Most of the keywords of this passage suggest, in an allusive contrast, the ways in which the Maharshi's teachings have often functioned as a welcome counterpoint to what is perceived by some as religious limitations inherent to Abrahamic monotheism. The use of the adjective 'rationalistic' is particularly significant in this respect, as it entails major implications and ambiguities. The term normally denotes an exclusive epistemological reliance on reason as a foundation for reaching knowledge, whether religious or other. In the context of Chadwick's development, this is probably intended to mean that 'religious faith' does not enter into the argument provided by the Maharshi, by contrast with Christianity, whose reliance on faith as a divine dispensation is paramount. The Maharshi does not explicitly ask his listeners to engage in an act of religious faith of the kind that is called upon by Jesus. It bears noting, however, that the basis of the Maharshi's claim does not lie in reason but in experience. Ramana does not claim to have established Self-knowledge through a rational inquiry, but rather through psycho-spiritual practice and above all through a supra-rational intuition, or let us say a recognition of That which is inherent to consciousness. This is not a discursive analysis, even though a meditational practice was involved in the form of an inquiry. Although it could be argued that the overall style of the inquiry is one characterized by objectivity and detachment, this is in no way to be equated with rationalism as such, since the latter is normally defined as confining legitimate knowledge to the domain of reason. Now, on the other hand, it appears that the very disposition that may lead one to take heed of the Maharshi's words and proceed on the path of Self-inquiry, pertains to something like an act of faith. In other words, the Maharshi's extraordinary recognition must strike a chord in one's consciousness in order for it to inspire a desire for Self-knowledge. *Advaita* itself lists *śraddhā* as one of the preliminary requirements for engaging oneself thoroughly in the path of discrimination. Shankara lists faith, *śraddhā*, among the 'means' of discrimination, together with cessation of worldly actions (*uparati*), 'patience in suffering' (*titikṣā*), and 'attention' (*samādhāna*).[45] Faith is primarily directed at scriptures and the *guru*. Even though the modalities of *śraddhā* are characteristically different from what the word faith may conjure up in Christian minds, there is little doubt that it cannot be exclusively understood as a rational conviction. Indeed *śraddhā* entails an assent that transcends purely rational, and *a fortiori* rationalistic, categories. Moreover, the 'lack of sentiment' that Chadwick identifies as one of the characteristics of the Maharshi's teachings might be misleading if understood as excluding the human ability from the spiritual equation. There is no question that the Maharshi does not found his teachings on religious sentiments—his perspective is definitely not sentimentalist—but religious feelings have been one of the preludes of his vocation, particularly with the first discovery of the *Periya-purānam*. But even following his foremost experience of Self-realization, the two ways characterizing his new state of being were mentioned to be spiritual introspection and 'the habit of emotional tears when visiting the Meenakshi temple', while still leaving in Madurai. Moreover some of the Maharshi's compositions are suffused with religious emotions that sometimes echo the most impassionate tone of David's *Psalms* or Christian mystics.[46] Thus in these verses from *Aksharamanamalai*: 'O Arunachala! Without letting me fall to the viles of those who are cruel and deceitful, bestow thy grace on me and be in union with me.'[47] Finally, Chadwick's remark that 'he never preached or laid down the law' reflects a profound reality of spirituality and mysticism in general and reflects an understanding of Hinduism that focuses on Self-knowledge rather than legal prescriptions, which also have their importance in the tradition as testified by the *Mānava-Dharmaśāstra*.

At any rate, the inner path cannot be preached, because it flows from an internal predisposition and vocation. As such, it transcends the domain of religious law, which is prescriptive and not vocational. In the case of the Maharshi, moreover, the diversity of paths is highlighted, making thereby prescriptions and proscriptions all the more relative. As we have seen, however, this does not amount to a rejection of rules and regulations on his part. One cannot but sense, therefore, that, for better or for worse, Chadwick is eager to distance the Maharshi's teachings from any religious associations that may be evoked in a Western seeker's mind.

It is incontestable, nonetheless, that, far from any kind of confessional and dogmatic intricacies, the Maharshi's teachings are characterized by an extreme simplicity and directness. However, the scope of the Maharshi's spiritual teachings is much richer and circumstantiated than it would seem from a mere consideration of *Ātma-vichāra*. This already appears in the fact that the Tamil sage did not encourage anybody from discontinuing their own religious or spiritual practice, nor indeed from renouncing their own religion. Notwithstanding this *de facto* spiritual 'pluralism', Ramana Maharshi's interviews reveal his consistent mention of a second spiritual approach besides *Ātma-vichāra*. As we have developed in a previous chapter, by virtue of his awareness of the diversity of qualifications and backgrounds, the Maharshi often mentioned the way of 'surrender' as an alternative to Self-inquiry. He deemed this inner disposition to be particularly appropriate for those whose intelligence and sensibility have been molded by the belief in the power and providence of God, from whatever tradition they may hail. In addition to Hindu sensibilities shaped by a bhaktic outlook, this would also be the case, in principle, for Western seekers whose intelligence and sensibility had been shaped by Judeo-Christian principles, values and reflexes. The Western religious outlook that derives from the Biblical tradition is theologically monist, in the sense of its affirming the unicity of God, but metaphysically dualist, since it does not reduce every reality to the Divine Essence, the duality of the soul and God remaining, by and large, the rule rather than the exception. As Frithjof Schuon has argued, this predisposition presents some major challenges when confronted with the Advaitin principle of the non-dual Self.[5] Ramana Maharshi appears to be aware of the latter, even though this awareness may not manifest at the forefront of his spiritual advice in most of the published accounts. In fact, Ramana sometimes stresses the principle that Self-inquiry is a steep path that presupposes rigorous qualifications. Thus, he refers to the point, taught in various scriptures, that Self-inquiry requires specific inner qualifications, spiritual practices over several lifespans, or at least years of meditation at the foot of a spiritual master.[49]

So why would the Maharshi so often refer to surrender? When asked about the weaknesses that hamper the search for the Self, and why the Lord does not remove the impediments that lie in the way of spiritual realization, Ramana Maharshi recommends that the practitioner surrender to the Lord. The fundamental spiritual alternative is clearly laid out in the following answer: 'If you believe that God will do all the things that you want Him to do, then surrender yourself to Him. Otherwise let God alone, and know yourself.'[50] What is recognized here implicitly is the traditional Hindu duality of path: *jñāna* and *bhakti*, spiritual knowledge and devotional love. There is a path that begins with the ego and its relationship with God, and another one that begins with the consciousness of Reality, or with an investigation into the nature of the Self, which amounts to the same, since inquiry underpins consciousness and the Self is the Real without qualifications. The way of devotion, which may also be considered as a stage on the way to Self-realization, is predicated on an identification with the body. The emphasis, therefore, is on the difference, *bheda*, between the devotee and God. As for the metaphysical path, it is fundamentally non-dual, postulates non-difference, *abheda*, and culminates in Self-realization. Besides religious devotion and metaphysical knowledge there is, however, a third way that may be referred to as mystical. In between the two ways, or as a kind of intermediary stage between them, lies the path of those who consider themselves 'a spark of the divine fire or as a ray of the divine sun.'[51] This path presupposes a measure of difference as fuel for its worshipping intensity, while reaching at the same time the horizon of union with the Divine, in a kind of ecstatic merging with the Beloved. It corresponds to *bhedābheda*, or difference-non-difference.

It is instructive to analyze the ways in which this basic distinction, which amounts to a fundamental spiritual typology, can be used, in the Maharshi's perspective, as a key to decipher and categorize religious traditions themselves. In this connection, one of the foremost Western devotees of Ramana Maharshi, Arthur Osborne, wrote a book that provides guidelines for such a comparative task on the basis of Hindu categories and on the background of the Maharshi's perspective. *Buddhism and Christianity in the Light of Hinduism* was first published in 1959, with Sri Ramanasramam.[52] In this work, Osborne presents the central thesis of a complementarity between Buddhism and Christianity, which he situates within the framework of a providential adaptation to the particular needs of diverse peoples, cultures and communities. Here is the substance of this thesis:

> Buddhism and Christianity are the two complementary aspects of a single process: the provision of a proselytising religion based on a Divine Founder in two forms, advaitic or metaphysical for the East and dualistic or devotional for the West, for the benefit of peoples whose own religions had lost their spiritual potency.[53]

Several points need to be highlighted here. One must note, first of all, a somewhat puzzling conjunction, at least from a Hindu point of view, between proselytizing on the one hand and the centrality of a Divine figure on the other. In Osborne's perspective, the 'Divine Founder' is by definition a 'delivered soul' or a *jivan-mukta*, as well as a Divine descent or *avatāra*. The Hindu tradition does not dissociate divinity and liberation from the realm of human relativity: in that sense the *avatāra* corresponds downward to what the *jivan-mukta* is upward. It must be noted that Ramana Maharshi himself does not seem to have ever answered explicitly the question of knowing whether he was an *avatāra*, bypassing the literality of the question in order to emphasise the innermost meaning of the avatāric identity: 'When the mind melts with love of Him [...] the subtle eye of pure intellect opens and He reveals Himself as Pure Consciousness.'[54] The Maharshi provides here the epitome of what the word 'Divine' may entail when applied to a human being: 'Melting' in the Self. Now, it cannot be missed that from an Advaitin point of view the reality of Self-realization is in a way incompatible with proselytization. So what is implicit in Osborne's point is the idea that Buddhism and Christianity represents adaptations of the principle of the 'Divine Soul' to religions destined to shape the outlook of large segments of mankind. This is the way in which the reality of the Self can provide guidance to the widest number through its 'embodiment' and radiance in the spiritual personalities of founders. This is normally not the mode in which the human realization of *Moksha* affects human collectivities, since within a Hindu context there is no question of any proselytizing dimension of the *mukti,* but rather a spiritual magnetism and radiance. The emphasis on the proselytizing power of the 'Divine Founder' is, needless to say, a double-edged sword, since it risks moving the focus of the Self-realization from inner search and assimilation to outer belonging and doing. In Buddhism, this tendency is much less evident in principle than it is in Christianity, as it is being understood that the Buddha's teachings point to *Nirvāna* and the spiritual duty of each soul, rather than to the Buddha himself. Still, the fact that much of Buddhism has gradually come to revolve around devotional practices could illustrate the fact that the proselytizing dimension of religious teaching tends to dilute its contemplative core, although such a dilution can also be assigned other causes in non-proselytizing contexts.

The second point that needs attention is the distinction between the metaphysical and the devotional, and the way Osborne makes it relevant to the economy of the two religious traditions, not without running the risk of attracting the reproach of absolutizing its reality. At any rate, the disjunction between East and West, which Osborne qualifies in other passages of his book in order to keep from simplistic categorizations, reflects to a large extent the ideas introduced by René Guénon in the first half of the twentieth century. The Guénonian outlook is based on the dichotomy of a contemplative East and an active West. For the French critic of the modern world, the distinction in question is grounded in history, although its foundations may be more than historical. Guénon sees in the Renaissance, the industrial revolution and the colonial enterprise, among others, evidences of the Western affinity with action. Many of the early Western devotees of Ramana Maharshi, whether influenced by the reading of Guénon or not, subscribed to these critical tenets, and saw the Western world as characterized by a civilizational extraversion verging on activism. In this vein, Guénon went so far as to get into generalizations in opining that Eastern people are more contemplative than Westerners.[55] At any rate, the connection to an active disposition appears not only in the fact that devotional practices tend to be more extroverted and 'active' than contemplative discipline, but also, and more fundamentally, in the principle that contemplativeness refers to a sense of unity whereas devotion presupposes duality, which is from a Hindu point of view the field of action.

It must be reiterated that devotion means, for the Maharshi, much more than what it refers to in common parlance. For one thing, its spiritual efficaciousness is contingent upon the total surrender of the ego. Complete abandonment to God's will, when perfected, cannot but reveal the Divine Reality as the true and only Self. The Maharshi likes to compare the way of the sincere and consummate *bhakta* to the attitude of the traveller 'putting his luggage in the cart which bears the load any way.'[56] By contrast, the imperfect devotee, on account of his 'spurious ego which presumes to bear that burden [the burden of the world that the Lord bears] is like a sculptured figure at the foot of a temple tower which appears to sustain the tower's weight.'[57] Surrender is so central in the teachings of Ramana Maharshi that it may be deemed to encapsulate the whole of religion. In fact, if there is a way in which the Maharshi's perspective may be properly characterized as religious, it is certainly in so far as it provides a synthesis of the whole of religious life as utter surrender to the Divine. One can think of Meister Eckhart's *Gelassenheit*.[58] One can also ponder the meaning of the Arabic word *islām* as perfect submission to God's Will, which is actualized, or perfected, through obedience to God's Law. In Sufism, as the culmination of the spiritual logic of Islam, the principle of surrender must ultimately lead to an extinction of the self into God, or *fanā'*.

It is no coincidence that the mystical reality of extinction appears in full light in Ramana's *Bridal Garland of Letters for Arunachala* (*Arunachala Aksharamanamalai*). Such verses as 'I sought refuge in Thee as my God, and Thou didst destroy me utterly', 'Thy fire burn me to ashes', 'Thou art, verily, Death to me!' are striking evidence of the inner call for annihilation of the ego that characterizes the peaks of the mystical path across traditions.[59] Thus, the *Garland* is like the epitome of a religious hymn in a non-dualistic context. In fact it could even be argued that the burning love of Arunachala that is expressed therein was for all practical purposes 'Ramana's religion.'[60] It also illustrates most powerfully the intrinsic integration of *bhakti* within *jñāna* or, if one wishes, of religion into spirituality. As mentioned in Chapter Two, the Maharshi confessed that the one hundred and eight distichs of this Tamil composition came to him as a pure inspiration: 'he himself later on said that it was not the result of any premeditation or conscious cogitation, but that it came out of his heart unexpectedly and spontaneously.'[61] The hymn came at the request of disciples as a means to help devotees be identified as such as they looked for food in the streets of Tiruvannamalai. Significantly, the first reaction of the Maharshi to this request was dubitative: what need is there to break silence to praise the sacred mountain while the devotional tradition already offers a number of hymns that are available to devotees? Moreover, the *mukta* does not need any exteriorization, whether aesthetic or ritual; his productions flow from the needs of others, on the one hand, and from divine inspiration, on the other. So the Divine response overwhelmed, as it were, human reticence, to provide a bridge between God and mankind. Keeping this in mind, one is tempted to say that the devotion to Arunachala was the 'religion' brought by Maharshi to his devotees, and that the *Bridal Garland* was its 'revelation.' Lest these terms be misunderstood or taken too literally, it is suitable to specify that, by using them, I am not implying that the Maharshi was intent on initiating a new religious tradition. I take the word 'religion' not as referring to a belief and salvation system, but merely as characterizing formal means of relating to the Divine. As for the word 'revelation', it does not point, here, to a Divine message of guidance and salvation, but simply to words inspired by Divine Grace. If religion is a link between the human and the Divine, what better symbol of this relation than a sacred mountain connecting the sky and the earth? And is not revelation a garland of sacred words expressing this transcendent bond?

6

WORLD AND MIND, WORLD IN MIND

Over the last half-century, the concept of objectivity has been questioned
both in intellectual circles and in popular discourse. The ontological and
epistemological realism of traditional philosophical teachings—their belief in
the reality of objects and concepts—has not been the only target of this critique,
as the modern narrative of scientistic progressivism and related ideological
inheritances of the eighteenth and nineteenth centuries have also come to be
considered with skepticism or suspicion. The postmodern deconstructivist
mood of the times, with its emphasis on deferment and displacement of
meaning—the idea that meaning is never fixed nor objective nor 'present'—
is indeed predicated not only on a rejection of the realist vision of a cognitive
adjustment between subject and object, but also on the contestation of the
very notions of a stable subject and a 'substantial' object. The rejection of the
principle of epistemological *adaequatio*, whereby the intellect and its object
are aligned, or even united, in the act of knowledge, has meant a breaking away
from the epistemological realism that had been by and large the inheritance
of the Western tradition since Plato.[1] This vision was solidly predicated on a
sense of ontological and epistemological *correspondence* between the knowing
subject and the known object. According to this traditional outlook, human
intelligence can know the objects of its intellection by virtue of the intelligible
nature of the universe. By contrast, while not necessarily reflecting the tenets
of a self-aware philosophical idealism, the pervasive claims of ambient
subjectivist relativism that are characteristic of the postmodern mood have

141

called into question the very reality of an objective field of intelligibility that could be universally recognized. In this cultural context, reality is *my* reality, and therefore alternative realities abound. This is all the more so when the private space of the virtual world increasingly encroaches upon the irreducible portions of objective constraints that constitute the shared daily duties of existence and the undeniable autonomy of fellow humans. New sophisticated or naïve forms of theoretical and practical solipsism have therefore arisen in the cultural ambience of the early twenty-first century. As a last zone of resistance to such relativistic sensibilities and assumptions, the cultural prestige and the practical benefits of the realizations of modern science and its technological applications have allowed scientific discourses, as relayed by scientistic ideology, to remain the quasi-exclusive foundation for any resilient sense of objectivity, if what is meant by this term can refer to the belief in a human ability to acquire reliable knowledge of the external world. However, in the development of science itself, some of the groundbreaking intuitions of the most recent theories have entailed a growing disruption of the notion of a radical distinction between subject and object.[2] Although such scientific theories are quite independent from ideological and cultural trends, and indeed in some ways opposed to them in their envisioning of the status of truth, their vulgarized forms have also contributed to the relativistic climate of the times.

The contemporary context is one in which a commonsensical and pragmatically necessary belief in the existence of objects goes in hand in hand with a pervasive skepticism vis-à-vis the objectivity of concepts and values. Thus, a form of pragmatic objectivism can paradoxically coexist with an ambient philosophical subjectivism. While a spontaneous and conventional sense of objectivity remains operative in the world of everyday experience, a prevalent cultural relativism leans toward considering representations of reality, that is beliefs, convictions, ideas, as mere subjective and self-made productions. Furthermore, the extent of this relativism—and we must leave aside in this context the contemporary phenomenon of 'fundamentalist' reactions to it—is such that it may imperceptibly lead to a growing receptivity to the principle of a subjective apprehension and understanding of the outer world itself. This trend could therefore be understood in the form of a kind of parody of the Buddhist distinction between 'conventional truth' and 'ultimate truth': while the daily affairs of the world are founded on a conventional acceptance of objective reality for the sake of 'business-related' expediency, the ultimate truth of the matter is the relativist non-recognition of any objective, universal reality. The postmodern view of an ever-receding meaning and reality—and the afferent principle of self-referentiality—has therefore provided arguments in favor of a cultural receptivity to the idea, rarely stated outright but underlying a variety of assumptions and forms of behavior, that the world is nothing more than a form of projection of the individual mind. When directed toward spirituality, this cultural bent finds in Asian metaphysical teachings such as *Advaita Vedānta* and *Madhyamaka* Buddhism what it conceives as validating spiritual antecedents. Indeed, one of the main characteristics of these metaphysical schools is their emphasis on the illusoriness of the objective field, whether it be couched in terms of unintelligible appearance, as the Advaitin *Māyā*, or as emptiness, or co-dependent origination, in Mahāyāna Buddhism. Needless to say, such metaphysical positions are but the negative side of various modes of reference to an absolute Reality, whether the latter be approached in affirmative or negative ways. Notwithstanding this fundamental grounding that postmodern readers of those traditions do tend to dispense with, Abrahamic religious teachings, by contrast, appear to offer nothing but dogmatic statements about objective realities, starting with the Reality of God as the most 'constraining' of all.

As has been noted previously, it is not only the notion of objective reality that is called into question, but also the stability of the subject itself. The traditional notion of the soul as an individual substance has become irredeemably obsolete in academic circles and prevailing schools of psychology.[3] Discontinuity, fragmentation, and distance have been set as hallmarks of what some proponents of postmodernity referred to as the 'zerological subject.'[4] Thus, the aforementioned characteristics of the postmodern subject are sometimes deemed to dovetail with metaphysical and spiritual insights into the self that originate from Asian traditions. The Buddhist doctrine of *anatta* or no-self, i.e., the negation of substantial and permanent selfhood, is particularly solicited in this regard, as it appears to confirm the need to dispense with any notion of a substantial and stable subject. In mainstream Buddhism, the self is considered to be a set of temporary aggregates or a nexus of co-dependently arisen conditions that has no substantial reality and permanence. Thus, in the *Anattalakkhana Sutta, The Characteristic of Not-Self,* the Buddha teaches 'feeling is not-self [...] perception is not-self [...] determinations are not-self [...] consciousness is not-self.'[5] In the Buddha's teachings this principle functions, methodically, as a way to de-identify from the very source of perishability and suffering. It has been argued that it is therefore less a metaphysical statement about reality than a principle of spiritual pedagogy.[6] The postmodern take on the self, naturally, is not determined by the same spiritual intent. Notwithstanding, the commonality of the two outlooks lies in a distrust of any substantialist understanding of selfhood. It bears highlighting, moreover, that this postmodern perspective on the matter, which amounts to a sort of dissolution of the self, can coexist with all manner of individualistic aspects of culture, including the aforementioned relativism. While the destruction of selfhood is expected to free one from constraining continuities and metaphysical accountability, it is far from being incompatible with the imperious needs of a present locus of idiosyncratic awareness. This is no doubt the reason why alternatives to the vacuum and inconsistencies left in the wake of deconstructivist postmodernity have arisen in the form of various reconstructivist discourses valuing interconnectedness over self-deconstruction.[7] Buddhist and Advaitin teachings are sometimes taken to task, in such contexts, in view of shaping a new holistic paradigm that would give a more positive direction to postmodernity, although not without serious metaphysical ambiguities.[8]

In addition to the theoretical ventures into postmodern interpretation of Asian forms of mysticism, popularized versions of 'practical' *Vedānta* and Buddhism resonate, particularly in the West, with the prevailing allure of relativism and its discarding of objective claims of reality. This stems from another dimension of the contemporary mood: the pervasive idea that doctrines are of no use, or may even function as impediments when it comes to the realm of 'inner experience.' This anti-intellectual bias is largely consistent with another general trend in neo-spirituality, namely a tendency to separate physio-psychological techniques from their traditional and metaphysical contexts. There is, therefore, great need to ponder the actual meaning, implications and limits of the apparent 'practical idealism' of many Asian metaphysical schools. This is particularly so in relation to *Advaita Vedānta*, which forms the framework of Ramana Maharshi's teachings, and is all-too-often expeditiously rendered as an idealist doctrine of illusion. Indeed Ramana's teachings are sometimes all too hastily considered to be representative of an extreme form of idealism, one in which the world is deemed to have reality only in relation to the mind, and even literally understood as a mere projection of the mind. Thus, when placed in parallel with the Maharshi's teachings, postmodern skepticism may superficially claim to find some corroborating evidence for its philosophical and cultural leanings. This is so in relation to several cardinal themes of the Maharshi's spiritual epistemology. First, there is the Maharshi's frequent reference to the non-existence of the mind, then there is the idea that the world is nothing but a projection of the mind, and finally there is the Maharshi's refusal to recognize an ontological distinction between dream and wakefulness. One must therefore further examine the meanings, context and implications of such seemingly postmodern positions and the ways they may intersect with, or differ from, the contemporary theme of the 'disappearance' of the subject.

Both commonsensical and philosophical forms of realism, which take the world as an undeniable reality, recoil at the consideration of a system of thought that would call into question the very objects of our human perceptions, inquiries and activities. This appears to be contradicting, moreover, the creationist teachings that are to be found not only in Abrahamic faiths but also in the Hindu tradition itself. These teachings assert that the world is, in one way or another, a production of the Divine Lord, which means that it cannot be reduced to a projection of the human psyche.[9] The questions and difficulties raised by these traditional references already suggest that there is much more to the Maharshi's assertions than what some hasty psycho-philosophical shortcuts would lead us to think. At any rate, our intention in the pages that follow is not so much to reach any definite conclusion on the perplexities that may arise from a discussion of the concepts at stake, but rather to contemplate the various vantage points from which they can be approached. In other words the goal of this exploration is not a mental resolution of the questions at issue, which would be quite nugatory, but a meditation of their various facets and implications.[10]

A fruitful way to start in order to delve into the complexity of the issue is to consider typical occurrences of the Maharshi's view on mind and world. We find particularly striking instances of the latter in the sixth and seventh stanzas of *Ulladu Nārpadu*:

'Tis the sense-objects that are termed the world;
And these that are perceived by senses five,
'Tis mind alone, which working through these five
Can know the Universe, and so it, too,
Is nothing more than mind. Or can you say
That it exists in absence of the mind? [...]
The world and its perceiver therefore rise
And fade together, for the world's no more
Than something we perceive. Where they arise,
The point in which they sink, this is the core,

From disappearance and appearance free,
'Tis ever Conscious, Perfect, Absolute.[11]

From one vantage point, to say that the world is but a perception of the mind amounts to stating that mind and world are interdependent. It is therefore a way to express their relativity, by contrast with That which is their source and destination, *Satcitānanda*. It must be noted, accordingly, that the question of the existence of the world in the absence of the mind is not in this case as much denied as it is deemed unanswerable from the point of view of the mind itself: whether or not the world exists in the absence of the mind, the mind itself cannot answer this question when absent. As for the Absolute Self, it is not simply 'free from disappearance' since it is pure Being, it is also free from appearance since the latter presupposes a state that would be prior to it. Now the Self is eternal light, and It cannot be preceded by anything from which, or following which, it could appear.

In response to a question about the reality of the world, the Maharshi invites his interlocutor to contemplate the way in which the world is a product of their own perceptions and actions: 'you are now producing [*kāram*] all these things, i.e., realizing these things, regarding as real all things, making real what is not real.'[12] The Sanskrit term *kāram*, from the root of causing or doing, is to be found, for instance, in the *Bhagavad Gītā* (17:15) in the sense of 'producing.' The well-known concept of *karma* belongs to the same etymon and it can be said, in light of this meaningful connection, that the world is like the karmic production of the individual. The individual creates the world, which is in a sense his world, by virtue of the consciousness, and therefore thoughts, words, and actions that are his own. This is the usual concept of *karma*. However, the Maharshi alludes to another production, which is the epistemological foundation for the very possibility of *karma*, and that is the 'making real of what is not real.' This is a production, or a creation, that suggests in what way the world is in the mind and, why, as the Maharshi puts it, when the ego disappears the world also disappears. Obviously the world does not disappear in its phenomenal reality—the *jivan mukta* could not even function in a world that is not—but it disappears as a set of discrete objects that would have reality in and of themselves.

It is to be noted, moreover, that, from this perspective, while the world has no reality except through the ego, the ego or the mind itself have no reality either without the world. In the absence of the mind, the world is none other than the Self; it is the Self since there is no other reality than the

Self. Analogously, in the absence of the world there is no mind in the sense that the mind-ego is 'created' by the world with which it is interdependent. This happens daily in deep sleep, which provides a direct symbol of what the disappearance of the world may mean for the *jivan mukta*. When the world vanishes, That which remains is the Self: 'Deep sleep can e'er be had while wide awake by search for Self.'[13] Saying that the world disappears may therefore be understood as another way of saying that phenomena vanish, as in the state of deep sleep, or that the world is no longer perceived as being different from the Self, and therefore also as other than the mind within the Self.

In other passages, Ramana Maharshi refers to the triad ego–world–God in order to illuminate the transcendence of non-dual Reality. This triad may be considered either from the point of view of the distinctions it entails, or in the perspective of the one Self. The first perspective is that of relativity and appearance, which is founded upon the qualitative differences between the three elements of the triad. In the same way as the world does not exist without the ego, in the sense that one is relative to the other, or that they are the two sides of appearance—or epistemologically ignorance of their non-dual Essence, there is no God without mind and without world: 'If the three, namely, the ego, world and God are considered to be distinct and separate from one another, they become illusory, like the silver in the mother-of-Pearl. These three are really one and identical. They are the one *Brahman* or *Ātman*.'[14] In *Advaita*, the concept of *Saguna Brahman*, or the Qualified *Brahman*, articulates the relativity, and therefore in a certain way 'illusoriness,' of 'God.' This subtle and delicate point, which may give rise to grave misunderstandings, is even expressed within some streams of Abrahamic religions, as evidenced by Meister Eckhart's bold statements such as:

> while I yet stood in my first cause, I had no God and was my own cause: then I wanted nothing and desired nothing, for I was bare being and the knower of myself in the enjoyment of truth. Then I wanted myself and wanted no other thing: what I wanted I was and what I was I wanted, and thus I was free of God and all things. But when I left my free will behind and received my created being, then I had a God. For before there were creatures, God was not 'God': He was That which He was.[15]

Eckhart's view is obviously not akin to the idea that God is unreal, but simply means that the 'formal and relational God' or 'God'—which is the only God from a purely human point of view—has no reality when considered from the vantage point of the non-dual Self, which is God as God, or God as Essence, independently from any relationship with other-than-Itself, God as All. This means, moreover, that the distinction that is conventionally, or humanly, established between the ego, the world and God, is based on qualitative formal differences among them. This explains why Ramana Maharshi can therefore approach the meditation on this triad in terms of the predominance of a particular cosmic quality. In the perspective of *Sāmkhya*, one of the six *darshanas* or orthodox points of view, the concept of *guna* refers to the three cosmological qualities that are constitutive of the whole of existence. In a response to a question, the Maharshi states that 'the world, individual soul and God *(jagatjiveswara)* are the embodiments of the three qualities or *gunas*.'[16] These are *sattva, rajas* and *tamas*.[17] Thus, the Maharshi does not only take the three qualities to be integral components of cosmic reality, but he also identifies each of them with one of the three elements of the fundamental ternary: 'In that group, goodness *(sattvam)* is the personal God *(Īśvara)*; activity *(rajas)* is the individual soul *(jīva)*; and heaviness *(tamas)* is the world *(jagat)*.' As for the Self, which is normally referred to as *Nirguna,* or beyond qualities, the Maharshi assigns to it, in the same passage, the quality of 'pure goodness' *(suddha sattva)*. This is obviously 'goodness beyond goodness' or '*sattva* beyond *sattva*' since it can in no way be relative to other *gunas*. Conceived in this way, the distinction between the triad of God, man and the world clearly preserves a hierarchy of ontological degrees in which God lies at the summit, as a most direct 'reflection' of the Self, and the world on the lowest ring, since it crystallizes the highest density of opacity, as it were. Human consciousness stands in between and its dynamic, or rajasic, character may take it in any direction, whether upward or downward; and this leads us back to the multifaceted question of its relationship with the world.

As was highlighted from the outset, the elliptical idea that the world is a projection of the mind is to be found in numerous texts and interviews with the Maharshi. This understanding of the mind-world relationship has sometimes been equated with forms of radical subjective idealism such as George Berkeley's and his standard formula *esse est percipi*.[18] It is also a position that has often been attributed to *Advaita Vedānta* in general, even though the reality of the matter is actually much more complex. At any rate this type of idealist position appears to confine to a kind of solipsism that denies any objectivity to the world, and flies in the face of ordinary experience and common sense. T.M.P. Mahadevan has effectively refuted the all too expeditious identification of the Advaitin perspective with 'subjective idealism.' The heart of his argument, which is developed in several of its implications in the current essay, is that this erroneous identification stems from a mere confusion between the individual soul and the Divine and universal Self. *Advaita* may be considered as a form of subjective idealism only inasmuch as one understands the real subject to be the Self of all selves, and not, in its perspective, the limited ego or mind. According to Mahadevan the idealist literality, or tone, of some Advaitin teachings is purely pedagogical, and not metaphysical.[19] It has two intents: one is to refute realism, while the second is to facilitate the spiritual assimilation of the doctrine. In other words, the brand of realism that is criticized herein is the one that affirms the full reality of the world. It is therefore akin to *dvaita* in one form or another. Thus, as a pedagogical or spiritual response, some forms of *Advaita* have adopted a point of view that echoes the Buddhist *Vijñānavadins'* so as to dispel in the mind of the disciple the attachment to the idea of the reality of the world. This appears to be, by and large, the perspective of the Maharshi, who may see this doctrine less as the ultimate truth about reality than as a means whereby the bond with the idea of the duality of a subject and an object is broken. Subjectivist idealism might function, in other words, as corrective excess to an abusive belief in the reality of the world. Such a position functions as a kind of *kōan*, these Zen perplexing riddles that are intended by Masters to precipitate a mental revolution within the disciple by dispelling conventional perceptions of reality. In other words, the Maharshi intentionally bypasses the pedagogical realism of Shankara's *Vedānta*. From another point of view, as I will develop it further, the 'idealist' bent of the Maharshi's teachings results from their being based in spontaneous realization rather than being the outcome of a metaphysical doctrine and its methodical complement.

Practically speaking, the world that disappears is the world-as-object-of-the-mind, because it is the only world that concerns the mind. The subject precedes the object since the latter presupposes the former, even though the subject may also be conceived as relative to, or co-dependent with, the object. At any rate, the world without a subject is not truly an object, hence the aforementioned question from *Ulladu Nārpadu*: 'can you say that it exists in the absence of the mind?' This is the view that is referred to in Hindu metaphysics as *drishti-srishti-vāda,* 'the doctrine of creation through perception'. This understanding of *Advaita* is post-Shankarian, and was particularly articulated by the sixteenth-century Prakashananda.[20] However, Shankara himself was not a subjective idealist. In his *Commentary on the Brahma Sūtras*, he writes that 'Non-existence [of things external] is not [true], on account of their being experienced.'[21] For Shankara the only unreality is of the kind of the 'horn of a hare', which means one that cannot be experienced, and therefore not dispelled. The external world is obviously not unreal in that sense, 'no one says that Devadatta is like the son of a barren woman.' Moreover Shankara insists on the limits of the analogy between the illusoriness of the world and the dream state by stating that, by contrast with spiritual awakening, the waking state annuls the phenomenal reality of the dream. While his opponents would object, in an analogy with waking up from a dream, that when the Self is realized, the world experienced during the waking state is also shown to be illusory, this does not mean, however, that the world vanishes since, as Shankara states, it continues to be experienced. All that could be said is that it is not taken for full reality anymore, or that its actual reality is indissociable from its being none other than *Ātman*. In a sense, it could be said that the realization of the Self makes the world truly real, while it was only illusorily so before Self-realization. It is plausible that the apparent disagreement between Shankara and Ramana on this point— the Maharshi being more amenable to recognizing the epistemological merits of *drishti-srishti-vāda*—is due to a difference of inflection. This difference of accent derives to a large extent from the diverse historical contexts in which respective statements were made. In the commentaries on the *Brahma Sūtras* Shankara is involved in a metaphysical dispute with Buddhists and other idealists. Such subjective idealism undermines the very foundation of the Shankarian outlook, which is the discrimination between the Reality of the Self and the appearance of reality of the phenomena as *upadhis*. Shankara emphasises discrimination between degrees of reality, and this discrimination is compromised, indeed made impossible, by radical idealism. The Maharshi's teachings developed in quite a different context. For most of the Maharshi's visitors, philosophical idealism was less an obstacle than was a worldly type of realism hampering spiritual realization.

The teaching of *drishti-srishti-vāda* must be distinguished from *ajātivāda*, or non-causality, or non-creation, which the Maharshi found more satisfactory but more difficult to assimilate for most. He gave a Tamil translation of Gaudapāda's *Māndūkya Upanishad Kārikā* that encapsulates the meaning of the doctrine: 'There is no creation, no destruction, no bondage, no longing to be freed from bondage, no striving to be free [from bondage], nor anyone who has attained [freedom from bondage]. Know that this is the ultimate truth' (2:32).[22] This is, of course, ultimate in that it expresses the truth from the point of view of the highest Reality, with no concession made to appearances. From this highest vantage point everything is cancelled out from the outset, as it were: this is the purest and simplest affirmation of Reality. In this view, the whole causal chains of creation and emancipation presuppose an inadequate perception of Reality as the sole reality. The idea of creation presupposes that the Creator is in a way ultimate; but that which is related to the world cannot be ultimate in a true sense. Therefore the Self, which is the Essence of everything, cannot be taken as an element in a causal chain. It is not strictly speaking the Cause of the world, but the world itself *as* Self. An interesting point to note is the convergence of this point of view with the ultimate truth, or *paramārtha satya*, as expressed in Buddhist texts such as the *Lankāvatāra Sūtra*: 'there is no time, no *Nirvāna*, no *dharma*-essence. And there are no Buddhas, no truths, no fruition, no causal agents, no perversion, no *Nirvāna*, no passing away, no birth.'[23] In both cases, the apparent reality of everything, including the most central tenets and realities of the path of emancipation, is revealed to be naught, and this constitutes the most fundamental metaphysical statement on Reality. The obvious difference, however, is that the Maharshi's negations do not include a negation of the Self. Quite the opposite, since this Reality is the fundamental ground upon which negations can arise and reveal their meaningfulness. Mahāyāna Buddhism goes a step further by conceiving the idea of the Self as a potential obstacle to the realization of Emptiness, or the Buddha nature, since it may itself be mentally turned into an object of attachment.

It is therefore only downstream of the *ajāti-vāda* that the issue of the status of the reality of the world, and that of the ego, may arise. Although the Maharshi himself clearly indicated that his was the truth of *ajāta*, or non-creation, he also adjusted his teachings to the needs of a variety of seekers by expounding both *srishti-drishti* and *drishti-srishti*.[24] Thus, according to the sage, there are in fact three possible perspectives on reality, one being ultimate, and two being pedagogical or expedient. Schematically they correspond to beyond-subject-object, object-subject and subject-object. While the second, *srishti-drishti,* could be coined 'naive realism', the third, *drishti-srishti* could be deemed to amount to a 'naive idealism.' The term naivety refers, here, to an inability to consider reality strictly as it is. It connotes lack of spiritual experience and discernment. At any rate, on such an unultimate level of consideration, it is possible to distinguish the world-in-itself, in its 'absoluteness' or objectivity, its existence too—independently from the relationship subject-object—and the world-object as one term of the relationship between human subject and object. From the first point of view, there is obviously, and by definition, a reality of the world independently from any perception. This is the perspective of *srishti-drishti*, in which the universe of creation, *srishti*, 'precedes' the 'gaze' of the subject, *drishti*. It is on account of this 'absoluteness' of the world that there exists a possibility for individuals to agree on the existence, or truth, of phenomena. When it is said, from this objective point of view, that 'the world is a projection of the mind,' it cannot mean, therefore, that it is a mere production of the individual psyche. As Kapali Sastriar has noted, such perspective can only refer to the principle that 'the mind is meant as cosmic principle (*Tattva*) manifest in the individual as well as in the Universal.'[25] In this sense the world that is contemplated is nothing but the 'gross form of the mind, which is subtle.'[26]

From the second point of view, the world is totally relative to a human subject who perceives and experiences it. This is another way of saying that the subject itself is relative to the aspect of reality that it 'evokes.' This approximates the Buddhist teaching of emptiness or *pratītya-samutpāda*, i.e., co-dependent origination. According to this principle there is no *svabhāva*, or self-nature, because nothing can be, and therefore can be defined, in and of itself, given that its 'reality' entails, intrinsically, an indefinite number of relationships without which it cannot 'be.' In and of itself, it is empty, which means that it is more no-thing than something. It appears that Ramana Maharshi considers both aspects, or rather either one depending on the context. To a question as to how the 'world' subsides, the Maharshi answers: 'If the mind subsides, the whole world subsides, the natural state presents itself.'[27] This amounts to saying that the mind and the world are co-dependent. Co-dependency does not mean causal origination, however, for as T.M.P. Mahadevan has noted, 'the entire world appears only *with* the ego, though not *from* the ego.'[28]

The various vantage points that have been evoked in the previous pages are sometimes related by the Maharshi to the three notions of *chidākāsha*, *chittākāsha* and *bhutākāsha*, as they correspond to three different 'worlds.' *Chidākāsha* is the field of pure consciousness, or the 'space' or ether of the *Ātman* itself. Spiritually speaking, it means the realization of the non-manifested and absolute reality. In the enumeration of the three, or four, states of consciousness, it corresponds to deep sleep, *sushupti*. From that point of view, deep sleep is a passive reabsorption into the Self. The second space, *chittākāsha*, is the field of consciousness experienced through the individual mind. This is the world as projected by the mind. The third realm is the space of consciousness as physical element, *bhutākāsha*. *Chittākāsha* includes *bhutākāsha*, but *chidākāsha* embraces both the latter and the former. In a text by the Tamil scholar Kannudaiya Valallar entitled *Ozhivil Odukkam: Eternal*

Repose upon Annulment, to which Ramana Maharshi liked to refer, these three spaces are alluded to in the context of a narrative. A temple elephant, while resting, dreams that he is in rut in a strange forest. There, he comes face to face with a lion, and consequently awakens. The commentary of this parable indicates that the resting elephant, untouched by dreams, is none other than the non-dual Self. It is *chidākāsha*. The elephant in rut is the Self appearing as the individual self in this world, while the forest is also the Self, but appearing as the waking world of the mental self. In the forest of the physical world the self of the elephant in rut appears, and in the latter the subtle or psychic space of the world emerges, both of them being none other than appearances within the spiritual or Ātmanic space. As René Guénon has indicated, one may consider the sequence between the three spaces from two different points of view. The first one is the immediate or conventional human point of view that starts with *bhutākāsha,* and then proceeds to *chittākāsha,* and finally to *chidākāsha.* The second point of view, by contrast, is in conformity with the metaphysical order of things, beginning with the *Ātman* and ending with the physical reality.[29] In the story, the lion corresponds to the Self appearing as the *guru,* that is the manifestation of Reality in appearance. The mind creates the world as a projection: in essence this *chittākāsha* is the outcome of the tendencies and desires of the individual self.[30] There is no mind without a world projected by the mind, since the nature of the mind is to be aware of objects, whether internal or external, which it 'imagines' as being other than itself. The question of the hierarchy between *bhutākāsha* and *chittākāsha* brings us back to a matter of points of view. René Guénon notes that in the perspective of the needs of ordinary life *bhutākāsha* is superior to *chittākāsha* in the sense that it provides more stability and continuity. However, this relative superiority, which is the bulwark of ordinary 'realism', does not mean that *chittākāsha* is in all respects subordinate to *bhutākāsha.* First of all, the very distinction between the two is annulled, essentially, by a consideration of *mahākāsha,* the fourth space of no-space, the pure Unconditioned. This is the universal space of the Self in Itself, if one may say so, by contrast with *chidākāsha,* which would refer in this case to the Self in so far as it is considered one of the three spaces or worlds, that is, in a sense, relatively. So, in this perspective the very difference between *bhutākāsha* and *chittākāsha* is moot. Secondly, the fact that *chittākāsha* comes in second, following *chidākāsha,* when contemplated from a metaphysical point of view, already indicates its aspect of relative eminence over *bhutākāsha.* René Guénon points out the fact that the 'possibilities of the state of dream are wider that than of the state of wake, and it allows the individual to escape, to a certain extent, some of the limiting conditions to which it is submitted in his corporeal modality.'[31] This is the reason why, in many religious traditions, dreams can provide the space for encounters with higher realms of reality; in Islam for example, the Prophet is said to have asserted that dream 'constitutes one forty-sixth of prophethood.'[32] This does not refer to just any dream, however, but to lucid oneiric experiences that are believed to originate in the spiritual world, and for the manifestation of which the dream state provides suitable conditions. It is evident, however, that this is in no way an exclusive privilege of the dreaming state, since celestial and spiritual manifestations do also take place frequently in a waking state. While the dream state corresponds, from a certain point of view, to a higher and subtler realm of reality, the state of wakefulness, for its part, holds the eminence of being a direct symbol of *chidākāsha*. For one thing, and indeed most importantly, Self-realization does not normally occur in the dream state. In other words, while its formal expanse is potentially greater than that of wakefulness, *chittākāsha* involves an element of passivity that does not agree with the demands of Self-awareness. It is noteworthy, in this regard, that the term Awakening is used by Indian spiritual traditions, to refer to the supreme spiritual experience, as already indicated by the Indo-European etymon of *buddhi* and *Buddha* that conveys the meaning of being awake, or aware. *Chidākāsha* is indeed Awakening, which led Muruganar to write that 'Ramanāshramam is *chidākāsha*' and extends therefore everywhere since, as the Maharshi corroborated, 'time and space do not exist.'[33] It is probably in the same way that one must understand the Hindu traditional idea that dying in Varanasi amounts to spiritual liberation, *Moksha*. Here the sacred place, or the spiritualized place, becomes a theurgic symbol of *chidākāsha*. Like Kashi, Ramanāshram is *chidākāsha* in the sense that its very foundation is *Ātman*, and *chidākāsha* is everywhere for there is no space—whether *bhutākāsha* and *chittākāsha*—that is not within *chidākāsha*, as pure Consciousness encompasses everything. Verses from Ganapati Muni's *Sri Ramana Gita* articulate the way in which the three spaces stretch in sequence, with *chidākāsha* corresponding to the Heart (*hridaya*), *chittākāsha* to the mind and *bhutākāsha* to the physical universe: 'The whole universe is nothing but the mind, and the mind is nothing but the Heart. Thus the entire story of the universe culminates in the Heart.'[34] We can begin to understand, through these verses, how the identification of mind and world is nothing but the external ring of the identification of mind and Heart. The universe of forms is not a projection of the individual mind but a manifestation of the

Self, or the Heart, or *chidākāsha,* through the mind. In this regard, Ramana Maharshi explicitly distinguishes between causality and co-dependence: the world does not exist because of the self but with the self, adding that 'by the *self* the body, subtle or gross, was not meant.'[35] One can therefore distinguish between the world as 'expanding' from the Self and the world as set by the mind in ignorance of the Self. The world is what it is within the Self, but it is only an illusion when perceived by the mind severed from the Self. Paradoxically the world perceived from the Self is 'objective', in the sense of being what it is within the Self, while it is 'subjective' when experienced as co-dependent with the mind.

An analysis of the Maharshi's reoccurring symbol of the moving picture is also particularly fruitful in order to reach a deeper understanding of the nature of *chidākāsha.* The symbol appears, for instance, in the *Upadesha Manjari—A Catechism of Instruction* composed by Sri Natanananda, a devotee of the Maharshi, in 1939 and comprising questions and answers. The second book of this compilation includes a rich development of the analogy between consciousness and moving pictures in response to a question on the relation between pure Consciousness and 'the relative knowledge of the phenomenal world.'[36] In this parallel between the world of consciousness and the picture show, the core analogy lies in the equivalence between the *Ātman* and the lamp as source of light. Without Consciousness nothing can be, the Self is the Witness of everything and this witnessing is the *conditio sine qua non* of the existence of any and all things. At the same time, the existence of the multiplicity of things does not affect in the least the reality of the *Ātman,* as all elements and objects involved in the projection of the film have no bearing whatsoever on the source of light itself. The second analogy is that of the lens in front of the lamp with the 'sattvic mind in close proximity to the *Ātman.'* The cosmological notion of *sattva* refers in essence to all that which, within the world of duality of *Māyā,* is in closest proximity to *Ātman.* The *Bhagavad Gītā* refers to sattvic realities in several ways, but the most enlightening one is probably to be found in verses 17 and 18 of Song XIV: 'From *sattva* knowledge is born' and 'those established in *sattva* go upward.'[37] The sattvic association with knowledge and upwardness lies in contrast with rajasic desire on the one hand, and tamasic ignorance and downfall on the other hand. *Rajas* is the fire of passion that keeps one moving along peripheral samsāric cycles, while *tamas* is the gravity of ignorance and existential torpor that precipitates one in lower realms. The 'sattvic mind' reflects the light of the *Ātman* without interferences in the same way as the lens refracts the light of the lamp. A lens can focus or disperse light, and this is exactly what the mind does in relation to the Self. On the one hand, the mind 'gathers' the infinite light of the Self on a particular point that is the source of individual consciousness, on the other hand, it 'disperses' this light in the sense of making a multiplicity of units of consciousness out of the single, non-dual *Ātman*. It limits and divides. The sattvic character of the mind and its proximity to the Self differs from its rajasic and tamasic states in that it entails an ability to refract the light in a clear and effective manner. The Maharshi specifies further the way in which the mind and the *Ātman* merge together to crystallize an individual unit of consciousness. The light is considered on three different levels: that of the lamp which is the *Ātman* as its source, that of the rays of light passing through the mind functioning as a lens, and that of the same rays as passed through the lens and appearing on the screen. It is on the screen that the subjective becomes objective, if one follows this example, even though from another point of view the objective world retains its character independently from the subjective realm. The analogy between the screen and the 'insentient world of matter' is most important in this regard.[38] It indicates that the objective world is not only a projection of the mind but also a kind of substratum, and it bars thereby a literally and unilaterally idealistic understanding of the Maharshi's perspective. The contact of the material world with mind consciousness lends to the former a higher or greater reality through its being 'illuminated' through the latter.

The third analogical element is constituted by the *vāsanās*. These are the latent dispositions that have been accumulated through past experiences. They are innately inherited through one's *karma*. In themselves they are independent from objects, as is evidenced by one's experience of them in dreams.[39] However, as indicated by Shankara in his *Commentary on the Brahma Sūtras*, they presuppose objects as their initial foundations, without which their very reality would be unexplainable.[40] The Maharshi compares these *vāsanās* to the 'film with pictures that run in succession.' This analogy is all the more adequate in that the predispositions need mind consciousness in order to be actualized. Their permanence is also connected to their replicability, as in the case of the film that functions as a kind of 'storehouse' for future projections. Ramana Maharshi emphasises the subtlety and elusiveness of these tendencies, which escape most of one's perception and control. These characters lie at the foundation of the seeming ineluctability of the *vāsanās* that run apparently of their own accord as the moving picture. The *vāsanās* are also associated by the Maharshi with the 'divine law' that introduces them to the mind. The aspect of law conveys the sense of ineluctability that has been mentioned; it also suggests the implacability of the mechanisms of individual consciousness. The divinity of these laws refers, moreover, to the fact that karmic necessity is ultimately identifiable to the Lord. As suggestively put by Natalia Isayeva, the Lord functions as a kind of 'embodiment of *karma* [... who] allocates the fruits of actions according to the efforts of living beings.'[41] The Maharshi draws a parallel between this divine law of karmic tendencies and 'the machine that moves the film.' The image is indicative of a sense of merciless causality and retribution that is exclusive of any grace. The Advaitin perspective does not ignore or reject the principle of Divine grace, since the latter is a requirement for any spiritual awakening, but its relevance and power becomes more apparent as the *jīva* moves forward in freeing itself from its own conditioning.

The Self is sometimes compared to a lamp, as in the previously analyzed example, sometimes compared to a screen as in the following: 'Consciousness is the screen on which all the pictures come and go. The screen is real, the pictures are mere shadows on it.'[42] When the screen-like quality is emphasized, what is highlighted is the reality of the Self, or its absoluteness, its ontological status of necessity. This absoluteness also means that the Self is utterly independent from any limited or relative state of consciousness, in the same way that the screen remains totally unaffected by the pictures that are projected upon it. This is also why, at times, the Maharshi identifies the screen as a symbol of the state of *turīya*; this is the fourth state of consciousness that both transcends and contains the three states of wake, dream and deep sleep.[43] When the Self is identified with the lamp, it suggests, by contrast, the productive power of the Self, or its infinity, the boundless extension of its diffusiveness that is the core reality of everything and radiates in and through everything. Things are not inasmuch as they are not the screen, and they are, as the Self, inasmuch as the lamp gives them being, or in so far as their existence is purely dependent upon its light. The screen represents the transcendence of the Self, or more precisely the transcendent aspect of its immanence. As for the light of the lamp, it is more univocally symbolic of the immanence of the Self. In one way the pictures are shadows, or mere projections on the screen; they are not, only the Self is. In another way they are light, and it is as such that they are; they are none other than the Self. Were the 'projector light' of the Self to go out, the whole 'moving picture' of the phenomenal world would disappear. This symbolic analogy leads Shuddananda Bharati to assert that 'the world is nothing but the objectified mind.'[44] The analogy is quite imperfect, though, since the source of the 'moving picture' is not the prism of the lamp, or the film, but the light itself. The world is projected by the Self, not by the mind, and the mind is but a limited point of view on the phenomenal universe.

The relationship between Reality and appearance lies at the very core of any discussion of the Hindu concept of *Māyā*, and the Maharshi, like other sages, is often asked about the perplexing nature of this principle. In his responses the sage of Arunachala tends to follow in the footsteps of the Advaitin tradition: *Māyā* is *anirvachanīya*, its ontological status is inexplicable and indefinable.[45] Its unexplainable character has to do with the fact that *Advaita* does not account for the appearance of ignorance from the Self or in the Self. Since the Self is everything, *Māyā* has to be somehow inherent to the Self without it being possible to provide an explanation for its presence. The indefinable aspect of *Māyā* is entailed by its being neither *Ātman*, the Real, nor unreal, since humans do experience it. *Māyā* is not nothing, it is not unreal, but it is not real either, and therefore its status is not decidable. The most relevant aspect of *Māyā* for our current purpose, however, pertains to its being utterly dependent upon the mind that perceives it.[46] *Māyā* appears to the mind as a result of a mistaken superimposition (*adhyāsa*) whereby the mind experiences itself as separated from its objects, by virtue of being confused with the Self. It is in this mistaken perception that *Māyā* resides and thrives, at least epistemologically, even though from another point of view, one that is more ontological in nature, *Māyā* can be considered as a kind of extrinsic dimension of *Ātman*, or the illusory play of the Divine.

When *Māyā* is translated as 'the world', one is in a position to understand how the latter is 'produced' by the mind. The world as world, that is, as separated from the Self, is founded on a radical misperception of reality. In other words, when we say 'the world' we already presuppose a reality that is severed from the unity of the Self. This reality has actually no reality except for the dualistic mind. It is actually appearance. It is that which appears to a mind that does not grasp Reality as it is. The Maharshi is quite aware of the fact that such an understanding of the world as a projection of the mind does not necessarily entail, from other points of view, the utter negation of its existence. Thus, he can recognize the aspect of reality of the world within the Self:

> It is not at all correct to say that Advaitins of the Sankara school deny the existence of the world, or that they call it unreal. On the other hand, it is more real to them than to others. Their world will always exist whereas the world of the other schools will have origin, growth and decay, and as such cannot be

real. They only say that the world as 'world' is not real, but that the world as *Brahman* is real. All is *Brahman*, nothing exists but *Brahman*, and the world as *Brahman* is real.[47]

Thus, the argument according to which *Advaita* would be a denial of the existence of the world on account of its doctrine of *Māyā* is rebuffed by Ramana Maharshi. In fact, he argues for the opposite position: the world is more real to the Advaitin than it is to others, precisely because 'the world as *Brahman* is real' whereas the world considered by dualists has a beginning and an end, and cannot therefore be called real in a proper sense. This demonstrates, by extension, that the world is not literally, or merely, a projection of the mind. If it were so, the world would have no more reality than the mind itself, and it would therefore be subject to the same ontological limitations as the latter. The world, inasmuch as it is none other than *Brahman*, cannot be considered as a projection of the mind.

There are, therefore, three ontological degrees of reality to consider with respect to the world. The first is the 'world as *Brahman*', which is none other than the Self. The second is the world as a projection, or a representation, of the mind. The third is the world as an interpersonal and interactive reality that results from the sum of all experiences. The second world must be considered as a principle of attachment, in a way analogous to the acceptation of the word in traditional Christianity. In this sense, the world is not an objective realm of reality, which would be a synonym of the universe, but rather a set of values and priorities that are the foundations of a rejection of God and a subjective worship of other-than-God. In the Gospel of John, Jesus refers twice to the 'prince of this world'. One of these instances, 'Hereafter I will not talk much with you: for the prince of this world cometh, and hath nothing in me' (John 14:30), clearly establishes the incompatibility between the world and Jesus. On the other hand, in other passages of the Gospel, Jesus characterizes himself as the Light and the Life of the world, and he affirms that he has not come to condemn the world: 'Then spake Jesus again unto them, saying, I am the light of the world: he that followeth me shall not walk in darkness, but shall have the light of life' (John 8:12). The same Greek word *kosmos* is used in both types of occurrence, but it is done in different contexts and from different points of view. A corresponding implicit distinction is present in the Maharshi's teachings. Thus, from one point of view, Ramana is intent on stressing that it is actually not possible to leave the world. In response to a question about renunciation he states: 'If the objects have an independent existence, i.e., if they exist anywhere apart from you, then it may be possible for you to go away from them. But they don't exist apart from you; they owe their existence to you, your thought. So, where can you go, to escape them?'[48] Here we find again the appearance of a solipsist conception of the world, whereby the objects have no existence except in the mind of the one who experiences them; but this very example shows that this apparent radical idealism amounts to a spiritual statement, not a metaphysical one. It is obviously always possible to leave objects, in the sense of renouncing them for a life of retreat and asceticism, and indeed Hinduism knows a kind of institutionalization of this possibility with *samnyāsa*. The world that one cannot leave is therefore not the world as *bhutākāsha* but the world as *chittākāsha*. In the latter, the 'objects' are compared to the shadow of a person, and they therefore cannot be escaped.[49] This is 'the world in the mind', and this is the only world that prevents one from realizing the Self. The image of the shadow is all the more meaningful in that it conveys not only the aspect of projection and inseparability, but also the suggestion of an obstruction of the light by the ego, by the individual outlines of the person who identifies with the body. In this sense the world that is created by the ego is none other than the reflection of the fundamental misidentification of the Self with the limitations of the *jīva*. Take away this mistaken identification and the world disappears. Thus, the world that disappears when the Self is realized is obviously not the world as physical reality but the world as psychic craving.

The question of the ontological status of the world is sometimes treated by the Maharshi in a way that is reminiscent of the Buddha's 'unanswered questions' (*avyākrita*), such as the eternity and infinity of the world, the identity between self and body, and the *post mortem* destiny of a Buddha. Answers to these questions, assuming that they are possible, do not facilitate the process of spiritual awakening, and are even likely to detract from it. Similarly, the Maharshi sometimes pushed aside questions aiming at a mental understanding of whether the world is real or not real by urging the interlocutor to prioritize spiritual work over dialectical investigation.[50] Once Self-realization is obtained, then the question of the reality of the world or lack thereof will be solved. This means, presumably, that the intellective perception of reality that results from spiritual awakening lies beyond the dichotomies of unaided reason.

Perhaps the most enlightening and direct treatment of the multifaceted question of the existence of the world is to be found in *Sat Darshana*, the

Sanskrit version of *Ulladu Nārpadu*. It goes as follows: 'To the ignorant and the wise alike the world exists. To the former, the world observed alone is real. To the wise, the formless source of the visible is the one world, Real and Perfect.'[51] There is no doubt that the world does exist, since the sage himself considers it so. The non-existence of the world can only have meaning from a point of view that is either mystically hyperbolic or spiritually heuristic. If by 'the world is only in the soul' is meant that the world is but a figment of one's mental life, then such a statement would be incompatible with the conclusion and perception of wisdom. On a basic level, the world exists for the ignorant who does not know the Self. Indeed, for the mind under the spell of *avidyā* the world is the only reality. The reality of God, for instance, is only at best an abstraction that has no direct and profound bearing on the ordinary mode of perception of the world. Conventional existence could be actually defined as a kind of crystallization of the belief that the world fully exists, and that it only exists. This is what René Guénon has referred to as 'the illusion of ordinary life,' which is a result of what the French metaphysician calls a materialism *de facto*, or a 'practical' materialism that evicts spiritual realities from the realm of existence, the latter being reduced to phenomena as mere objects of sensory perception.[52] The illusion does not lie in the belief of the existence of the world, but in the intimate conviction that this world is the only existence, or rather that it is another word for existence. For Guénon, ignorance is self-reinforcing, since it solidifies its limitations through the negation of what lies beyond it, therefore 'suggesting' or 'creating' a reality. This is, in a way, another application of the idea that the 'world is in the mind': it would be more accurate to say that the world as understood and shaped by the outlook of metaphysical ignorance is a projection of the limitations of the latter. This is how Guénon characterizes the modern world inasmuch as it is based on a negation of that which transcends the domain of sensory experience, and, therefore, the field of investigation of science. By contrast, the vision of the *jñanī* is focused on the essential substratum of existence, that in which the world is entirely 'contained': 'He sees in it [the world of forms] the formless *Brahman* that permeates all existence.' These various understandings and perceptions of the world can be related to the three stages of Enlightenment as they are sometimes symbolized in Zen meditations. 'In the beginning the mountains are mountains, and the rivers are rivers,' then, 'the mountains are not mountains anymore and the rivers are not rivers,' and finally, 'the mountains are mountains again and the rivers are rivers.' These three stages correspond to ways of perceiving the world that can be termed 'affirmation according to ordinary life,' 'negation by virtue of discernment or ecstasy,' and 'affirmation with *Brahman*.'[53] In other words, first the world is a projection of the ordinary mind, then the world and the mind are negated—there is no world and no mind—and finally the world is apprehended within the Self.

The question of the reality or unreality of the world is often connected, in the Maharshi's teachings as in many other mystical paths, to analogies with the dream state, in which the whole perceived reality is nothing but a projection of the dreamer: 'all that you see depends on the seer. Apart from the seer there is no seen. This is called *drishti-srishti vāda*, or the argument that one first creates out of his mind and then sees what his mind itself has created.'[54] The analogy is obviously only partial, and it is to be contemplated as a symbolic key rather than as the affirmation of a literal equivalence. It is a suggestive way of providing people who are totally determined by the belief in a kind of density of the world with an accessible way of envisaging what the illusory character of *Māyā* might mean. However, the question of the ontological status of the dream state in relation to the waking state is in several ways perplexing.

In response to several questions by devotees, and in a stark rebuke to the conventional view, the Maharshi repeatedly denied that there is any difference between the two states of wakefulness and dream. *Prima facie* this runs contrary to one's ordinary experience, since we can indeed identify differences between the two states in several respects. The question remains, obviously, of knowing what is meant by 'no difference;' and in this respect it seems evident, from the context of the Maharshi's statements, that what is at stake is a matter of ontological as well as epistemological difference. What the Maharshi denies is that the world experienced during the dream state would be more or less real than that of the waking state; but this has evidently to be contemplated within the context of the Maharshi's understanding of the words 'reality' and 'real.' From the point of view of *Advaita*, the question of the status of the dream state appears both simple and complex. It is simple when referred to the fundamental discernment between *Brahman* and *Māyā*, since the former reduces everything, including both dream and ordinary wakefulness, to the status of appearance.[55] It is complex when considering the plurality of cognitive vantage points that are *de facto* part of the human experience. More generally, it is averred that mystical metaphysics can sometimes make use of the distinction between dream state (*svapna*) and wakefulness (*jāgrat*) as an analogue with the relationship between the illusory superimpositions of the ego, which are akin to somnambulic dream, and Self-

Awakening.[56] The very term awakening is frequently used by mystics to refer to the ultimate goal of the path, particularly in Buddhism. Spiritual awakening dispels the appearance of unenlightened life in a way that can be transposed symbolically in the ordinary experience of waking up. This didactic and symbolic distinction is itself annulled, however, when the emphasis is placed on the unconditioned transcendence of the Self and its non-relatability.

By and large the principle of a distinction between dream and wake is akin to a realist philosophical outlook. It posits both the existence and the cognizability of a realm of external objects. It is on the basis of this position that it can assert the aforementioned distinction, and therefore assign superiority to the waking state over the oneiric realm. A denial of the difference between the two states is akin, by contrast, to an idealist position. In such a view, what we call objects are reduced to, and indeed sublated into, the subject. From this point of view there would be no significant difference between dreaming and being awake. In the context of this debate the Shankarian position deserves to be briefly outlined in order to contrast it with the Maharshi's. However, Shankara's argument on dream and the waking state must be understood within its context, that is, by contrast with the Buddhist outlook of the *Vijñānavadins,* which the Advaitin metaphysician strives to refute. In Chapter Three of his *Commentary on the Brahma Sūtras,* Shankara developed a rebuke to the *Vijñānavāda,* or *Yogācāra,* Buddhist position on the non-distinction between dream and wake on idealist grounds. The purpose of *Vijñānavāda* Buddhists was to show, on the basis of the cognitive features of dream, that objects are not necessary to cognition. Independently from the specific *Vijñānavāda* positions Buddhism tends, as a whole, to lower the ontological degree of reality of objective phenomena by depriving them of any sense of substantiality. This is, by and large, the meaning of the pervasive notion of Emptiness, or co-dependent origination. In a more specific context, and in response to the idealistic stand of the *Vijñānavādins* and other idealists, one of Shankara's chief points is that the world of dream is in fact an illusory creation of the individual, whereas the world experienced awake is a creation of the Lord.[57] In other words, in order to refute Buddhist idealism, Shankara situates his argument within the dualistic framework of scripture-based religion. This echoes the analogous Shankarian position that recognizes in the dualism inherent to scriptural accounts of creation a Divine pedagogical concession to the limitations of ordinary consciousness. In both cases, a form of empirical and propaedeutic realism serves as a founding ground for the Advaitin path. Moreover, even from the point of view of the directly non-dualistic core of Advaitin knowledge, there is a clear conceptual difference between the phenomenal dispelling of the dream objects in the waking state, and the metaphysical reduction of relative objects in intellective discrimination. The former entails the cancellation of the phenomena of the dream world, while the latter does not annul the world of *Māyā*; it simply reveals its nature of ontological appearance.[58] It appears, therefore, that Shankara's take on the nature of dreams is, at least in his commentary on the *Brahma Sūtras*, significantly different from the Maharshi's. When asked about this difference of outlook, the Maharshi would suggest that Shankara distinguished the dreaming state and the waking state for the 'purpose of clearer exposition.'[59] This is probably a way to indicate that Shankara's intent was primarily pedagogical, and therefore connected to the requirements of the Advaitin *sādhanā*, which the Maharshi himself never followed nor taught. In other words, the traditional Advaitin perspective must assign a sufficiently objective reality to the waking world in order to base its path on solid scriptural, moral and didactic grounds. By contrast, the dream state does not afford the degree of objectivity, consistency and determining activity required for the unfolding of a *sādhanā*.

To sum it up, Shankara's position could be encapsulated as a kind of provisional realism within the encompassing perspective of an ultimate, non-dual, transcendent idealism.[60] The provisional aspect of Shankarian realism can be approached from a variety of points of view. It could be explained in terms of traditional imperatives, with the need to account for the scriptural realism of the Vedas. It could also be envisaged as grounded in the spiritual considerations of the ethico-spiritual prerequisites of the *sādhanā*, which presuppose the requirements of the waking state. It could be, finally, taken as being determined by the need for a refutation of Buddhist positions, and therefore as a metaphysical emphasis intended to offer a contrasted exposition.

One of the close early devotees of the Maharshi, Alan Chadwick, who confessed that 'some doubts always remained for [him]' on this matter, took the question of the non-difference between the dream and waking states to the Maharshi on many occasions. As he relates it in an article published in *The Call Divine* in March 1954, Chadwick was deeply puzzled and unsatisfied by the Maharshi's repeated assertion that there is no difference between dreams and the waking state. The sage considered the conventional arguments supporting the superiority of the waking state to be characteristic of an illegitimate absolutization of the conditions of a limited state in relation to another. He reproached Chadwick for studying 'one limitation from the point of view of another limitation.'[61] In other words, he appeared to deny thereby that any real difference or superiority could be affirmed from a single relative vantage point. This is so because the only Reality from which one could derive absolute difference lies precisely beyond all differences, and therefore cancels out all differences; and this is indeed the 'vantage point' of the Self, which actually knows of no point and no vantage, and sublates every state into Itself. For the Maharshi, any relative perspective has only validity within the limits of the reality it entails. As a consequence, when Chadwick argued his point concerning the perceived 'unreality' of dreams, the Maharshi would retort by referring to a similar feeling of 'unreality' that may at times seize one in the midst of the waking state. Deciding upon the reality or superiority of a particular state over another one would presuppose an ability to jump over the two, so to speak, in order to be able to compare them from a site that is limited by none; hence the Maharshi's recommendation: 'go beyond all limitation, then come here with your doubts.'[62] Now it is plain that when it comes to a matter of consciousness, a limited perspective cannot account for the full reality. This is the reason why the Maharshi would consistently invite his interlocutors to reach beyond all limitations into the Self. The question of dream was therefore but one instance of a more general call to absolute consciousness and an invitation to transcend thereby all duality. Thus the Maharshi seems to have envisaged the question from the point of view of subjective consciousness, both in the relative domain and in the absolute field. On the one hand, he would deny that any state has not its own reality; on the other, and that was his main point, he would invalidate the very question of a difference among states by situating the matter from the point of view of the Self. In other words, any perceived difference is not a real difference when referred to Consciousness as such, since the latter is actually the only underlying Reality of all differentiated vantage points.

One might say that the Maharshi was pointing at the fact that the world of dream and the waking world are 'the same' inasmuch as they are envisaged as 'created' by the mind that lives in them and of them; and this is the reason why they are both incompatible with Self-realization, which is a kind of 'decreation' of the world.[63] Waking and dreaming are the same inasmuch as they think themselves different from the Self, and hamper Self-realization. The only other way to relate a mode of limited consciousness to the Self would consist in assessing the extent to which it affords a spiritual entrance point into Realization. And this is precisely the point of view of Shankara when he asserts the difference between the waking and dreaming states in favor of the former.

Chadwick's hitherto confounded account ends with an anecdote that remains more suggestive than conclusive:

> I was arguing philosophy [in a dream] with someone and pointed out that all experience was only subjective, that there was nothing outside the mind. The other person demurred, pointing out how solid everything was and how real experience seemed, and it could not be just personal imagination. I replied, 'No, it is nothing but a dream. Dream and waking experience are exactly the same.' 'You say that now,' he replied, 'but you would never say a thing like that in your dream.' And then I woke up.[64]

Without being explicit about it, Chadwick appears to suggest that the reference to the dream state from within his dream itself ended up blurring the lines between wakefulness and dream. This point would be analogous, in a way, to the famous passage from Zhuang Zi in which the Chinese sage, when dreaming he was a butterfly, wonders whether he might actually have been a butterfly dreaming he was Zhuang Zi.[65] The 'transformation of things' envisaged by the Taoist philosopher corresponds to a recognition that a single essential Reality is both the agent and the object of universal transformation, all boundaries fizzling down into fragile relativities. It remains, however, that Zhuang Zi had to wake up in order to contemplate this very possibility, which appears to indicate that the apologue should not be taken too literally. In Chadwick's account, by contrast, the principle of the inherent subjectivity of experience is independent from its subjective conditions, since it is validated both during the dream and upon waking up. This sounds like a contradiction, of course, since it appears that the principle itself is denied by its seeming independence from any specific subjective state: the point that 'all experience [...] is only subjective' seems to escape, as a universal truth, from the limitations of subjectivity. It must be noted, however, that what is at stake here is not a metaphysical or mathematical truth, but an empirical content.

An extremely interesting aspect of the same question was raised by a devotee who asked the Maharshi whether the vivid interaction he had with him in a dream was indeed an initiation. In his response, the Maharshi stressed that the external appearance of the *guru* and the internal *guru*, or the Self, are one. However, a predominant consideration of the *guru* as external means that the various instructions and initiations received by him 'have a relative meaning and significance.' This amounts to saying that the full actualization of the *guru's* grace coincides with the realization of the *guru* within, the very Self. When understood in this essential light the spiritual influence of the *guru* is, therefore, determining both in the waking and dreaming states. The states of *jāgrat,* wake, and *svapna,* dream, are intermittent, and they therefore cannot be equated with the permanent Self which can pierce through both and any of them by the grace of the *guru.* This relativizes both of them, and explains on what ground the Maharshi was reticent to assign any ontological eminence to the waking state. His purpose seems to have been to highlight the 'unreality' of the waking state by refusing to grant it a kind of epistemological or ontological superiority or independence. The question remains of determining what the sentence 'dream and waking experience are exactly the same' may mean. It cannot be taken literally without falling into absurdity, since the very consideration of dreams and wakefulness as two realities subject to comparison evidently entails that they are in some way different. The statement must therefore be read either as a hyperbole, or as referring to the adjective 'different' in the strictly technical sense of *bheda.* In the first case the statement could be taken to fulfill the function of a *kōan.* Significantly, it may be proposed that the Maharshi's perspective is, on this particular point, closer to some forms of Buddhism than to Shankara. This is so inasmuch as his emphasis lies on the subjective dimension of spirituality, that is to say Self-realization. The intent is therefore to open the mind of the devotee to the single Reality of the Self by 'subverting' the illusory certitudes of his ordinary consciousness. The Maharshi's intent is spiritual rather than metaphysical, to the extent that these two terms may be contrasted to highlight the difference between applied metaphysics, as in Shankara's path, and implied metaphysics, as in the Maharshi's realization.

Finally, it may be particularly fruitful to consider passages from Muruganar's *The Garland of Guru's Sayings—Guru Vachaka Kovai,* a work that received the full *imprimatur* of the Maharshi, and which synthetizes in 1,282 stanzas (of which twenty-eight are actually the Maharshi's) the whole teachings of the sage in a way that 'equals the *Talks* in comprehensiveness and authenticity.'[66] The first stanza contemplates the gift of reality from Reality to the world:

> From cause alone proceeds effect.
> The big world, which the scriptures say
> Is only names and forms, proceeds
> From Pure Awareness which is real,

Clear as the berry in one's palm.
Hence you may say this big world too
Is real.[67]

The second stanza draws a distinction between the apparent reality of the world as Divine *līlā* and its illusoriness in light of the Self:

For those who take the world appearance
As real and enjoy it, it is
The Lord's creation. But for those
Who, free from fear, have known the Truth,
The undeluded Self, it is
No more than a mere mental image
Projected by desire.[68]

The third and fourth stanzas reduce the world to naught within the Reality of the Self:

The world of trivial names and forms
Perceived by the five senses is
A mere appearance in the Self,
Awareness pure. It is the sport
Of *Māyā*, of images projected
By the mind, itself a thought
Arising in Being-Awareness.[69]
The world by the illusive mind
Perceived, is not, by the mind's source,
The Self, perceived. How can it, then,
This poor world, claim reality.[70]

A purely idealist interpretation of those statements that reduce the world to the status of a projection of the mind must therefore be qualified, indeed revoked, by others that explicitly differentiate the world as creation from the world as it is perceived by the mind. We find a glaring confirmation of the limitations and flaws of any one-sided idealist reading in another passage from *Guru Ramana Vachana Mala,* a selection from Sri Muruganar's *Guru Vachaka Kovai (Garland of the Guru's Sayings)* published as a collection of more than eight hundred sayings in 1939: 'God's creation does not bind; that which does so is the *jīva's* own creation; this is illustrated by the story in which through false news the one whose son was kept alive wept, and the one whose son was dead rejoiced.'[71] The story refers to two men on a pilgrimage, one of whom perished, and relates the confusion resulting from the mistake of an informant, whereby the father who had lost his son thought the latter to be surviving, and conversely. The sorrow of the latter, like the joy of the former, was totally disconnected from the reality of the matter. The world of each of the two fathers was truly a projection of their own respective minds, and bereft of an accurate correspondence with the actual state of reality. This is the 'binding world' that results from the superimposition of the ego upon the Self. On the other hand, if 'God's creation' is not binding, it cannot be the mere projection of the mind, for it is the latter and the latter only that is the principle of binding. If the world is to be weighed as a creation of the mind it is not, therefore, on account of a kind of solipsist epistemology, but quite the contrary by way of recognizing the absolute vantage point from which it is realized to be none other than the Self, and therefore utterly independent of the mind. This means that the essence of the subjective, the Self, is also objective, in the sense of being freed from individual biases and distortions. By contrast, the patterns of displacement and deferment that underpin the deconstructivist critique of metaphysics never reach any ground that would restore mountains as mountains and rivers as rivers; for them there is not ever any mountain, not ever any river. There is nothing relativistic, nothing nihilistic, in the Maharshi's worldview; his is an absolutist non-dualism that reduces every moving relativity and partial subjectivity to ashes, and which no mere discourse of postmodern reconstructivist interconnectedness can fathom. While it can be argued that the teachings on the world as projection of the mind were intended as a kind of shock therapy in the form of what Buddhists would call an *upāya*, a pedagogical device, or perhaps even a *kōan*, a perplexing theme of meditation, the Maharshi's point of view on the reality of the world was both definitive in its being grounded in the Self and multifaceted as a response to the diversity of contexts and needs. Ultimately, the question of the reality of the world and its relationship to the mind can be reduced to a simple alternative within the fold of which many points of view and intents may arise: 'the world is unreal if it is perceived by the mind as a collection of discrete objects, and real when it is directly experienced as an appearance in the Self.'[72] The supreme paradox lies in that perceiving the world as real 'makes' it unreal, while perceiving it as unreal 'makes' it real: 'The world seen as world through ignorance is false, but the same world seen as *Brahman* through knowledge is real.'[73]

7

THE EYE OF THE SELF

The question of the impermanence of the personal self is one that marks a divide between Abrahamic religions and most metaphysical traditions of Asia. In the world of the Bible and the Qur'ān, the substantiality and continuity of the soul is demanded by the very nature of the relationship between human and God; indeed, without it, the whole economy of salvation would be meaningless. There has to be a *real* soul who relates with God, and which God saves in His Mercy. Although Christian and Muslim mystics have sometimes noted the fact that the human soul changes from instant to instant in order to emphasise, by contrast, the permanent immanence of God's Presence or God's creative act, as well as the utter dependence of the soul upon the latter, the general economy of the traditions entails a sense of free will, ethico-spiritual accountability and post-mortem continuity that appears to be contingent upon the full reality of the individual soul.[1] The eternity of God guarantees the permanence of the human self, the relationship between the two being paramount and the very *raison d'être* of the religious message itself. The perspective of the metaphysical traditions of Asia, such as Advaita, Buddhism and Taoism, is much more intent on relativizing, or even questioning and negating, the reality of the human self. The spiritual goal of these traditions is to unveil the only Reality that lies underneath layers of ontological and epistemological appearance. Thus Buddhism undermines the belief in the soul as a substance and highlights the emptiness of the self, *anatta*. This keen 'de-substantialization' provides the metaphysical basis conducive to detaching the human subject from the illusory principle of craving and suffering, which is intrinsically associated with the erroneous assumption that phenomena and the subject that perceive them are substantial realities. Buddhists are particularly keen on analyzing and decomposing the aggregates that form the apparent self, in order to free themselves from alienating conditionings. Taoism, in a very different way, underlines the universal transformation of the 'ten thousand things,' which it perceives as the unending and ever-changing flow of the Tao within existence. The unceasing transformation that flows from the Tao makes it impossible to delineate a stable and permanent subjective entity. The Taoist self is an ever mobile becoming grounded in the Eternal Tao.[2] It is like an echo, or a shadow. As for Advaita, we have seen that it basically considers the *jīva* as a kind of optical delusion connected to the superimposition of finite phenomena onto the infinite Self. It is not literally inexistent, like the horn of a hare, but it is not metaphysically real. Irrespective of the important differences of outlook that differentiate these traditions, as well as the diversity of schools within each of them, the core of the teaching lies, in all three cases, in unveiling a universal substratum of Reality that shatters the conventional belief in one's own empirical reality. This emphasis on individual impermanence, or lack of reality, does not preclude Asian metaphysical traditions from considering some sort of continuum in existence, without which the very notion of spiritual path, their eschatology, and the traditions themselves, would be both meaningless and useless.

As was suggested in the introduction of this book, the seemingly non-substantial and de-centered characters of the illusory self of *Advaita* would seem to make it akin, in some ways, to postmodern deconstructionist projects. Thus, much of the postmodern intellectual bent revolves around a deconstruction of the classical understanding of the self as a substance and as a unified field of cognition, volition and affections. While the classical Western concept of self is characterized by words such as substance, permanence and centering, the postmodern self has been variously referred to as 'zerological', 'dispossessed' and 'de-centered.' In the Western philosophical tradition the self is a substance that undergoes accidents, and this substantial character is the basis of permanence in time and centering in space. It is also a principle of continuous identity and the source, or site, of a perspective on reality. This substantial concept of self could be seen as being challenged by the Maharshi's perspective in ways that may find echoes in postmodern thought. Does not the Maharshi evoke the 'inexistence' of the self as mind when he emphasises it constantly escaping one's attempts at reaching or grasping it? Is not the mind around which the self is crystallized, constantly deferred, is not it discontinuous and ephemeral as it moves from object to object without any apparent permanence? Finally, is not the self constantly de-centered by virtue of its being displaced by its inherent relativeness? Moreover, such categories could, *mutatis mutandis,* also be applied to the Self. The Self is a kind of void that transcends all determinations. It is Self-effulgent, ever renewing itself as *aham sphurana,* and it is always escaping any relative position, therefore any relative centering.[3] The traditional universe is one in which God is 'an infinite sphere whose centre is everywhere and whose circumference is nowhere'.[4] This could be applied to the Maharshi's teachings, since the Self is at the center everywhere and the periphery, or *Māyā,* has no reality on its own, and therefore no real ontological 'place.' In the postmodern world, by contrast, it could be argued that the center is nowhere and the periphery everywhere. The negation of any center is actually one of the possibly most direct ways of defining the postmodern outlook. As for the periphery it is in a way this *'différance'* that is the very origin of reality; it is like *Māyā* both inconceivable and necessary, and it is also like a 'trace' of that which is untraceable, the origin without origin.[5] Discussing Mark C. Taylor's postmodern 'disappearance of the self' as 'the absence of a permanent self, an absence that is always present, a mere trace,' Carl Olson remarks judiciously that 'from Shankara's perspective, it is only possible to discover the absence of a permanent self by means of ignorance' and 'moreover, it is nonsensical to discuss the disappearance of the self, a self-luminous and timeless reality'; hence, 'according to Śankara, Taylor is writing about the self from the perspective of lower knowledge (*aparā vidyā*), whereas the Indian philosopher is more concerned with the self from the standpoint of higher knowledge (*parā vidyā*).'[6] In other words, the postmodern disappearing self is like the shadow projected by ignorance: that which is not present to itself is not the Self, it is a superimposition on the Self. The *jīva* inasmuch as it is ignorant of the Self is always deferred in its selfness, as it were, but the real Self lies above any possible deferment, or *différance,* it is pure Presence to Itself, and it remains therefore altogether untouched by the postmodern outlook.

A fruitful way in which the question of the nature of the Subject can be approached is through the symbolism of the eye. The eye implies some sort of essential and perspectival identity. However the eye is both a substance—in the literal sense of standing 'below' any visual perceptions, as the basis for them—and a sort of emptiness, in that it has no content or character in itself, being simply the source of all perceptions. The eye is also permanent in its ability to see and impermanent in the actualization of its vision in relation to objects. Finally, the eye is the center of any visual perspective, while this centering position is always challenged by its inability to see itself.

The eye is a widespread mystical and contemplative symbol. This is particularly true in paths that emphasise knowledge, and even more so in those that are grounded in non-dualistic foundations. Whether in Plato or in the Upanishads, the eye has been an apt symbol of a direct apprehension of reality which, while presupposing empirically a distinction between the seer and the seen, entails a sense of immediacy and unity by virtue of suggesting a kind of absorption of the seen in the seer. That which I see is within me, as it were, inasmuch as it is included in my field of vision. Analogous statements could be made about some other senses, of course, but in a much more partial manner, one that does not involve the entire field of reality. In other words, there is much more to see than there is to hear or to taste— at least from a human point of view. This is the case to such an extent that the objective universe appears all to be seen, with microscopes and telescopes extending this vision toward the 'infinitely small' and the 'infinitely large', as Pascal would put it. One will not be surprised, therefore, to consider how recurrent the image of the eye and sight is recurrent in the Maharshi's teachings and writings.

The question of the 'vision' of the Self is central when it comes to understanding the dialectics of transcendence and immanence in the Maharshi's perspective; for the Self can be conceived both as the seer and the seen, the eye and its field of vision. This is so inasmuch as it both founds everything and embraces everything. This seemingly twofold dimension of *Ātman* is directly evoked by a verse of *Arunāchala Pancharatma*, which connects seeing the Self with seeing the whole world as Its form: 'He who dedicates his mind to Thee, and seeing Thee, always beholds the universe as Thy figure, he who at all times glorifies Thee and loves Thee as none other than the Self, he is the master without rival, being one with Thee, O Arunachala! And Lost in Thy Bliss.'[7] This raises the question of what it may mean for a figure or a form to be figure of the figureless or form of the supra-formal, since the Self obviously lies beyond all figures and forms. To a query concerning this difficulty the Maharshi's answer is that one must first see the Self within before being able to see it in everything.[8] The first 'seeing' is characterized by a reduction of everything to the Self. It is why it is inward. This reduction through knowledge sees a coincidence of transcendence and immanence. There is transcendence in the sense that it is known that nothing is except the Self, the Self 'transcends' everything. But this knowledge is also immanent in that it is inward, the essence and source underlying all reality that is 'discovered' within the heart. This is, as it were, transcendence in immanence. Having recognized the Self within as the only Reality, one cannot but recognize it in the world as being such, since there is only one Reality. To say that the world is the 'figure' of the Self is just a way of saying that there is only the Self, and that to the extent that the world is not unreal it cannot but be the Self. In no way can it mean that the Self has any form, or is limited by forms. The Self is and is not the world, depending upon whether one considers the latter in relation to it, or—illusorily—independently from It.

When stating that the Self is the world the Maharshi also implies that, in a sense, it cannot 'see', because anything that could be seen would have to be other than the Self to be seen as an object. Hence the Maharshi's distinction between ordinary consciousness, which constantly sees things and others— and which is only 'seeing'—and the Self that sees without seeing since 'for the Self, the Infinite Eye, what can be seen?'[9] Ordinary consciousness is only and constantly 'seeing' because it is essentially consciousness of otherness. It is intrinsically dualistic and turns its attention away from 'finding out the obvious seer, but run[s] about analyzing the seen.'[10] By contrast the Self, although being the only Seer in the sense that it is the only Consciousness, does not 'see' anything as other than Itself: 'He sees all things as but himself.'[11] It therefore literally does not see if by seeing is meant a perception of an object that would be exterior to oneself. From another point of view, it could be said that, by contrast with human consciousness, it is the only Reality that sees Itself.

There is, however, a point of view according to which the Self is the Eye par excellence, indeed the only Eye. This view of the Self is particularly developed in the fourth stanza of *Ulladu Nārpadu, The Forty Verses on Existence*:

> If Self has form then God and world as well
> Appear accordingly. Yet if 'tis true
> The Self is formless, then by whom and how
> Can any shapes be known? Without the eye
> Can there be vision? But the Self's the Eye,
> And this same Eye is infinite as well.[12]

This is, in a way, the classical Advaitin distinction between *Saguna Brahman*, the Divine with forms, and *Nirguna Brahman*, the Divine without forms. The first unfolds the space of relationality, whereas the second folds back everything into non-duality. But there is also a sense in which the Self is form, but not 'with form,' inasmuch as form is perceived as no different from the Self. At any rate what the Maharshi implies is that it is impossible to see the world as form of the Self if one has not first recognized that there is none but the Self. Since the Self is the most intimate reality, the very source of one's being, it cannot be found nor realized out there in the world. It is from within that the question of vision comes into play. For the Maharshi, there are two kinds of vision, and therefore two kinds of eyes. The first eye relates to the formal domain, and to one's identification with form. To the extent that the principle of one's consciousness lies in one's identification with the body, then we cannot but see the world, and everything else including God, in and through forms. This means, among other things, that the Advaitin notion of *Saguna Brahman* is intrinsically connected to the *jīva* as principle of identification with forms. The second eye is the Witness of everything, but a Witness that is no different from the witnessed, and therefore does not witness anything; the eye that sees without seeing anything. The latter highlights an important aspect of the symbolism of the eye: its ultimate inadequacy to account for the non-dual perspective. The eye, the organ of vision, presupposes one that sees and one that is seen. There is, therefore, in the very symbol of the eye, a presupposition of duality. The idea of contemplation is in that sense intrinsically dualistic. It is for this reason that the Maharshi expresses reservations vis-à-vis the idea, often expressed in mystical texts, that 'one must see *Brahman* in everything and everywhere.' There is no vision of *Brahman*. *Brahman* in its essence is *Nirguna*, non-qualified. A vision implies something that is seen, and pertains therefore to the formal realm, the realm of *gunas*, or qualities. For the Maharshi the ultimate knowledge transcends the very conditions of form, which are space and time. It also transcends the polarity of a subject and an object. The triplicity of perceiver, perception and perceived disappears in non-dual knowledge, and 'the only thing that exists then is the infinite eye.'[13] The eye of God is the only eye that sees without seeing: it sees without anything being seen, in a way that is analogous to Franklin Merrell-Wolff's 'Consciousness-without-an-object.'

Thus, while Self-realization can be symbolized as an all-encompassing vision of everything, it can also be considered as a kind of superior blindness, in a way that is analogous to the mystical *Cloud of Unknowing*.[14] Devaraja Mudalia narrates that the Maharshi was once visited by a blind scholar called Dilip Kumar Roy. It is in this context that, out of compassion, he developed an analogy between the situation of the *jñanī* and that of the blind man.

The crux of the matter is that neither the viewer nor that which is viewed exists in an ultimate sense. We have seen that this duality is cancelled out in Self-realization. The comparison of the Self with a screen upon which phenomena, including the ego, are projected, emphasises the point of view according to which that which is seen and the seer are just but shadows. The fact that the screen does not 'see' does not constitute in the least a negative factor, since there is nobody to see and nothing to be seen.[15] All there is to see is the Self, and thus blindness can be, in that sense, a symbol of knowledge, in a way that is the reverse of sight and vision.

While blindness is an imperfect but suggestively potent symbol of the non-objectification of the Self, witnessing is one of the all-encompassing consciousness of *Ātman*. The notion of witness has been used in a number of traditions to refer to the Self, to God, or to the human being bearing witness to God. In Hinduism the concept of *Sākshin*, or Witness, refers to pure consciousness. The Self, pure Consciousness, being the innermost Subject, cannot but be witnessing everything else, including the ego. In *Advaita*, this is illustrated by the *Mundaka Upanishad*'s symbol of the two birds: 'Two birds of the same kind and inseparable as friends, cling to the same tree. One of them eats the sweet fruit, the other looks on without eating' (3.1.1–4).[16] The pure witness is not engaged in the action nor its enjoyment, but it is fully aware of all the constituents of the experience from which it is utterly independent. Other traditions refer to analogous concepts of ultimate witnessing, like Islam, which assigns to God the Name *al-Shahīd*, the One-who-witnesses. This is all the more significant, in this tradition, that the central element of the Muslim's creed is the uttering of the *shahādah*, the profession of faith, a term that relates to the same Arabic root as *al-Shahīd*. A Muslim is one who bears witness to God. Islamic theology also refers to the world itself as *'alam ash-shahādah*, from the same family of words, because it is 'manifest,' and constitutes thereby a means whereby God is witnessed. But what does it mean for God to be Himself the One who witnesses? The various occurrences of this Divine Name in the *Qur'ān* mostly allude to the fact that God is the best—and ultimately only—witness of the truth of the Books and the veracity of the Prophets. In other terms, God is the best guarantor of the truth, because He is Himself the Truth, *al-Haqq*, which is another Name of God. In some passages of the *Qur'ān* it is even said that God is the sufficient proof of Himself, by contrast with the signs (*āyāt*) of His existence that are to be found in the *shāhid*, the world as manifest. God bears witness of His own Being better than any other reality: 'We will show them Our signs in the horizons and within themselves until it becomes clear to them that it is the truth. But is it not sufficient concerning your Lord that He is, over all things, a Witness?' (41:53). This is probably the closest one can come, in Islam, to recognizing God as the Self of all selves. One extremely important consequence of this passage, moreover, is that, to the extent that the *shahādah* is the fundamental witnessing in Islam, God is Himself the very subject, metaphysically speaking, of this witnessing. Hence the notion of *wahdat ash-shuhūd*, or Unicity of Witnessing, which is, in some schools of Sufism, the highest spiritual realization, and the closest approximation of the Advaitin view of the Divine *Sākshīn*. The principle behind this conception is that only God can bear witness to Himself, therefore the most sincere and consummate witnessing amounts to an ecstatic extinction of the kind experienced by the ninth-century mystic Mansūr al-Hallāj (858–922), and epitomized by his theopathic statement 'I am the Truth' or 'I the Truth,' *Anā al-Haqq*,' for which he was put to death. It is not a coincidence that *Anā al-Haqq* is considered by Muruganar as the *mahāvākya* of Islam, in a way that explicitly includes the 'I', echoing thereby *Aham Brahmāsmi* and 'I Am That I Am'.[17] By contrast with the climate of Hindu *Advaita* this kind of enunciation is, in Sufism, quite exceptional and often deemed problematic. This is mostly because the spiritual economy of Islam is characterized by an emphasis on the transcendence of God, and consequently by the centrality of the law—two emphases that constitute the basic self as individual. The idea that the Divine would be immanent to the human self cannot be the central statement of a tradition that is defined by the need to submit to God through actions, *islām*, thereby implying an emphasis on one's distance vis-à-vis the Divine Object of worship. However, the serenity that emanates from sincerely worshipping the One offers, within Islam, a direct reflection of blissful Self-realization 'by putting out the raging flames of anguish for life's sins and sorrows.'[18] In this we see how the focus and structure of a particular religion can at the same time give access to the notion of the non-dual Self and limit the ways it is manifested.

At any rate, and despite its traditional backing in the world of Hinduism, Ramana Maharshi cautions against an indiscriminate use of the term 'witness', precisely because it appears to entail, in its very concept, the triplicity of one who witnesses, one before whom one witnesses, and something one witnesses.[19] Muruganar goes as far as to utterly dismiss the very concept of Self as Witness on account of the unity of the latter:

Tis a foolish fancy to ascribe
The role of 'witness' to the Self,
The luminous Sun, the mighty sky
Of Pure Awareness. In the Self
Immutable there is no room
For *maya's* darkness void. The Self
Is one sole whole without a second.[20]

This is the reason why the Maharshi prefers to refer to the light as a proper symbol of That which is beyond this triplicity, while being at the same time the only Reality within which they unfold as three. In this regard, the first stanza of *Ulladu Nārpadu* is particularly instructive: 'From our perception of the world there follows acceptance of a unique First Principle possessing various powers. Pictures of name and form, the person who sees, the screen on which he sees, and the light by which he sees: he himself is all of these.'[21] In reference to the 'light by which' the person sees, the Maharshi explains that the light that is mentioned here—even though it is essentially none other than the light of the Self, the First Principle which *is* all the elements involved in the vision—is more specifically and exclusively to be identified with the light of the *manas*: 'a reflected light, the light of pure *manas*, and it is this light which gives room for the existence of all the film of the world which is seen neither in total light nor in total darkness, but only in the subdued or reflected light.'[22] This light that is the intermediary between the 'white light' of the Self and the darkness of ignorance (*avidya*), constitutes the world as an object, since the pure light of the Self knows of no object, as does also ignorance, but in a completely opposite way. The Sanskrit term *manas* is etymologically akin to the Latin *mens,* which is the root of the adjective 'mental', referring thereby to activities of the mind. The light of the mind is subdued in the sense that it is not pure consciousness but consciousness of limited objects, and it is reflected in so far as it is essentially no different from the light of the Self, of which it is but a prolongation.

What precedes accounts for the fact that the mind can never know the Self: 'There are not two *Ātmas*, one to know and one to be known.'[23] The *Ātman* cannot be an object, since it is intrinsically and universally the source of any consciousness and knowledge, being therefore absolutely unobjectifiable. One can be the *Ātman*, but not know the *Ātman,* at least not in the way one knows an object. But even as a subject, indeed as the Subject, the Self is not consciousness of an object that would be other than itself. This is why the Maharshi reiterates that, for the Self, to be conscious simply means to be. The perfection of knowledge is being. As the Maharshi puts it: 'Seeing is only being.'[24] The word 'seeing' implies an object that is looked at, or sought, whereas Self-realization is merely repose in one's being. Symbolically speaking, this also means that the eye cannot be known because it is the very subject of the vision: one must be the eye that includes the objects into its vision as the light contains that which it enlightens.

The Maharshi translated into Tamil a number of texts attributed to Shankarāchārya, as well as other scriptural excerpts. One of the most significant of these translations is the *Drik Driśya Viveka*, a title that can be translated by the *Discrimination of the Seer and the Seen*. The terms *drik* and *driśya* are derived from the root that means 'to see' and 'to look.' These terms are therefore akin to the word *darshan*, which denotes seeing a god or a saint. We know from several testimonies that seeing the Maharshi sometimes culminated in being seen by him in a way that would ultimately abolish the scission between seer and seen. G.V. Subbaramayya writes as follows about his *darshan* of Ramana Maharshi in 1933: 'I had *darshan* of Sri Bhagavān in the Hall. As our eyes met, there was a miraculous effect on my mind. I felt as if I had plunged into a pool of peace, and with eyes shut, sat in a state of ecstasy for nearly an hour.'[25] The term *darshan* reveals its most powerful meaning here: it refers to a direct connection with one's true being.[26] The sight of the sage, or the vision of the divine being, leads into a discovery of the Divinity within.

Perhaps the most synthetically meaningful expression of the symbolism of the eye in the Maharshi's non-dualistic perspective appears in verse 15 of *Aksharamanamalai*: 'O Arunachala! Being the Eye of the eye, without eye Thou seest. Who can see Thee? See!'[27] Arunachala is Śiva himself, and the mountain is the center of the world that is identified with the Self. It is as such that it can be referred to as 'the Eye of the eye.' One of the main caves on Arunachala is Virupaksha cave, situated on the southeast slope of the mountain, where the Maharshi lived for seventeen years. The name Virupaksha refers to the three-eyed Śiva. According to T.M.P. Mahadevan, 'the third eye assigned to Lord Śiva is a symbol of the fact that the Supreme is the eye of the eye.'[28] One of the most famous scriptural statements, from the *Kena Upanishad*, teaches that 'it [*Ātman*] is the ear of the ear, the mind of the mind, the speech of speech, the breath of breath, and the eye of the eye.'[29] It is therefore not the eye itself but that by which the eye can see, the very principle or source that is not itself vision in the ordinary sense of the term. This is a sight 'without eye' because it does not pertain to the visual, nor to the mental, realm, but to That which makes vision and the visual world possible. This vision, by contrast with physical sight, cannot be impaired, and there is nothing than can hamper its ability to see. The rhetorical question 'Who can see Thee?' alludes to the impossibility of objectifying the Self that is a key teaching of *Advaita*. The paradoxical exclamation 'See!'—paradoxical in that there is no-one left to 'see'—is the shortest, most direct, expression of the nature of the Self; the verb has no grammatical object, since there is nothing 'objective' to see, and points to the pure Act of Being Conscious that is the essence of the *Ātman*.

In the second of the *Eight Stanzas to Sri Arunachala*, we read: 'Who is the seer? When I sought within, I watched the disappearance of the seer and what survived it. No thought arose to say, "I saw", How then could the thought "I did not see" arise?'[30] Here the seer 'within the mind' is not ultimate since it can be the object of a scrutiny (*nāda*). This investigation results in the disappearance of the seer itself. However something remained after this disappearance to be seen; but by whom could that which remained be seen? What is sure is that the mind did not rise to claim this vision, nor therefore could it claim either a non-vision. This is the mystery of *Ātma-vichāra* whereby the seeker disappears in the process of seeking himself, leaving That which is found without seeking, the blinding evidence of the Self.

EPILOGUE

Given the most intimate identification of Ramana Maharshi with the inquiry 'Who am I?', and the extraordinary diffusion of his presence and teachings throughout the world, one cannot but reflect upon the significance of this question for the age when it was raised as a synthesis of all spiritual paths. It is precisely inasmuch as it is like the quintessence of all ways that it may be deemed most suitable for our age. Synthetic simplicity and universality are welcome in a world weighed down by growing complexities and chaotic fragmentation. The time of intellectual and spiritual traditions and their intricate and integrated elaborations has waned. Human intelligence has largely deserted the field of religions in the widely illusory endeavor to capitalize on the uncertain promises of science and technology, as well as in countless other earthly tasks, the analytic profusion of which often looks vertiginous. Thus, religious traditions have lost their sway, in different ways and proportions, or else have been replaced by unmediated spiritual and devotional improvisations that shun metaphysical and ritual forms inherited from the past in the name of what they regard as a renewed and free experience of selfhood or transcendence. There is therefore great urgency in providing syntheses that distill the sap of tradition without having to embrace the profusion of its treasures and the ambiguities of the totality of its productions, including the most contingent ones. On the other hand, inter-civilizational communication and religious encounters do provide a context that is radically different from anything that has been normatively lived in the past. Thus, the question 'Who am I?' brings back any religious life to its core essentials while lying at the crossroad of existing religions. This does not mean, quite obviously, that most believers would recognize this core as theirs—far from that. The Maharshi thought it necessary to make his message available for all those who have ears to hear. Most Christians do not readily reflect upon the most fundamental implications of the admonition 'The Kingdom of God is within you,' nor are most Muslims disposed to delve into the depth of meaning of the verse 'We are closer to you than your jugular vein,' but some do, or might, when confronted with the profound insight and transforming presence of the Maharshi's quintessential teaching. The sage's fundamental question is a reminder that the heart of religion, if it is to be a truly and deeply transformative way, lies with the realization, or rather the actualization, of a mystery that transcends our individuality while being its innermost secret. Christian faithful will no doubt remember Saint Paul's striking witnessing in Galatians 2:20, 'I live, yet not I, but Christ lives in me.' Even though most believers would take this statement to mean that Christ's grace through faith is more operative in them than their own will, and would likely shun an assertion of Divine immanence within the human self, it remains nevertheless true that the experience of Divine proximity that is arguably inherent to any interiorized form of religion opens onto an innermost domain of ineffability that cannot but echo intimations of the 'God within', the Self.

The Maharshi's Self-realization may also inspire a complementary lesson with respect to the crisis of meaning that has characterized postmodern times. Identity is at the forefront of contemporary conflicts and malaise. The quest for identity has never been as intense as it is today in the modern world, both collectively and individually. Grievances resulting from past or present social and political oppressions have reached an intensity that has been rarely matched in previous times. Groups and individuals are keen to emphasise the rights that they attach to their identity as the very condition of their existence and development. There is no doubt that this widespread protestation is both the symptom of a sense of identity in disarray, and the distant reflection of the foundational reality of the Self as Self of all selves. The Maharshi would say that the source of our unhappiness dwells in our inability to situate selfhood where it truly and ultimately belongs. While modern individualism is a symptom of the collapse of most, if not all, forms of organic sense of belonging, the postmodern collapse of the individual calls for new forms of group belonging that virtually any cultural, ethnic, ideological, or religious symbol can mobilize. From the point of view of Self-knowledge, what could be opportunities to undo the shackles of some limitations all too often result, therefore, in the opposite: a hardening of the boundaries within which the individual or collective ego binds itself.

The idea of surrendering to the Self probably sounds like quite an enigmatic formula to most contemporary ears. First, the term 'surrender' is not uncommonly associated with a sense of alienation. One surrenders to that which overcomes us, and this is already an indication that an external necessity weighs upon us, and prevents us from being what we want to be. Since we consider ourselves as masters and makers of our own life, any surrender threatens and jeopardizes our very integrity. It makes us other than what we are, or think we are. Accordingly, surrendering implies that the world of objectivity constrains us in a way that contradicts and alters the virtually unlimited freedom that we claim for ourselves. From such a perspective, 'surrendering' to one's self sounds like an oxymoron. Needless to say, capitalizing the word Self can help one realize that what is at stake here is something infinitely greater than our own individuality, since the latter is actually a limitation, and in a way a negation, of real Selfhood. While we are used to consider the other as an interlocutor or an object outside of ourselves, the Maharshi teaches that the Other is in us, that It is us. It is no doubt here that devotional religion and spiritual seeking meet. When understood this way, the Buddhist distinction between power of the self (*jiriki*) and power of the Other (*tariki*) becomes a mere question of perspective. Still it might be argued that the point of view of surrender, akin to *tariki*, is more specifically adapted to the needs of our times. The way of surrender is intrinsically metaphysical in the sense that it presupposes transcendence. Self-investigation, when not properly understood by qualified devotees as also implying transcendence, may confine, especially outside of religious and traditional contexts, to a form of psychological exercise that is far from being guaranteed against the most sterile or dangerous delusions of psychic life. This is, no doubt, one of the reasons why the Japanese novelist Hiroyuki Itsuki has been able to encapsulate what may perhaps appear *prima facie* as a paradox: '(*Tariki*) is, in my opinion, a more realistic, more mature, and more quintessentially modern philosophy than self-Power, and it is a philosophy that can be a great source of strength to live in our world today.'[1] Many modern readers might disagree with this assessment, which makes it perhaps sound, by a twist, all the truer. The power of the Other can sound 'unrealistic' in the sense that it may conjure up religious images of God that many contemporaries find unreal or de-realizing. Atheistic ideologies would consider the power of the Other as a mythical cover for fear and helplessness; but it is precisely this fear and helplessness that is claimed by surrender, as the fear of death that suddenly gripped the young Ramana. Itsuki's 'realism' is another way to evoke the 'reality' of our finitude, mortality and wretched limitations. And while turning to the Other might sound infantile to some, it is most mature for the one who surrenders. Immaturity stems from a lack of awareness of the reality and scope of one's being: a deficit in one's appreciation of what is possible, and what is not. While it might be paradoxical to consider as 'quintessentially modern' that which appears to run contrary to the individualistic impulses, and indeed also Promethean tendencies, of modern mankind, a closer examination might reveal that postmodern responses to modernity flow in many ways from coming to terms with the limitations of human knowledge and human endeavors. By 'quintessentially modern' might be meant what remains when the modernist illusions of self-power born in the nineteenth century, scientific progress and political promises, have revealed their cruel boundaries. By contrast, in a way, with Itsuki's assessment of the modern predicament, Arthur Osborne considered that the message of the *Ātma-vichāra* was a reaffirmation of the way of knowledge in our times.[2] He set off this view against the traditional Hindu point of view, which tends to see *japa-yoga* as the most fitting spiritual method in the days of the Kali-Yuga, the final age characterized by an obscuration of spirituality. The two points of view are far from being incompatible, however, as has been suggested in Chapter Three, which is devoted to *japa-yoga*.[3] Both approaches can be combined in several ways, and the Maharshi sees them as converging on the experience of the Self. While Osborne's opinion points to a need that must be fulfilled in order to compensate for the virtual disappearance of the way of knowledge in the religious field—unless knowledge be taken in a merely academic or perhaps, in some traditions, in a legal sense, it also brings out questions on how what is most needed, i.e., knowledge, is equally less likely to be assimilated, by want of qualifications and supporting contexts.[4] Close disciples of the Maharshi such as Annamalai Swami have asserted, in this regard, that 'most people have to follow other paths until they are ready for the final path.'[5] Showing that the path of knowledge and the way of surrender, far from being contrary, are like the two sides of the same reality is, in that sense, the most beneficial task possible. This conjunction is all the more important to stress that Self-inquiry on its own has never been as fraught with perils and more problematic an approach in the absence of a religious and ethical culture that would provide it with foundations and help purify spiritual intentions. While simplicity, synthesis and essentiality are the order of the day, it must also be acknowledged that the conditions for its bearing fruit have never been so lacking as a whole. One of the *leitmotifs* of this book has been to highlight these two *de facto* contradictory, but also in other ways complementary, observations.

As for the Maharshi himself, his 'modernity' is just another name for his perennity: 'he is in all that was, that is and will be. He is the ancient and yet the only modern.'[6] If modernity is understood as relevance to the current times, Ramana Maharshi is indeed more modern than modernist thinkers or activists might fancy themselves to be. The Maharshi's present cannot become obsolete, differently from the 'ways of today' that will be soon tomorrow's past. If presence is the state of being present, then there is no doubt that the Maharshi is indeed a sage for the present, since his has been above all an action of presence, and to the extent that he has always emphasised the most essential nature of the Self as ever present. Granted, this action of presence was most vividly documented during his terrestrial life, and the various testimonies that have been included in this book bear witness to it, but it knows no place and no time, being that of the Self. As he stressed it in many occurrences the real *satguru* is the Self, which amounts to saying that the question 'Who am I?' is the essence of all paths. Hence, the Maharshi's message is a reminder of the core and goal of all spiritual ways, enlightening their means and deepening their reach.

NOTES

INTRODUCTION

1. It is worth noting that *Life* was for decades the first American news magazine, with peaks of over 13 million weekly sales.

2. Here is what Sargeant wrote about his meeting with the Maharshi: 'Sri Ramana would have looked like a superior being in any surroundings. He had the quietly assured look of a man who has experienced a great deal and thought everything through to a final, unshakable, conclusion. Even an unbeliever could see that he possessed a sort of personal serenity that is rare even in the contemplative Orient.' *Life Magazine*, May 30, 1949, pp. 99-100. Sargeant became a Sanskritist and is mostly known for his remarkable translation of the *Bhagavad Gītā* published by the State University of New York Press in 1994.

3. John Grimes, *Ramana Maharshi The Crown Jewel of Advaita*, Varanasi: Indica, 2010, p. 93.

4. 'Pre-occupation with theory, doctrine and philosophy can actually be harmful insofar as it detracts a man from the really important work of spiritual effort by offering an easier alternative that is merely mental, and which, therefore, cannot change his nature. "What use is the learning of those who do not seek to wipe out the letters of destiny (from their brows) by enquiring: 'Whence is the birth of us who knows the letters?' They have sunk to the level of a gramophone. What else are they, O Arunachala?"' Arthur Osborne, Editor, *The Teachings of Ramana Maharshi*, London: Rider, 2014, p. 2.

5. Grimes, p. 11.

6. T.M.P Mahadevan, *Ramana Maharshi and His Philosophy of Existence*, Tiruvannamalai: Sri Ramasramam, 2015 (First Edition, 1959), p. 145.

7. '*Nididhyāsana* [...] means fixing the mental gaze on the principle of reality to determine its true nature, like one examining a jewel.' Sri Swami Satchidānandendra, *The Method of the Vedānta—A Critical Account of the Advaita Tradition*, New Delhi: Motilal Banarsidass, 1997, p. 147.

8. Michael James, *Happiness and the Art of Being—An introduction to the philosophy and practice of the spiritual teachings of Bhagavan Sri Ramana*, 2006, p. 334. James

based this insight on the first verse of *Ulladu Narpadu*, which he translates as follows: 'If the Reality "I" did not exist, could there exist the consciousness "am" (the consciousness of one's own existence)? Since (that) Reality exists in the heart devoid of thought, how to (or who can) meditate upon (that) Reality, which is called the Heart? Know that abiding in the Heart as it is (that is, without thought, as "I am"), alone is meditating (upon the Reality).' p. 5.

9. John Grimes, *Ramana Maharshi The Crown Jewel of Advaita,* Varanasi: Indica, 2010.

10. T.M.P Mahadevan, *Ramana Maharshi and His Philosophy of Existence,* Tiruvannamalai: Sri Ramanasramam, 2015. First Edition, 1959.

11. *Essays on Individualism: Modern Ideology in Anthropological Perspective,* Chicago: University of Chicago Press, 1992.

12. 'Ramana alighted from the train in Tiruvannamalai on September 1, 1896, the holy mountain and the temple lay before him in the morning light. [...] One of the barbers who practised his trade at the Ayyankulam tank, cut off his beautiful black locks and shaved his head. He gave the barber some money and threw the rest of the 3½ rupees away. Then he tore up the *dhoti* he was wearing and kept only one piece as a loincloth.' Gabriele Ebert, *Ramana Maharshi—His Life—A Biography*, Stuttgart: Lüchow Verlag, 2015, p. 35.

13. 'When, after his three-day journey, Ramana alighted from the train in Tiruvannamalai on 1st September 1896, the holy mountain and the temple lay before him in the morning light. It is worth noting that he identified Arunachala first with the temple and only later with the mountain.' Ebert, p. 32.

14. 'Absolutistic Hinduism believes in ultimate reality as an Absolute and is closely associated with the form of Hindu thought known as *Advaita Vedānta*. It is the preeminent form of intellectual Hinduism in our times. About three-fourths of Hindu intellectuals subscribe to this form of Hinduism in one way or another. The main exponent of this form of Hinduism in modern times was Ramana Maharshi (1879–1950).' Arvind Sharma, *Our Religions*, New York: HarperOne, 1993, p. 14.

15. This is the *Viśishtādvaita* of Rāmānujā (1017–1137), which is non-dual only to the extent that it conceives of the world and the soul as emanating from God, while keeping the distinction between the three of them irreducible in conformity with its bhaktic perspective.

16. Author's translation. Henry Corbin, *En islam iranien I: Le Shî'isme duodécimain, aspects spirituels et philosophiques*, Paris: Gallimard, 1971, p. 33.

17. Frithjof Schuon, *Spiritual Perspectives and Human Facts*, Bloomington, Indiana: World Wisdom, 2007, p. 37.

18. Here is how the Maharshi describes his utter lack of traditional knowledge at the time of his spiritual awakening: 'As for *Brahman*, the Impersonal Absolute, I had no idea then. I had not even heard the name "*Brahman*". I had not read the *Gita* or any other religious work except *Periya-purānam* and the *Bible*; in the religion class, the four Gospels and the Psalms in the *Bible*.' *Arunachala Ramana Eternal Ocean of Grace, Volume 1, Biography*, Tiruvannamalai, India: Sri Ramasramam, 2018, p. 31.

19. On the question of the global standardization of religion see Olivier Roy, *Holy Ignorance—When Religion and Culture Part Ways,* London: Hurst, 2010.

20. Prince Dārā Shikūh (1615–59), a grand nephew of Emperor Akbar, convened representatives of Sufism and Vedānta at his court, and he translated some fifty Upanishads into Persian. Cf. Dārā Shikūh Muhammad, *Majma'-ul-Bahrain, or, The Mingling of the Two Oceans*. Translated by M. Mahfūz-ul-Haqq, Calcutta, Asiatic Society, 1982. One may also consult with profit Shankar Nair's study *Translating Wisdom—Hindu-Muslim Intellectual Interactions in Early Modern South Asia*, University of California Press, 2020.

1. WHOSE LIFE?

1. Suri Nagamma, *Letters from Sri Ramasramam*, Tiruvannamalai: Sri Ramanasramam, 2014, p. 472.

2. 'I want to be left alone, therefore I welcome the libellous pamphlet.' Godman, *Living By The Words of Bhagavān*, p. 141.

3. Grimes, p. 291.

4. Ganapati Muni went to the Maharshi in desperate search of *tapas*, or spiritual practices, for Self-realization. The Maharshi's response was the following: 'Find out wherefrom this "I" springs forth and merge at its source; that is *tapas*. Find out wherefrom the sound of the *mantra* in *japa* rises up and merges there; that is *tapas*.' The following day Ganapati Muni wrote to his disciples: 'I have found my Master, my *Guru*. [...] He is a great Seer, a mighty spiritual personality. To me and to you all he is Bhagavān Sri Ramana Maharshi. Let the whole world know him as such.' S. Shankaranarayanan, *Bhagavan and Nayana*, Ramanasramam, Third Edition, 2014, pp. 6–7.

5. Notwithstanding a deep reverence for the Maharshi I shall refrain from using the term Bhagavān in this book, and refer to the sage simply as the Maharshi or Ramana Maharshi. This is nothing but a matter of convention and usage in the context of an academic publication.

6. *Arunachala Ramana Eternal Ocean of Grace, Book 1, Biography*, Tiruvannamalai: Sri Ramanasramam, 2018, p. 28.

7. Ibid.

8. '*Viveka* is the capacity to distinguish between the timeless (*nitya*) and the timebound (*anitya*). *Advaita* commentators generally elaborate by explaining that *viveka* is recognition that *Brahman* alone is eternal and everything else is non-eternal.' Anantanand Rambachan, *The Advaita Worldview*, Albany, New York: State University of New York Press, 2006, p. 21.

9. 'All this was not dull thought; it flashed through me vividly as living truth that I perceived directly, almost without thought process.' *Biography*, p. 28.

10. David Godman, *Living by the Words of Bhagavān*, Pondicherry: Sri Annamalai Swami Ashram Trust, 1994, p. 1.

11. *Biography*, p. 32.

12. Mahadevan, p. 127.

13. 'Other thoughts might come and go, like the various notes of music, but the "I" continued like the [single] fundamental "*śruti*" note [in Indian music] that blends with all the other notes. Whether the body was engaged in talking, reading or anything else, I was still centered on "I".' *Biography*, pp. 28–9.

14. *Biography*, p. 4.
15. *Biography*, p. 23.
16. *Biography*, p. 23.
17. 'He was an abnormally heavy sleeper and once they had to break open the door of the room in which he slept before they could wake him up. His friends took advantage of this abnormality, they would pull him off his bed while still asleep and take him with them, buffeting him and playing on him every trick they would not dare to try when he was awake.' A.W. Chadwick, *A Sadhu's Reminiscences of Ramana Maharshi*, Tiruvannamalai: Sri Ramanasramam, 2012, p. 1.
18. 'Getting to know about this quality of his, some schoolmates who were earlier beaten up by Venkataraman but were afraid to retaliate, would take him while asleep to a lonely spot, thrash him and bring him back to his bed. By their words and hints on the following day, Venkataraman would guess what had transpired the previous night.' *Biography*, p. 16.
19. Arvind Sharma, *Sleep as a State of Consciousness in Advaita Vedānta*, Albany, New York: State University of New York Press, 2004, p. 49.
20. Suri Nagamma, *Letters*, p. 358.
21. Paul Brunton, *Conscious Immortality - Conversations with Sri Ramana Maharshi*, Tiruvannamalai: Sri Ramanasramam, Fifth Edition, 2015, p. 145.
22. In his *Forty Verses in Adoration of Sri Ramana* Ganapati Muni considers that this eloquence of silence proceeds from the goddess Sarasvati through Ramana Maharshi. As goddess of literature, the arts and eloquence, Sarasvati's power manifests on different levels of reality, including its lowest level as *vaikhari*, or articulated word, but in the case of the Maharshi, the goddess manifests as *parā vāk*, the unmanifest seed of sound, the secret womb of silence.' Sri Kavyakantha Vasishtha Ganapati Muni, *Forty Verses in Adoration of Sri Ramana*, Tiruvannamalai: Sri Ramanasramam, 2012, p. 47.
23. *Sat-Darshana Bhashya and Talks with Maharshi by K.*, Sri Ramanasramamam, Tiruvannamalai, 2015, First Edition 1931, p. 1.
24. Dominic Goodall, edit. *Hindu Scriptures*, New Delhi: Motilal Banarsidass, 1996, p. 72.
25. In Hindu chanting, the *Omkara* or sacred syllable formed by the three letters A, U and M, is the alpha and the omega of any performance; it is also its underlying note. AUM is also a kind of articulation of silence, proceeding from it and ending in it. It lies at the articulation of silence and sound, and therefore in a way, as suggested by the *Maitri Upanisad*, serves as a transition between *Brahman*-Sound and *Brahman*-the-Supreme, without sound, the *Saguna Brahman* and the Nirguna *Brahman*.
    'Two *Brahman*s are to be known, the Sound-*Brahman* and the Supreme; he who is versed in the Sound-*Brahman*, attains to the Supreme. It has been said elsewhere: The syllable Om is Sound; its end is silence, soundless, [...] To attain this state other than all else, let a man worship these two.' *The Maitri or Maitrāyanīya Upanishad*, translated by E.B. Cowell, London: W.M. Watts, 1870, p. 271.
26. 'Lectures may entertain individuals for a few hours without improving them. Silence, on the other hand, is permanent and benefits the whole of humanity. [...] By silence, eloquence is meant. Oral lectures are not so eloquent as silence, silence

is unceasing eloquence.' *Talks with Ramana Maharshi—On Realizing Abiding Peace and Happiness,* Carlsbad, California: InnerDirections Publishing, 2001, p. 14.

27.   In a tradition that is not given to emphasise withdrawal from the world, quite the contrary, Muhammad's retreats in a cave of Mount Hira before his receiving the revelation, as well as Ghazālī's withdrawal from his family and professional duties during the several years he spent in retreat, suggest that the alternation of spiritual retreat and presence in the world are not as antinomic as they may appear to be on the surface.

28.   Suri Nagamma, *Letters from Sri Ramanasramam,* Tiruvannamalai: Sri Ramanasramam, Eighth Edition, 2014, p. 498.

29.   *Letters,* p. 490.

30.   *Letters,* p. 477.

31.   *Letters,* p. 466.

32.   This is according to F.H. Humphreys: 'The most touching sight was the number of tiny children up to about seven years of age, who climb the hill, all on their own, to come and sit near the Maharshi, even though he may not speak a word or even look at them for days together. They do not play, but just sit there quietly, in perfect contentment.' *Face to Face with Sri Ramana Maharshi,* Compiled and edited by Laxmi Narain, Hyderabad: Sri Ramana Kendram, 2009, p. 246.

33.   *Face to Face,* pp. 13–14.

34.   *Day by Day With Bhagavan—From the Diary of A. Devaraja Mudaliar,* Tiruvannamalai: Sri Ramanasraman, 2002, p. 29.

35.   'Frank Henry Humphreys' in 'Sixty-three Devotees', *Arunachala Ramana, Book 4,* p. 55.

36.   *Face to Face,* pp. 246–7.

37.   *Day by Day,* p. 25.

38.   'Bhagavān Sri Ramana Maharshi has often been compared to Sri Dakshinamurti, who sits silently under the banyan tree on the north slope of Arunachala, and there is much ground for this comparison. Moreover, it is more than just a comparison. Actually the two are identical, although their bodies may seem different to us who are bound by the limitations of time and space.' A.W. Chadwick, 'Sri Dakshinamurti and Sri Ramana', *Arunachala Ramana, Book 7,* pp. 38–9.

39.   '(Dakshināmūrti) [refers] to that Incarnation of Śiva in which He is represented as a *Guru* teaching spiritual wisdom at the foot of a fig tree with His face turned to the South.' Alladi Mahadeva Sastry, *Dakshinamurti Stotra of Sri Sankaracharya,* Chennai: Samata Books, 2001, p. 213.

40.   'This whole Universe, moving and non-moving, from Brahmā to the blade of grass, is enchanted by that Unborn and Incomprehensible *Māyā.*' *The Srimad Devi Bhagawatam,* Oriental Books Reprint Corporation, 1977, p. 582.

41.   'Now pay attention! So one and simple is this citadel in the soul, elevated above all modes, of which I speak and which I mean, that that noble power I mentioned is not worthy even for an instant to cast a single glance into this citadel; nor is that other power I spoke of, in which God burns and glows with all His riches and all His joy, able to cast a single glance inside; so truly one and simple is this citadel, so mode- and power-transcending is this solitary One, that neither power nor mode can gaze

into it, nor even God Himself! In very truth and as God lives! God Himself never looks in there for one instant, insofar as He exists in modes and in the properties of His persons.' Meister Eckhart, *The Complete Mystical Works of Meister Eckhart*, translated by Maurice O'C Walshe, New York: Herder & Herder, 2009, Sermon 8, p. 81.

42. Mercandante, Linda A., *Belief without borders: Inside the minds of the spiritual but not religious*, New York, NY: Oxford University Press, 2014.

43. 'The pot is a god. The winnowing fan is a god. The stone in the street is a god. The comb is a god. The bowstring is also a god. The bushel is a god and the spouted cup is a god. Gods, gods, there are so many there's no place left for a foot. There is only one god. He is our Lord of the Meeting Rivers.' Basavanna, *Speaking of Śiva*, translated by A.K. Ramanujan, Baltimore, Maryland: Penguin Books, 1973, p. 28.

44. *Bhagavān Ramana The Friend of All Creation, Offerings by the Devotees of Bhagavān At His Lotus Feet*, Tiruvannamalai: Sri Ramanasramam, 2008.

45. In the triad of the goddesses who are the consorts of the gods of the Trimūrti, Ganapati Muni sees Lakshmi as having 'her play in (his) [the Maharshi's] face [...] as the face resembles a full-blown lotus, full of ethereal beauty and charm [... as] she spreads concord, harmony, beauty and charm all around.' *Forty Verses*, p. 47.

46. 'A devotee asked a Mahatma "Swami! How do we know a *Jnani*?" The Mahatma answered, "One who has a balanced tranquil mind in any kind of situation, one who has universal vision of equality towards all beings; one who has love, care, compassion and solicitude for all beings; irrespective of whether it is a plant, animal, bird, insect or human being, he is a Jnani."' *The Friend of All Creation*, p. 16.

47. *The Friend of All Creation*, p. 104.

48. Sermon Eighty-Seven, *The Complete Mystical Works of Meister Eckhart*, translated by Maurice O'C. Walshe, New York: Crossroad Publishing, 2009, p. 422.

49. 'Devotees of Siva consider this divine mountain as the form of Siva who appeared in the midst of Brahma and Vishnu as a column of fire without beginning or end in order to dispel their ignorance after both failed to realise his Presence with the aid of their physical efforts.' Lucia Osborne, 'Arunachala' in *Arunachala Ramana Eternal Ocean of Grace, Book 7 The Guiding Presence*, p. 2.

50. 'The *tīrthas* are primarily associated with the great acts and appearances of the gods and the heroes of Indian myth and legend. As a threshold between heaven and earth, the *tīrtha* is not only a place for the "upward" crossings of people's prayers and rites, it is also a place for the "downward" crossings of the gods. These divine "descents" are the well-known *avatāras* of the Hindu tradition. Indeed, the words *tīrtha* and *avatāra* come from related verbal roots: tr.., "to cross over," and avatr.., "to cross down". One might say that the *avatāras* descend, opening the doors of the *tīrthas* so that men and women may ascend in their rites and prayers.' Diana Eck, *Banaras City of Light*, Princeton, New Jersey: Princeton University Press, 1982, p. 35.

51. 'The symbolist mind sees appearances in their connection with essences: in its manner of vision, water is primarily the sensible appearance of a principle-reality, a *kami* (Japanese) or a *manitu* (Algonquin) or a *wakan* (Sioux); this means that it sees things, not "superficially" only, but above all "in depth", or that it perceives them in their "participative" or "unitive" dimension as well as in their "separative"

dimension.' Frithjof Schuon, *The Feathered Sun*, Bloomington, Indiana: World Wisdom Books, 1990, p. 9.

52.   *Arunachala Ramana*, Osborne, p. 7.

53.   'As soon as I saw him [Ramana Maharshi] I was at once convinced that God Arunachala Himself had come in human form to give salvation to all who approached Him.' Varanasi Subbalakshmiamma, 'My Life, My Light', *Arunachala Ramana, Book 7*, p. 22.

54.   The two notions of extinction and permanence are drawn from the vocabulary of Sufism, *fanā'* and *baqā'*. Cf. Eric Geoffroy, *Introduction to Sufism*, Bloomington, Indiana, World Wisdom, 2010, p. 15. They offer deep areas of correspondence, however, with the *kevala* and stages of *samadhi*.

55.   One may find more on this point in David Godman's reflections in *The Power of the Guru I*, https://www.youtube.com/watch?v=Pz-KNGbec30

56.   'To some he would grant a special vision, invisible to others; with some he would openly discourse. Crows would gather round him and each would see him differently. Even his pictures differ. A stranger would not guess that they are all of the same person.' Varanasi Subbalakshmiamma, 'My Life, My Light', *Arunachala Ramana, Book 7*, p. 27.

57.   'One who accustoms himself naturally to meditation and enjoys the bliss of meditation will not lose his *samadhi* state whatever external work he does, whatever thoughts may come to him. That is *sahaja nirvikalpa*. *Sahaja nirvikalpa* is *nasa* [total destruction of the mind] whereas *kevala nirvikalpa* is *laya* [temporary abeyance of the mind]. Those who are in the *laya samadhi* state will have to bring the mind back under control from time to time. If the mind is destroyed, as it is in *sahaja samadhi*, it will never sprout again. Whatever is done by such people is just incidental, they will never slide down from their high state.' *Ramana Maharshi, Be As You Are*, edited by David Godman, Penguin UK, 1991, p. 159.

58.   *Face to Face*, p. 84.

59.   This is narrated by David Godman in his video *The Power of the Guru I*, https://www.youtube.com/watch?v=v8wDe4ngpDw

60.   *Arunachala Ramana, Book 3*, p. 101.

61.   *Face to Face*, p. 234.

62.   Vishwanata Swami, 'Activity, Help not Hindrance', *Arunachala Ramana, Book 7*, p. 18.

63.   Godman, p. 144.

64.   Annamalai Swami remarks that the only aspect of the entreprise in which the Maharshi declined to be involved was the financial one. This was no doubt on account of his '*samnyāsa*.' Godman, p. 155.

65.   *Arunachala Ramana Book 7*, p. 31.

66.   Ibid.

67.   The quotes are from D.T. Suzuki. Albert Welter, *The Linji lu and the Creation of Chan Orthodoxy*, Oxford University Press, 2008, p. 18.

68.   Mahadevan, p. 143.

69.   'Speak little. Hold to your own nature. A strong wind does not blow all morning. A cloudburst does not last all day. The wind and rain are from Heaven and Earth and

even these do not last long. How much less so the efforts of man?' Jonathan Star, *Tao Te Ching The Definitive Edition*, Jeremy P. Tarcher/Putnam, 2001, p. 36.

2. GRACE AND DEVOTION

1. The use of this compound adjective refers to the fact that the Self-investigation advised by the Maharshi pertains, at least initially, to an activity of the mind—hence it is *a priori* 'psychic', although its goal is obviously transcendent in relation to the latter—and therefore better characterized as 'spiritual'.

2. 'To this level belong those rare, highly spiritual souls who are born fully enlightened and come into the world to show others the way to attain their liberated state. For them *Anupāya* literally means that they do not need to practice at all.' Mark Dyczkowski, *The Doctrine of Vibration-An Analysis of the Doctrines and Practices of Kashmir Shaivism*, Albany, New York: State University of New York Press, p. 178. 'We have said that there are four types of means to realisation. Although this is quite true from one point of view, the fourth and ultimate means is not one in the same sense as are the others. Considered to be the highest form of the Divine means (*sāmbhavopāya*, for which see below), it is the end of all practice and is accordingly called "No-means" (*anupāya*). It is the uninterrupted consciousness the absolute has of its own nature [...] spontaneously and completely realised in an instant.' Ibid. p. 257.

3. It is probably not an exaggeration to suggest that the testimony of I.S. Varghese, a devotee of the Maharshi, is quite representative in this respect: 'Though I have always been vitally concerned with religion, the position I had come to in middle age was one of agnosticism. I had totally lost faith in the Christian dogma which had been taught to me as a child. The nearly one hundred denominations of Christianity nauseated me. All external forms of religion I held in utter contempt as the domain of old women and fools.' *Arunachala Ramana Book 7*, pp. 182–3.

4. Paul Brunton, *Conscious Immortality—Conversations with Sri Ramana Maharshi*, Tiruvannamalai: Sri Ramanasramam, Fifth Edition, 2015, p. 12.

5. Some, like René Guénon, thought of such contacts with Asian wisdom traditions not so much as 'conversions' as to ways of revivifying the Western traditional heritage: '[...] certain Western elements would have to bring about this [intellectual and spiritual] restoration with the help afforded by a knowledge of the Eastern doctrines; this however could not for them be quite direct, since they would have to remain Westerners, but it might be obtained by a sort of second-hand influence working through intermediaries [...].' René Guénon, *The Crisis of the Modern World*, Hillsdale, New York: Sophia Perennis, 2001, p. 111.

6. After his enlightenment Ramana started to visit the temple regularly. He recalled, 'Formerly I would go there rarely with friends, see the images, put on sacred ashes and sacred vermilion on the forehead and return home without any perceptible emotion. After the awakening into the new life, I would go almost every evening to the temple. I would go alone and stand before Śiva, or Meenakshi or Nataraja or the sixty-three saints for long periods. I would feel waves of emotion overcoming me. The former hold on the body had been given up by my spirit, since it ceased

to cherish the idea I-am-the-body. The spirit therefore longed to have a fresh hold and hence the frequent visits to the temple and the overflow of the soul in profuse tears. This was God's (Īśvara's) play with the individual spirit. I would stand before Īśvara, the Controller of the universe and the destinies of all, the Omniscient and Omnipresent, and occasionally pray for the descent of his grace upon me so that my devotion might increase and become perpetual like that of the sixty-three saints. Mostly I would not pray at all, but let the deep within flow on and into the deep without. Tears would mark this overflow of the soul and not betoken any particular feeling of pleasure or pain.' Gabriele Ebert, *Ramana Maharshi: His Life*, p. 25.

7. In Hindu *Advaita* this is known as the classical distinction between the Non-Qualified Absolute, *Nirguna Brahman*, and the Qualified Absolute, *Saguna Brahman*; now the latter is Īśvara, or God as a Person, indeed as the Supreme Person.

8. This point of view is expressed, for instance, in Qur'ān 23:115, 'Did you think that We had created you in play (without any purpose), and that you would not be brought back to Us?' Muhammad Saed Abdul-Rahman, *Tafsir Ibn Kathir*, volume 6 of 10, London: MSA Publication Ltd., 2011, p. 406.

9. '[The *līlā*] metaphor is that of the consummate artist manifesting her skill in creation. This suggests an everyday world pervaded not only by a sense of divine action, but also by a divine beauty produced in the play of reality [...]. To understand the nature of art and of the creative act is to understand the nature of reality.' Nalini Bhushan and Jay L. Garfield, *Minds Without Fear—Philosophy in the Indian Renaissance*, Oxford University Press, 2017, p. 245.

10. *Arunachala Ramana, Book 1*, p. 33.

11. 'From that moment onwards the "I" or Self focused attention on itself by a powerful fascination. Fear of death had vanished once and for all. Absorption in the Self continued unbroken from that time on.' *Arunachala Ramana, Book 1*, p. 20.

12. Thus, here is the way Franklin Merrell-Wolff distinguishes between what he calls 'recognition' and experience: 'I say "Recognition" rather than "experience" for a very definite reason. Properly it was not a case of experiential knowledge, which is knowledge from the senses whether gross or subtle, nor knowledge from deduction, though both forms, particularly the latter, have helped in a subsidiary sense.' *Pathways Through To Space*, New York: Julian Press, 1973, p. 4. Merrell-Wolff, following a meditation of Shankara's writings, recognizes that the search for an experience is actually antithetical to Self-realization: 'Then, as I sat afterward dwelling in thought upon the subject just read, suddenly it dawned upon me that a common mistake made in higher meditation—i.e., meditation for Liberation—is the seeking for a subtle object of Recognition, in other words, something that could be experienced.' Ibid.

13. *Arunachala Ramana, Book 1*, p. 33.

14. Ibid.

15. 'If we receive this gift—a gift which surpasses all others—then through weeping we will enter purity; and when we have entered there, it will not be taken away from us again; right up to the day of our departure from the world. Blessed, therefore, are the pure in heart, who at all times enjoy this delight of tears and through it see our Lord continuously.' Saint Symeon the New Theologian, in Maria Jaoudi, *Christian*

Mysticism East and West—What the Masters Teach Us, Mahwah, New Jersey: Paulist Press, 1998, p. 26.

16. Born in England in 1953, David Godman was librarian of the Ramanashraman between 1978 and 1985. He is one of the most authoritative and prolific writers on the Maharshi. One of his most rewarding books is comprised of his recordings of interviews he had in 1987 with one of the advanced devotees of the Maharshi called Annamalai Swami (1906–95). The account of the interviews, duly checked and authorized by Annamalai Swami himself, is accompanied by Godman's annotations. It was published under the title *Living By The Words Of Bhagavān*, Tiruvannamalai: Sri Annamalai Swami Ashram Trust, 1994.

17. Godman, p. 25.

18. Ibid.

19. 'Selections from *Guru Ramana Vachana Mala*', *Arunachala Ramana, Book 5*, p. 56.

20. 'It is only knowledge that actually brings liberation, but action is an indirect aid and is spoken of as a cause figuratively.' Sri Swami Satchidānandendra, *The Method of the Vedānta—A Critical Account of the Advaita Tradition*, New Delhi: Motilal Banarsidass, 1997, p. 180.

21. 'The thought "Who am I?" will destroy all other thoughts, and like the stick used for stirring the burning pyre, it will itself in the end get destroyed, Then, there will arise Self-realization.' *The Collected Works of Ramana Maharshi*, Sophia Perennis, San Rafael, CA, 2006, p. 35.

22. *Sat-Darshana Bhashya and Talks with Maharshi by K.*, Sri Ramanasramamam, Tiruvannamalai, 2015, First Edition 1931, p. 85.

23. '[According to Shankara] [...] the realization of *Brahman* completely annihilates [...] those accumulated past *karmas* that have not yet begun to produce effects. [...] It does not destroy the *karmas* that have been producing the effects of the current life, *prārabdha karma*, but allows them to work themselves out. The realizer, free from unfructified *karma* and from the possibility of any new *karma*, but not free from *prārabdha karma*, [...] the *jīvan-mukta*. The persistence of the body for the *jīvan-mukta* does not in any way constitute a state of bondage, but merely a working out of *prārabdha-karma*.' Daniel P. Sheridan, 'Direct Knowledge of God and Living Liberation in the Religious Thought of Madhva', in *Living Liberation in Hindu Thought*, edited by Andrew O. Fort and Patricia Y. Mumme, Albany, New York: State University of New York Press, 1996, p. 95.

24. 'The absence of thoughts is the measure of your progress towards Self-realization.' Godman, *Be As You Are*, p. 67.

25. *Brahma-Sūtras According to Sri Shankara*, translation and commentary by Swami Vireswarananda, Kolkata: Advaita Ashrama Publication Department, 1936, p. 10.

26. *Sat-Darshana Bhashya*, p. 16.

27. 'Decreation: to make something created pass into the uncreated. Destruction: to make something created pass into nothingness. A blameworthy substitute for decreation.' Simone Weil, *Gravity and Grace*, Routledge: London and New York, 2003, p. 32.

28. The Greek and Sanskrit words are etymologically cognate: 'Interestingly, this is one word whose root or basic form remains recognizable in virtually all Indo-European

languages: Skt: *jñāna*, Greek: *gnosis* or *gignoskein,* Latin: *gnoscere, noscere*; *cognitio,* French: *connaître,* Eng: know, etc. The Sanskrit *jñ-* becomes *kn-* in English, as in German it becomes *kennen, Kenntnis* (Old High German: *bi-chāan,* Old English: *cnāwen,* Middle English: *knowen*). In other language groups such as Semitic (Hebrew: *da'ath*) or Chinese (*chih*), no similarities with the Indo-European root are found.' Dan Lusthaus, *Buddhist Phenomenology: A Philosophical Investigation of Yogācāra Buddhism and the Ch'eng Wei-shih lun,* New York: Routledge-Curzon, 2002, p. 195.

29. *Conscious Immortality,* p. 165.
30. *Sat-Darshana Bhashya,* p. 5.
31. On the theological notions of sufficient, prevenient, cooperating and efficacious grace see Thomas P. Flint, 'Two Accounts of Providence' in Michael Rea, edit., *Oxford Readings in Philosophical Theology Volume II,* Oxford University Press, 2009, p. 28.
32. 'Of course, nothing is impossible to God, but everything happens according to the order established by God's will or plan and exceptions are few.' Quoted in A. Devaraja Mudaliar, *The Mountain Path,* Volume 4, number 2, April 1967, p. 114.
33. Ibid., p. 115.
34. 'Your life becomes a needle drawn to a huge mass of magnet and as you go deeper and deeper, you become a mere center and then not even that, for you become a mere Consciousness.' *Sat-Darshana Bhashya,* p. 21.
35. *Sat-Darshana Bhashya,* p. 5.
36. Ibid.
37. 'V.: It is said only some are chosen for Self-realisation and those alone could get it. It is rather discouraging. B.: All that is meant is, we cannot by our own *buddhi,* unaided by God's grace, achieve realisation of Self.' *Day by Day,* p. 4.
38. Grimes, p. 229.
39. *Arunachala Ramana Book 7,* p. 145.
40. 'The Master [...] appears as a man to dispel the ignorance of a man, just as a deer is used as a decoy to capture the wild deer. He has to appear with a body in order to eradicate our ignorant "I am the body" idea.' *Arunachala Ramana Book 7,* p. 143.
41. *Talks,* p. 300.
42. Ibid.
43. '[...] In *Advaita* the method is not *just* to engage the Text through reading, but the method is to listen to the text from the mouth of the *guru,* to hear it orally transmitted and explained; and to present it as primarily an exercise of study, of "reading", is to deprive it of the methodology that it articulates for itself.' Michael Comans, *The Method of Early Advaita Vedānta,* New Delhi: Motilal Banarsidass, 2000, p. 183.
44. Here is the way Thamus responds to the god Theuth's invention of written characters: 'for this discovery of yours [writing] will create forgetfulness in the learners' souls, because they will not use their memories; they will trust to the external written characters and not remember of themselves. The specific which you have discovered is an aid not to memory, but to reminiscence, and you give your disciples not truth, but only the semblance of truth; they will be hearers of

many things and will have learned nothing; they will appear to be omniscient and will generally know nothing; they will be tiresome company, having the show of wisdom without the reality.' *Phaedrus*, 154, translation Benjamin Jowett (1871), New York: Cosimo, 2010.

45. 'The Ordainer controls the fate of souls in accordance with their past deeds. Whatever is destined not to happen will not happen, try how hard you may. Whatever is destined to happen will happen, do what you may to stop it. This is certain.' Ebert, p. 55.

46. 'If the initiatic role of the *guru* or spiritual master is often spoken of [...], there is on the other hand another notion that is generally passed over in silence: what the Hindu tradition designates by the word *upaguru*. This term must be understood to signify every being, whatever it may be, with whom an encounter is for someone the occasion or starting-point of a spiritual development; and, in a general way, it is not at all necessary that this being itself be conscious of the role it plays.' René Guénon, *Initiation and Spiritual Realization*, Hillsdale, New York: Sophia Perennis, 2004, p. 104.

47. It must added, however, that the grace of the Self, *Ātma-kripa*, is sometimes understood as referring to the means actualized by the *jivātman* on the way to spiritual realization: 'Then you need *atma kripa*, the grace of your Self, which takes the form of committing yourself to your practice. Sincerity, regularity, staying away from useless things and useless people, and being strong in one's decision in *atma kripa*.' Rajmani Tigunait, *The Himalayan Masters—A Living Tradition*, Honesdale, Pennsylvania: Himalayan Institute Press, 2002, p. 146. In this sense, what Japanese Buddhists would call the 'power of the self' (*jiriki*) ultimately points to the immanence of the Self, of which it is but a prefiguration.

48. *Talks with Ramana Maharshi*, Carlsbad, California: Inner Directions, 2000, p. 199.

49. *Talks*, p. 206.

50. 'Another aspect of Self-inquiry that became apparent after some months of practice was the assurance of being taken care of by some Higher Power. There was a feeling of power all around, but always subtle power. In very complex situations totally unexpected solutions have automatically appeared. Some experiences which may be classed as miraculous have also come unbidden.' I.S. Varghese, 'Light on the Path', *Arunachala Ramana. Book 7*, p. 183.

51. A number of accounts of miraculous interventions attributed to the Maharshi are included in books about him. The following report is representative of the ways in which bhaktic consciousness, or human consciousness inasmuch as it is bhaktic, relates to the *guru*'s presence and reads the world in his light: 'Bhagavān, I have got a letter from Shanta (the Maharani of Baroda). Bhagavān has performed a miracle and she is writing about it. It seems she went out in a car and on the way the car broke down and the driver could do nothing about it. So, it seems, he took the Rani's permission and went to phone for another car. Meanwhile, it seems a striking-looking and mild sadhu suddenly appeared on the scene and touched the car and said, "You can go on now." The driver returned and when he started the engine, the car moved on without any trouble. The Rani thinks it was all Bhagavān's grace.' Devaraja Mudialar, *Day by Day*, p. 295.

52. 'Ramana Himself would [...] dismiss these visible signs of His Grace as being only the automatic intervention of a higher power when matters are brought to the notice of a *jnani*.' A.R. Natarajan, 'Secret Operation of Ramana's Grace'. *The Mountain Path*, Volue 19, number IV, October 1982, p. 228.

53. Ibid.

54. 'This (self) was indeed *Brahman* in the beginning. It knew only Itself as "I am Brahman." Therefore It became all. And whoever among the gods knew It all became That; and the same with sages and so on.' *Brihad Aranyaka Upanishad* I, 10, in *The Upanishads*, Swami Nikhilananda, New York: Harper and Row, 1964, p. 191.

55. 'Now that which is that subtile essence, in it all that exists has its self. It is the True. It is the Self, and thou, O Svetaketu, art it.' *Chandogya Upanishad*, 6, 9, 4. Max Muller, *The Upanishads*, Part I, Oxford University Press, 1900, p. 101.

56. *The Song of Ribhu: The English Translation of the Tamil Ribhu Gītā*, translated by Dr. H. Ramamoorthy and Mone, Santa Cruz, California: Society of Abidance in Truth, 2000, p. 91.

57. In the case of one who is not a perfect *jñanin* prayer for another person is a possibility, indeed a necessity, by virtue of a lingering identification with the individual state.

58. *Arunachala Ramana. Book 7*, p. 157.

59. 'D.: They speak of the four Ashramas or prescribed vocation in life. What is their meaning? M.: To go by stages is a social rule intended for the generality. But if one is a *pakvi*, a well developed being, he need not mind this rule. Young or old, man or woman, Brahmin or outcast, if one is *paripakvi*, fully ripe, he or she can and does go straight to the goal, without minding the stages.' 'Conversations with Kapali Sastry as an Introduction to *Sat Darshana Bhashya*', *Arunachala Ramana, Book 5*, p. 50. The term '*paripakvi*' literally means 'fully cooked,' which brings to mind Rūmī's verse: 'I was raw, I became "cooked", I was burnt up.' Annemarie Schimmel, *A Two-Colored Brocade—The Imagery of Persian Poetry*, Chapel Hill, North Carolina: The University of North Carolina Press, 2004, p. 250.

60. *Talks*, p. 186.

61. Ebert, p. 184.

62. *The Spiritual Teaching of Ramana Maharshi*, Boulder, Colorado: Shambala, 1998, p. 59.

63. Suri Nagamma, *Letters from Ramanasramam*, Tiruvannamalai: Ramanashramam, 2014, p. 2.

64. Henri Le Saux, *Souvenir d'Arunâchala*, Paris: Epi-Desclée de Brouwer, 1978-1980, p. 23.

65. Ibid., p. 24.

66. Ibid., p. 45.

67. 'Before my thought was able to recognize it nor above all express it, the intimate aura of this Sage had been perceived by something in me, at the deepest of myself. Unknown harmonies were awakening in my heart. A chant let itself be divined, and above all a *bass* that enveloped everything.' Ibid., pp. 27–8.

68. *Arunachala Ramana, Book 3*, 58.

69. Ganapati Muni attributes this power of the Maharshi's eyes to the action of the goddess Durgā who 'destroys all evil forces, puts an end to all the miseries and dispels

the darkness and ignorance [...] she takes her station in the eyes of Bhagavan and acts through his penetrating gaze.' *Forty Verses*, p. 47.

70. *Living by the Words of Bhagavan*, p. 301.
71. *Letters*, p. 2.
72. 'Ramanuja argues that it is those who constantly devote themselves to the Lord with worship and love, who receive that knowledge by which they are able to attain him, knowledge by which they are liberated from their bondage. [...] He then describes this knowledge of the supreme Being as having the character of "immediate presentation" (*sāksātkāra*), even though the devotional relationship remains intact, and the God-soul distinction remains unblurred.' Eric Lott, New York: Palgrave MacMillan, 1980, *Vedantic Approaches to God*, p. 78.
73. *Day by Day*, p. 193.
74. Ibid.
75. Ibid.
76. Sri Muruganar, *The Garland of Guru's Sayings—Guru Vachaka Kovai*, Tiruvannamalai: Sri Ramanasramam, Fourth Edition, 2016, p. 138.
77. *Vivekacūdāmani of Śrī Śankarācārya*, translated by Svāmī Turīyānanda, Madras: Sri Ramakrishna Matt, 1991, p. 13.
78. *Brihadāranyaka Upanishad* 2.4.2–4, in *A Source Book in Indian Philosophy*, edited by Sarvepalli Radhakrisnan and Charles A. Moore, Princeton University Press, 1967, p. 80.
79. Verses composed by Ramana Maharshi in *The Garland of Guru's Sayings*, p. 140.
80. Alison Williams, 'Sunk in an Ocean of Bliss: Learning from Ramana', *The Mountain Path*, July 2003, p. 15.
81. 'I used to go and weep before those images and before Nataraja that God should give me the same grace He gave to those saints. But this was after the "death" experience.' *Day by Day*, p. 327.
82. Godman, p. 1.
83. *Arunachala Śiva, Arunachala Aksharamanamalai* (*Bridal Garland of Letters for Arunachala*), Translation and Commentary by T.M.P. Mahadevan, Sri Ramanasram, Sixth Edition, 2014, p. 37, p. 41, p. 56.
84. S.S. Cohen, *Guru Ramana*, Tiruvannamalai: Sri Ramanasramam, 2009, p. 10.
85. The reverse is not necessarily true since *bhakti* can, and indeed most often does, constitute a path in and of itself.
86. David Godman, *The Power of the Presence*, Part Three, Boulder, Colorado: Avadhuta Foundation, 2002, p. 127.
87. 'The Hindu keeps the eleventh-day fast, eating chestnuts and milk.
He curbs his grain but not his brain, and breaks his fast with meat.
The Turk [Muslim] prays daily, fasts once a year, and crows "God!, God!" like a cock.
What heaven is reserved for people who kill chickens in the dark?
of kindness and compassion, they've cast out all desire.'
Linda Beth Hess, *Studies in Kabir: Texts, Traditions, Styles and Skills*, University of California Press, 1980, p. 201.

88. J.N. Mohanty, *Classical Indian Philosophy*, Lanham, Maryland: Rowman and Littlefield, 2000, 129.

89. On an extensive academic study of *prapatti*, see Srilata Raman, *Self-Surrender (Prapatti) to God in Srivaisnavism—Tamil Cats and Sanskrit Monkeys*, Routledge, 2007.

90. In monastic practice, the 'making space for God' appears to follow self-awareness and to be the pre-condition for reaching spiritual wisdom. '*Tibi vaco*, William of Saint-Thierry advises, "Give your attention to yourself", but this is only a preparation for the activity par excellence [*negotium negotiorum*], the proper activity of solitaries: *vacare Deo, frui Deo*. Gilbert of Hoyland places *vacatio* between investigation [*vestigatio*] and the vision of wisdom.' Edith Scholl, *Words For The Journey: A Monastic Vocabulary*, Collegeville, Minnesota: Liturgical Press, 2009, p. 81.

91. 'This is the virtue of spiritual poverty, detachment, and an emptiness making way for God's presence. It is the great spiritual virtue of the Prophet in relation to God. Among the mystics *faqr* is the central virtue, emblematic of all the virtues.' Cyril Glassé, *The New Encyclopedia of Islam*, Lanham, Maryland: Altamira Press, 1989, p. 134.

92. *The Mountain Path*, January 1981.

93. 'Surrender to Him and abide by His will whether he appears or vanishes. [...] His is the burden, you no longer have any cares. All your cares are His. Such is surrender. This is *bhakti*.' *Talk with Ramana Maharshi*, p. 349.

94. A. Devarajar Mudaliar. 'God and Destiny', *The Mountain Path*, 1967, Volume 4, Number 2.

95. *Arunachala Ramana*, p. 364.

96. Ibid.

97. *Arunachala Ramana*, p. 365.

98. 'Can God be deceived? The man thinks that God accepts his *Namaskāra* and that he himself is free to continue his old life. They need not come to me. I am not pleased with these *Namaskāras*.' *Arunachala Ramana*, p. 366.

99. *Arunachala Ramana*, 7, p. 376.

100. '[The intermediate practice of surrendering one's problems to the external "Higher Power"] is not a dilution of his notion that surrender must be complete and total to be effective, it is more an admission that for some devotees, such a massive step is impractical without some lesser intermediate stage.' Editorial, *The Mountain Path*, Volume 18, 1981, p. 2.

101. 'But who is meditating, eating, sleeping? What advantage is there in meditating for ten hours a day if in the end that only has the result of establishing you a little more deeply in the conviction that it is you who are meditating?' *The Mountain Path*, Volume 18, 1981, p. 3.

102. *Guru Ramana Vachana Mala*, in *Arunachala Ramana, Book 5*, p. 60.

103. *Padamalai*, p. 24.

104. '*Tariki* stands in contrast to "Self-Power," or *jiriki*. Since its beginning in India, Buddhism has taught a long and arduous path of practice to reach enlightenment. This personal effort made to achieve enlightenment is a manifestation of Self-Power. *Tariki*, on the other hand, is the recognition of the great, all-encompassing power of the Other - in this case, the Buddha and his ability to enlighten us - and the

simultaneous recognition of the individual's utter powerlessness in the face of the realities of the human condition.' Hiroyuki Itsuki, *Tariki*, Tokyo: Kodansha, 2001, p. xvii.

105. 'My personal view [...] is that *tariki* was probably based on the concept of *paratantra*, as it has been long claimed, or upon some closely related term. The word *paratantra* was translated into Chinese as *engi* (conditional arising) or *eta* (depending on others).' Takamaro Shigaraki, *Heart of the Shin Buddhist Path: A Life of Awakening*, Boston: Wisdom Publication, 2013, p. 91.

106. For parallels in the Christian world one may contemplate the meaning of Meister Eckhart's *Gelassenheit*. This is truly an abandonment of the will through which the human self is released into God's will. One of the most direct and striking expressions of this *Gelassenheit* is to be found in Eckhart's *Talks of Instructions*: 'For whoever has released his own will and himself has released the whole world, as truly as if it were his free property, as if he possessed it with full power of authority. Everything that you expressly do not desire—that you have forsaken and let go of for the sake of God. "Blessed are the poor in spirit," our Lord has said; and this means those who are poor in will.' Quoted in Bret W. Davis, *Heidegger and the Will: On the Way to Gelassenheit*, Northwestern University Press, 2007, p. 127.

107. Amir 'Abd al-Kader, *Spiritual Writings*, Albany, New York: State University of New York Press, 1995, p. 38.

108. Amir 'Abd al-Kader, p. 39.

109. 'The Divine Name, revealed by God Himself, implies a Divine Presence which becomes operative to the extent that the Name takes possession of the mind of the person invoking. Man cannot concentrate directly on the Infinite, but by concentrating on the symbol of the Infinite, he attains the Infinite Himself: for when the individual subject becomes identified with the Name to the point where all mental projection is absorbed by the form of the Name, then the Divine Essence manifests spontaneously, since this sacred form tends to nothing outside of itself. It has a positive affinity with Its essence wherein Its limits finally dissolve. Thus it is that union with the Divine Name becomes union with God Himself.' Titus Burckhardt, *Introduction to Sufism*, San Francisco: Thorsons, 1995, pp. 100–1.

110. *Padamalai*, p. 258.

111. 'The doctrine of Self-Knowledge [the mystical or esoteric dimension of religion] is dangerous, the great danger being, as one of the Shaikh's disciples has said, that the seeker, for want of the necessary sense of the Absolute, should unconsciously "deify a secret fold of the ego", imagining it to be the Self.' Martin Lings, *A Sufi Saint of the Twentieth Century: Shaikh Ahmad Al-Alawi, His Spiritual Heritage and Legacy*, Cambridge: Islamic Texts Society, 1993, p. 206.

112. *Padamalai*, p. 258.

113. This is what Annamalai Swami, one of the foremost 'disciples' of the Maharshi has highlighted in a very keen way: 'Those who meditate a lot often develop a subtle form of ego. They become pleased with the idea that they are making some progress. [...] When ego feelings are present, awareness of the Self is absent. The thought "I am meditating" is an ego thought. If real meditation is taking place, this thought cannot arise.' *Living by the Words of Bhagavan*, p. 271.

114. 'We do not say that a Jew or a Christian can never follow a Hindu *sādhanā;* we say that, if they follow it, they must—from a purely human point of view, not from the *jnānic* point of view which is above contingencies—take account of their own mental make-up. They are neither Hindus nor Brahmins; *Jñana* is more dangerous for them than for men belonging to the elite of India. Being Europeans, they think too much, which gives them an appearance of intelligence; in reality their thought, more often than not, is basically passionate, and has no contemplative serenity whatsoever.' Frithjof Schuon, *Language of the Self,* Madras: Ganesh and co, 1959, p. 55.

115. 'D.: How can the rebellious mind be brought under control?
    M.: Either seek its source so that it may disappear or surrender that it may be struck down.'
    Talks with Ramana Maharshi, 1958, p. 446.

116. *Living by the Words of Bhagavān,* p. 108.

117. The situation is analogous with methodical *dhikr,* which, in Sufism, normally requires some preliminary moral and spiritual qualifications and the authorization of a *murshid,* a spiritual guide.

118. *Arunachala Ramana, Book 5,* p. 71.

119. Ibid. p. 62.

120. Ibid. p. 62. This unity of all sages in the Self is beautifully suggested in the Maharshi's allusion to his identity with Shankara: 'Is the teacher Sankara, who grants the knowledge of the Self, other than the Self? Remaining in my heart as the Self, he who utters the Tamil today—who is he other than that one himself?' Mahadevan, p. 144.

3. *JAPA,* PRAYER AND SELF-KNOWLEDGE

1. '"Who am I?" is the best *Japa.* What could be more concrete than the Self? It is within each one's experience every moment.' *Talks,* p. 81.

2. 'What could be more concrete than the Self? It is within each one's experience every moment. Why should he try to catch anything outside, leaving out the Self?' *Talks,* p. 63.

3. 'Yes, when one is alone, either walking, sitting, etc., one should engage one's mind in stotras or *japa,* to prevent the mind from getting distracted. As far as possible one should see that the mind is kept introverted, and for that stotras and *japa* are the best aids.' In Darlene Delisi, 'Conversation with Sri Kunju Swamigal', *Arunachala Ramana, Book 7,* p. 385.

4. http://socialsciences.in/article/ramana-maharshi-differentiation

5. 'This world is a huge theatre. Each person has to act whatever role is assigned to him. It is the nature of the universe to be differentiated but within each person there should be no differentiation.' *Living by the Words of Bhagavān,* p. 99.

6. These 'great sayings' are sentences from the Upanishads that summarize the whole Advaitin vision, such as *Tat tvam asi* (That thou art) and *Aham Brahmāsmi* (I am *Brahman*).

7. It is the sixth song of the Śivaite *Śiva Rahasya Purāṇa*. An English version of excerpts from this text was given by N.R. Krishnamoorthi Aiyer and published by Sri Ramanasramamam.

8. 'The continued repetition of "I am Self-*Brahman*" constitutes the sole *mantra-japa* leading to *Mukti* (Liberation). All other *mantra-japas* connected with diverse gods should be firmly eschewed, as they aim at mundane objectives other than the Self. All other *mantra-japas* always entangle one inextricably in the bondage of worldly enjoyments.' (Ch.6, v.37) *Ribhu Gītā*, Tiruvannamalai: Sri Ramanasramam, 2001, p. 4.

9. *Day by Day*, p. 265.

10. The talk then turned to the names of God and Bhagavān said, 'Talking of all mantras, the *Brihadāranyaka Upanishad* says "AHAM" is the first name of God. The first letter in Sanskrit is A and the last letter Ha "h" and "Aha" thus includes everything from beginning to end. The word "Ayam" means that which exists, Self-shining and Self-evident.' *Day by Day*, p. 49.

11. Godman, p. 299.

12. 'He and his "name" are not different.' *Sayings of Ramakrishna Paramahamsa*, complied and edited by Deepanshu Jhari, New Delhi: Juggernaut Publications, p. 75.

13. 'Is not Arunachala *mantra japa* superior to this [Rāma *mantra japa*]? "No! No!" said Bhagavān vehemently. "Both are identical."' David Godman, edit. *The Power of Presence—Transforming Encounters With Sri Ramana Maharshi, Part One*, Boulder, Colorado: Avadhuta Foundation, 2005, p. 143.

14. 'He once gave a *harijan* devotee a *mantra* to repeat and on a few occasions he told visitors to repeat some or all of the poems that he had written about Arunachala.' Godman, *Living by the Word of Bhagavān*, 1994, p. 108.

15. '"Ra" means "that is" and "ma" means "thou". "A" in Arunachala means "that", "ru" means "thou", and "na" means "art".' Godman, *The Power of Presence*, p. 143.

16. When questioned about the fact that uneducated people may not be able to understand the meaning of his verses the Maharshi answered: 'They don't have to understand the meaning, [...] they will get some benefit from merely repeating the verses.' *Living by the Words of Bhagavān*, p. 109.

17. *Day by Day*, 170. 'In the afternoon G.V.S. asked, "What is the difference between *manasa japa* and *dhyana*?" Bhagavān: They are the same. In both, the mind is concentrated on one thing, the *mantra* or the Self. *Mantra, japa, dhyana*—are only different names. So long as they require effort we call them by these names, but when the Self is realized this goes on without any effort and what was the means becomes the goal.' *Day by Day*, p. 250.

18. Swami Adiswarananda, *Meditation and Its Practices—A Definitive Guide to Techniques and Traditions of Meditation in Yoga and Vedanta*, Woodstock, Vermont: SkyLights Paths, 2007, pp. 250–1.

19. In Kashmiri Shaivism *ajapa japa* is also called *hamsa mantra*. It is associated with the natural rhythm of respiration: 'The *mantra hamsah* is repeated by every *jiva* (living being) automatically in every round of expiration-inspiration. Normally it is repeated 21,600 times a day. Since the outgoing and incoming breaths repeat this naturally, automatically without any effort on any body's part, it is known as *ajapi-japa* i.e. a

repetition of the mantra that is going on naturally without any body's repeating it. Since the sounds of expiration and inspiration resemble *ham* and *sah*, therefore it is called *hamsa mantra*.' Jaideva Singh, *Śivas Sūtras—The Yoga of Supreme Identity*, New Delhi: Motilal Banarsidass, 1979, p. liv.

20. Although its emphasis is somewhat different, and less technical in a sense than the Hindu understanding, Pure Land Buddhism offers teachings that resonate with the spirit of *ajapa*, particularly in Shinran's works: 'Further, once one has entrusted oneself to Amida's Primal Vow, as the great teacher Master [Hōnen] has said, no working is true working. Thus, it is taught that as long as one's own working remains, it is not Other Power, but self-power.' *The Essential Shinran—A Buddhist Path of True Entrusting*, Alfred Bloom, editor, Bloomington, Indiana: World Wisdom, 2007, p. 94.

21. 'Using your mind as your mouth, let the name Rāma revolve continuously like Vishnu's *chakra* [discus-like weapon] within your mind. No others need know that you are doing *japa*.' Godman, *The Power of Presence*, 143.

22. This innermost form of prayer is known as the 'prayer of the heart' in the Eastern Orthodox tradition of Hesychasm: '[...] Those who by long custom or by the mercy of God have progressed from prayer of the mind and reached prayer of the heart, they do not break off their continuous prayer during profound mental exercises, nor even during sleep itself. As the All Wise has told us, "I sleep, but my heart waketh." (Cant. 5:2).' *The Way of a Pilgrim and The Pilgrim Continues His Way*, translated by R.M. French, London, 2012, p. 179.

23. 'Sacred Speech is personified as the goddess Vāc [...from the verb vac-, "to speak"] [...] In this way *Vāc* plays the role of a demiurge, the personified manifestation of a certain cosmogonic power. The specific form of her creative activity is rendered by the verb "to speak" (*vad-*) Her essential nature is manifested through her being forever identical with herself, despite the countless multitude of her temporary forms [...]' Tatyana J. Elizarenkova, *Language and Style of the Vedic Rsis*, Albany, New York: State University of New York Press, 1995, p. 107.

24. *Upadēśa Sāram (The Essence of Spiritual Instruction)—The Complete Version in Four Languages Composed by Sri Bhagavān (in Tamil, Sanskrit, Telugu and Malayalam) with Transliteration, Word-for-Word Meaning, Paraphrase and Commentary*, Tiruvannamalai, 2011, p. 106.

25. Cf. D.T. Suzuki, *The Zen Kōan as a Means of Attaining Enlightenment*, North Clarendon, Vermont: Charles E. Tuttle, 1994.

26. Quoted in Philip C. Almond, *Mystical Experience and Religious Doctrine*, Berlin, New York, Amsterdam, Moutons Publisher, 1982, p. 27.

27. After all this, Bhagavān said, 'Now you consider you are making an effort and uttering "I", "I" or other *mantrams* and making meditation. But when you reach the final stage, meditation will go on without any effort on your part. You can't get away from it or stop it, for meditation, *japa*, or whatever else you call it, is your real nature.' *Day by Day*, p. 345.

28. *Talks*, p. 415.

4. SELF-REALIZATION AND TRADITION

1. 'The experience of pure consciousness can be characterized as follows: The subject is awake, conscious, but without an object or content of consciousness—no thoughts, emotions, sensations, or awareness of any external phenomena. Nothing. During the event the subject is not even aware "Oh, I am experiencing X" or "I am having an extraordinary experience." Yet the subject is not asleep and may afterwards also report confidently that he or she was not asleep.' Stephen Bernhardt, 'Are Pure Consciousness Events Unmediated?' in Robert K. Forman, edit., *The Problem of Pure Consciousness—Mysticism and Philosophy*, Oxford University Press, 1990, p. 220.

2. 'Pushed to its logical extreme, a Hindu can claim that one is most a Hindu when least a Hindu. That is to say, one is most a Hindu when one has dissolved one's Hindu particularity into Hinduism's all-embracing inclusiveness and universality.' Arvind Sharma, 'Hinduism' in *Our Religions*, New York: HarperOne, 1994, p. 4.

3. This point of view has been argued by J. Glenn Friesen in *Ramana Maharshi: Hindu and non-Hindu Interpretations of a Jivanmukta*, 2006. http://citeseerx.ist.psu.edu/ viewdoc/download?doi=10.1.1.178.9171&rep=rep1&type=pdf

4. Thomas A. Forsthoefel, *Knowing Beyond Knowledge: Epistemologies of Religious Experience in Classical and Modern Advaita*, London and New York: Routledge, 2002.

5. 'Ramana's parents were Smarta Brahmins, an orthodox community that tended toward *Advaita Vedānta* for its conceptual framework, and their family deity was Shiva. According to B.V. Narasimha Swami, one of Ramana's early biographers, a family priest occasionally conducted domestic devotional rites (*pujas*), and Ramana's father, Sundaram Ayyar, occasionally visited the local temple and hosted evenings of spiritual reading.' Thomas A. Forsthoefel and Cynthia Ann Humes, editors, *Gurus in America*, Albany, New York: States University of New York Press, 2005, p. 41.

6. It is as if a name was given to a reality, but the name in no way affected that reality: 'Later, when I was in the Arunachala Temple, I learned of the identity of myself with *Brahman*, which I had heard in the *Ribhu Gita* as underlying all.' https://www. davidgodman.org/bhagavans-self-realisation/

7. Godman, p. 137.

8. 'Philosophically, Bhagavān's teachings belong to an Indian school of thought which is known as *Advaita Vedānta*. (He himself, though, would say that his teachings came from his own experience, rather than from anything he had heard or read.)' Godman, 1994, p. 24.

9. An English translation of a Tamil version of parts of the *Ribu Gītā* was published by Ramanasramam: N.R. Krishnamoorthi Aiyer, *The Essence of Ribhu Gītā - Selection and English Translation*, 2001.

10. 'Remaining alertly aware and thought-free with a still mind devoid of differentiation of self and non-self even while being engaged in the activities of worldly life is called the state of Sahaja Nirvikalpa—Samadhi (the natural state of abidance in the Self when all differentiation has ceased.' *The Essence of Ribhu Gītā*, p. 8.

11. *The Essence of Ribhu Gītā*, p. i.

12. See for instance the various shades of meaning of *Māyā* in a text like the *Devī Gītā, The Song of the Goddess: A Translation, Annotation, and Commentary*, C. Mackenzie Brown, State University of New York Press, 1998, pp. 92–3.

13. 'I know no such period (or purgatory or *sādhanā*). I never performed any *pranayama* or *japa*. I knew no *mantras*. I have never done any *sādhanā*. I did not even know what *sādhanā* was.' *Arunachala Ramana, Book I*, p. 35.

14. Godman, p. 137.

15. 'Of course this does not rule out certain extremely rare cases of individuals claiming to have reached spiritual enlightenment through direct divine intervention (the *majdhûb*)—e.g., as was claimed in various ways by Ibn 'Arabî and his famous 19th-century Algerian follower, 'Abd-al-Qâdir. But it is revealing that even these exceptional individuals, before undertaking to teach others, first consciously undertook to pass through the "normal" stages of the spiritual path under the guidance of other masters.' James Morris, 'Situating Islamic "Mysticism": Between Written Traditions and Popular Spirituality', in *Mystics of the Book: Themes, Topics and Typologies*, ed. R. Herrera, New York/Berlin, Peter Lang, 1993, pp. 293–334.

16. An 122 verses long abridgement of the text was translated by N.R. Krishnamoorthi Aiyer under the title *The Essence of Ribhu Gītā*, Tiruvannamalai, Sri Ramanasramam, 2018, eight edition.

17. Quoted in *Tattvālokah*, Volume 26, Sri Abhinava Vidyatheertha Educational Trust, 2003, p. 71.

18. 'The intricate maze of philosophy of the various schools is said to clarify matters and to reveal the Truth, but in fact it creates confusion where none need exist. To understand anything there must be the Self. The Self is obvious. So why not remain as the Self? What need to explain the non-self?' *The Teachings of Ramana Maharshi*, edited by Arthur Osborne, London: Rider, 2014, p. 3.

19. *Guru Ramana*, p. 50.

20. *Guru Ramana*, p. 51.

21. 'A French Doctor of Philosophy came for the day. He asked: "How should a seeker work?" Bh. Without taking himself to be the actor, that is he should work without motive or a hard-cast plan. For instance, when you started on a journey from Paris did you include this place in your itinerary?' *Guru Ramana*, p. 51.

22. Suri Nagamma, *Letters from Sri Ramanasramam*, Tiruvannamalai: Sri Ramanasramam, Eighth Edition, 2014, p. 102.

23. Theodore Gabriel, 'Muni' in Denise Cush, Catherine Robinson and Michael York, *Encyclopedia of Hinduism*, London and New York: Routledge, 2008, p. 513.

24. The Maharshi recognises this priority as the main foundation of the Buddha's non-theistic pespective: 'Buddha concerned himself more with directing the seeker to realise Bliss here and now rather than with academic discussions about God [...]' *Maharshi's Gospel, Books I and II*, Tiruvannamalai: Sri Ramanasramam, 2012, p. 42.

25. This refusal has been interpreted either as a wish not to mislead auditors or as a statement of the fact that there is actually no answer to these questions: 'According to one tradition of interpretation of the Buddha's refusal to answer these questions, he refused to answer because the questioner would have been misled by any possible answer because of the questioner's beliefs. By contrast, Candrakīrti's commentary

makes it clear that he interprets the Buddha's refusal to give a positive answer to any of these questions simply as the straightforward denial of the truth of any answer to the questions.' James Duerlinger, *The Refutation of the Self in Indian Buddhism*, New York: Routledge, 2013, p. 113.

26. *Padamalai*, p. 257.

27. Sadhu Natanananda relates that there was one exception to this rule, as the Maharshi was once approached by an untouchable in search of salvation. The Maharshi told this man : 'Go on saying, Siva, Siva, That will save you.' *Arunachala Ramana, Book 7*, p. 428.

28. *Living by the Words of Bhagavān*, p. 211.

29. 'This is who I truly am.' *Living by the Words of Bhagavān*, p. 211.

30. Osborne, 2006, 113.

31. '"Bhagavān gave initiation by look and by silence." Initiation by look was given to those who came to the ashram and were drawn to the use of the *vichara*,' *Arunachala Ramana, Book 7*, p. 416. It must be noted that such supra-traditional modalities are not the exclusive privilege of the Maharshi. Another great sage of the 20th century, Mā Ānanda Mayī, was also credited for instance by number of her devotees with an ability to initiate in silence and though her gaze: 'Twelve interviews describe receiving initiation from Mā, usually outside the formal setting, through her look, or *drik diksha*, which often occurred during their first *darshan* with Mā.' Lisa Lassell Hallstrom, *Mother of Bliss—Ānandamayī Mā (1896-1982)*, New York: Oxford University Press, 1999, p. 141.

32. 'The initiation by look was a very real thing. Sri Bhagavan would turn to the devotee, his eyes fixed upon him with blazing intentness. The luminosity, the power of his eyes pierced into one, breaking down the thought-process. Sometimes it was as though an electric current was passing through one, sometimes a vast peace, a flood of light. [...] Always it was followed by the feeling, the indubitable conviction, that one had been taken up by Sri Bhagavan, that henceforth he was in charge, he was guiding.' Arthur Osborne, *Ramana Maharshi and the Path of Self-Knowledge*, San Rafael, California: Sophia Perennis, 2006, p. 113.

33. 'Bhagavan wrote *Upadēśa Sāram* only when Muruganar wrote about the *lilas* of Lord Siva—about Siva blessing the *tapasvis* of Daruka Vana, isn't that so?' Bhagavan said: 'Yes, what he wrote was not merely about the story of the Daruka Vana tapasvis. He thought of writing about all the Avatars of the Lord as applying to me, in one hundred verses. He took up the folk song of "Undeepara" for the purpose and wrote up to seventy verses. Towards the end of those seventy verses he wrote about the story of the *tapasvis* of Daruka Vana and then requested me to write the remaining thirty verses as they pertain to *upadesa* (teaching). "You have done everything. What is there for me to do? You had better write that also," I said, but he did not write them for a long time. He insisted on my writing them, saying that he did not know anything about the upadesa portion of it and that Bhagavan alone could write them. What was I to do? I had no alternative but to write. After writing those thirty verses, we called them "*Upadesa Undiyar*". When that was done, Yogi Ramiah said he did not know Tamil and so pressed me to write them in Telugu, and so I wrote them in *dwipada*. After that, Nayana said, "What

about Sanskrit?" I agreed and wrote them in Sanskrit also. After I had written them in those three languages, Kunjuswami, Ramakrishna and others requested me to write them in Malayalam also, and hence I wrote them in Kummi Pattu style in Malayalam.' Suri Nagamma, *Letters*, p. 127.

34. *Ramana Maharshi's Essence of Self-Realization*, translation and commentary by David Frawley, Vedic Wisdom Press, 2018, p. 16.

35. 'Papaji' in *The Mountain Path*, Sri Ramanasramam, Volume 30, June 1993, 10.

36. One may mention such diverse figures as the American jazz musician and spiritual teacher Andrew Cohen (born in 1955), the Jamaican guru Mooji (born in 1954), and the American philosopher and neuroscientist Sam Harris (born in 1967), a figure of the New Atheist movement. On Neo-Advaita see James Swartz, 'What is Neo-Advaita?', http://www.advaita.org.uk/discourses/trad_neo/neo_vedanta_swartz.htm

37. 'What joins them (immediatists) all is not so much the enlightenment they urge their respective audiences toward [...] *it is how they claim that one can get there.* One gets there, the immediatist claims, not via sustained practice in a particular religious tradition [...] but spontaneously.' Arthur Versluis, *American Gurus: From Transcendentalism to New Age Religion*, Oxford University Press, 2014, p. 238.

38. Jean Klein, *Who am I? The Sacred Quest*, Salisbury, UK: Non Duality Press, 2006.

39. *The Song Celestial—Verses from Sri Bhagavad Gītā Selected and Reset by Bhagavān Ramana Maharshi*, Tiruvannamalai: Sri Ramanasramam, 2018.

40. *The Spiritual Teaching of Ramana Maharshi*, 2004, p. 55.

41. *The Song Celestial*, p. 63.

42. Ibid.

43. Ibid.

44. *The Bhagavad Gītā*, translated by Winthrop Sargeant, Albany, New York: State University of New York Press, 1994, p. 335.

45. *The Song Celestial*, pp. 63–4.

46. 'Such *karma* is not an obstacle in the way of attaining *Jñana*. Nor does *Jñana* stand in the way of discharging one's duties in life. *Jñana*, and *karma* are never mutually antagonistic; and the Realisation of the one is not an obstacle for the performance of the other, and vice versa.' *Arunachala Ramana—Eternal Ocean of Grace—Teachings Book 2*, Tiruvannamalai: Sri Ramanasramam, 2018, p. 264.

47. 'Moreover, so long as there is either the desire or effort, one is not a *Jñānī* at all.' *Arunachala Ramana—Eternal Ocean of Grace—Teachings Book 2*, Tiruvannamalai: Sri Ramanasramam, 2018, p. 273.

48. *Upadēśa Sāram—The Complete Version in Four Languages Composed by Sri Bhagavan*, p. 48.

49. Arvind Sharma, (1993), *The Experiential Dimension of Advaita Advaita Vedanta*, New Delhi: Motilal Banarsidass Publishers, 1993, p. xiv.

50. Cohen, 2009, p. 121.

51. Cohen, p. 123.

52. 'Reality is simply the loss of the ego. Destroy the ego by seeking its identity. Because the ego is not entity it will automatically vanish and reality will shine forth by itself. This is the direct method. Whereas all other methods are done, only retaining the

ego. In those paths there arise so many doubts and the eternal question remains to be tackled finally. But in this method the final question is the only one and it is raised from the very beginning. No *sādhanās* are necessary for engaging in this quest.' *Padamalai—Teachings of Sri Ramana Maharshi*, recorded in Tamil verse by Muruganar, translated by Dr. T.V. Venkarasubramanian, Robert Butler and David Godman, Boulder, Colorado, 2004, pp. 161–2.

53. 'This path (attention to the "I") is the direct path; all others are indirect ways. The first leads to the Self, the others elsewhere. And even if the others do arrive at the Self it is only because they lead at the end to the first path which ultimately carries them to the goal. So, in the end, the aspirants must adopt the first path. Why not do so now? Why waste time?' Ibid., pp. 200–1.

54. 'Truth (*satya*) implies love, and firmness (*agraha*) engenders and therefore serves as a synonym for force. I thus began to call the Indian movement Satyagraha, that is to say, the Force which is born of Truth and Love or non-violence, and gave up the use of the phrase "passive resistance", in connection with it, so much so that even in English writing we often avoided it and used instead the word "satyagraha" itself or some other equivalent English phrase.' Quoted in Richard L. Johnson, *Gandhi's Experiments with Truth: Essential Writings by and about Mahatma Gandhi*, Lexington Books, 2006, 71.

55. https://www.davidgodman.org/bhagavan-and-the-politics-of-his-day/2/

56. Ibid.

57. Godman, 2005, p. 109.

58. David Godman, *The Power of the Presence, Part Three*, p. 97.

59. *Conscious Immortality—Conversations with Sri Ramana Maharshi*, recorded by Paul Brunton and Munagala Venkataramiah, Tiruvannamalai: Sri Ramanasramam 1984, p. 165.

60. 'His plain, simple and unsophisticated philosophy vividly reflected in his day-do-day conduct serves as a key to unlock the mystery of life and solves in a practical way some of the complicated social, political and economic problems that confront us today.' Syed Hafiz, *Face to Face*, p. 49.

61. *Talks*, p. 200.

62. *Day by Day with Bhagavan, From the Diary of A. Devaraja Mudaliar*, Tiruvannamalai: Sri Ramanasramam, 2002, pp.133–4.

63. *The Power of the Presence, Part Three*, p. 205.

64. Godman, p. 74.

65. *Padamalai*, p. 319.

66. 'Since the moral and religious observances that have been laid down protect the *sadhaka* for a long distance [along the path], they deserve to be appropriately observed, but if they obstruct the practice of the excellent and true *Jñana vichara*, then give them up as deficient.' *Padamalai*, p. 318.

67. *Letters*, Suri Nagamma, pp. 719–20.

68. Here are Suri Nagamma's eight verses as quoted by herself: 'Oh Mother! this is a place where your son Ramana is living. Why are you assuming your *rajasic* and *tamasic* form instead of the *sattvic*? [...] Not only myself but your son, Ramana,

also feels sad and is grieved on hearing the slaughtered goat's bleatings.' *Letters*, p. 720.

69. 'Unless a person has finished (in this or previous births) the other paths, he will not pursue the Jñana path; and he need not bother himself that he has not done the various karmas prescribed by sastras. But he should not wilfully transgress the sastraic injunctions by doing things prohibited by them.' *Day by Day*, p. 341.

70. Ramana Maharshi actually translated the *Hastamalak Stotra* into Tamil. The English translation is available in *The Collected Works of Ramana Maharshi*, pp. 151–3.

71. *Hastamalakiyam of Hastamalaka, Disciple of Sri Shankara*, S.N. Sastri, Turlock, California: Dennis B. Hill, 2007, p. 8.

72. *Maniśā-Pañcakam*, with a commentary by Swami Chinmāyānanda, Mumbai: CCMT, 2014, p. 1.

73. *Maniśā-Pañcakam*, p. 8.

74. D.: Is the desire for *swarāj* (independence) right? B.: Such desire no doubt begins with self-interest. Yet practical work for the goal gradually widens the outlook so that the individual becomes merged in the country. Such merging of the individuality is desirable and the *karma* in question is *nishkama* (unselfish). D.: If self-government for India is granted after a long struggle and terrible sacrifice, is one not justified in being pleased with the result and elated by it? B.: In the course of one's work one must have surrendered oneself to the higher Power whose might must be kept in mind and never lost sight of. How then can one be elated? One should not even care for the result of one's action. Then alone the *karma* becomes unselfish. Gandhiji has surrendered himself to the Divine and works accordingly with no self-interest. He does not concern himself with the results but accepts them as they turn up. That must be the attitude of national workers. [...] Should we then not think of and work for the welfare of the country? B.: First take care of yourself and the rest will naturally follow. Q.: I am not speaking individually but for the country. B.: First surrender and then see.' *The Teachings of Bhagavan Sri Ramana Maharshi in His Own Words*, Arthur Osborne, edit., Tiruvannamalai: Ramanasramam, 2002, pp. 85–6.

75. *The Teachings of Bhagavan Sri Ramana Maharshi in His Own Words*, p. 85.

76. *Padamalai*, p. 320.

77. Sadhu Natanananda, *Sri Ramana Darsanam*, Sri Ramanasramam, 2002, p. 35.

78. Natanananda, p. 36.

79. *Padamalai*, p. 320.

80. *Padamalai*, p. 113.

5. RELIGION AND RELIGIONS

1. 'In him we see that glorious realisation which at once includes and transcends all religions.' Seyed M. Hafiz, *Face to Face*, p. 48.

2. The 19th century Bengali saint Ramakrishna was, among contemporary Hindu figures, probably the one who made most explicit references to such an inner unity of religions. On the one hand, Ramakrishna fully recognized the *Nirguna* and *Saguna* dimensions of the Divine, on the other hand he is said to have himself experienced, at least to some extent, various formal manifestations of the Transcendent. He is said

to have immersed himself in Christian and Muslim practices during some periods of his life. There was a bhaktic dimension in the spiritual personality of Ramakrishna that called for the penetration of various formal universes. Such was not the case with the Maharshi. Ramana Maharshi situated himself from the point of view of the highest Self-Identity that transcends the various paths of approach to it. One can hardly imagine the Maharshi practicing Christianity or Islam.

3. *Day by Day*, p. 268.
4. Thomas A. Forsthoefel, 'Weaving the Inward Thread to Awakening—The Perennial Appeal of Ramana Maharshi' in Thomas A. Forsthoefel and Cynthia Ann Humes, editors, *Gurus in America*, Albany, New York: State University of New York Press, 2005, pp. 37–8.
5. Like the Maharshi, Frithjof Schuon characterizes the perennial religion as a discernment between the Real and the unreal: 'The essential function of human intelligence is discernment between the Real and the illusory or between the Permanent and the impermanent, and the essential function of the will is attachment to the Permanent or the Real. This discernment and this attachment are the quintessence of all spirituality; carried to their highest level or reduced to their purest substance, they constitute the underlying universality in every great spiritual patrimony of humanity, or what may be called the *religio perennis*; this is the religion to which sages adhere, one which is always and necessarily founded upon formal elements of divine institution.' *Light on the Ancient World*, Bloomington, Indiana: World Wisdom, 2006, pp. 119–20.
6. *Brahmasūtrabhāsya* I, 3, 19, translated by George Thibaut, in Eliot Deutsch and Rohit Dalvi, *The Essential Vedānta—A New Source Book of Advaita Vedānta*, Bloomington, Indiana: World Wisdom, 2004, p. 212.
7. *Sat-Darshana Bhashya*, p. 104.
8. Ibid.
9. '[...] You believe in God without form; that is quite all right. But never for a moment think that this alone is true and all else false. Remember that God with form is just as true as God without form. But hold fast to your own conviction.' *The Gospel of Ramakrishna—translated int English with an Introduction by Swami Nikhilananda*, New York: Ramakrishna-Vivekananda Center, 1996, Sixth Printing, pp. 124–5.
10. *Sat-Darshana Bhashya*, p. 104.
11. Quoted in Arthur Osborne, *Buddhism and Christianity in the Light of Hinduism*, Tiruvannamalai: Sri Ramanasramam, Fifth Edition, 2016, p. 58.
12. Osborne, 2014, p. 124.
13. Osborne, 2014, p. 130.
14. 'D.: Has God a form?
    M.: Who says so?
    D.: Well, if God has no form is it proper to worship idols?
    M.: Leave God alone because He is unknown. What about you? Have you a form? [...] If you are the body why do they bury the corpse after death? The body must refuse to be buried.
    D.: No, I am the subtle *jiva* within the gross body.

M.: So you see that you are really formless; but you are at present identifying yourself with the body. So long as you are formful why should you not worship the formless God as being formful? The questioner was baffled and perplexed.' *Talks*, p. 121.

The perplexity of the Muslim questioner must stem from the fact that for him the formal requirement of religion are satisfied by the various physical actions that the religion enjoins. In other words, to be a 'formal' being means to worship the Formless by means of religious forms.

15. 'Q. Is there a separate Being, *Īśvara*, who is the rewarder of virtue and punisher of sins? Is there a God? A. Yes.' *Conscious Immortality—Conversations with Sri Ramana Maharshi*, recorded by Paul Brunton and Munagala Venkataramiah, Tiruvannamalai: Sri Ramanasramam, Fifth Edition, 2015, p. 10.

16. *Conscious Immortality*, p. 11.

17. Ibid.

18. Ibid.

19. 'Narrated Abū Hurayra: "I have memorized two kinds of knowledge from the Messenger of God. I have divulged one of them to you and I divulged the second, my throat would be cut." (Quoted by al-Bukhārī)'. *Spiritual Teachings of the Prophet, Hadīth with Commentaries by Saints and Sages of Islam*, edited by Tayeb Chouiref, Louisville, Kentucky: Fons Vitae, 2011, p. 92.

20. 'And with many such parables spake he the word unto them, as they were able to hear *it*. But without a parable spake he not unto them: and when they were alone, he expounded all things to his disciples.' Mark 4:33–34.

21. Victor P. Hamilton notes that the 'amount of secondary literature on Exod. 3:13-15, especially v. 14, is staggering.' Victor P. Hamilton, *Exodus: An Exegetical Commentary*, Ada, Michigan: Baker Books, 2011, p. 63.

22. *Talks*, p. 76.

23. Arthur Osborne, *The Teachings of Ramana Maharshi In His Own Words* Tiruvannamalai: Sri Ramanasramam, 2014, p. 88.

24. 'The One is God; indeed the fulfillment, the plenitude, of the Godhead is Oneness. The "One without another" is transcendence; it is not the "one" of a series, since every series is finite. "God is One without the essence of one and number"; is "without all number and supranumber."' C.F. Kelley, *Meister Eckhart on Divine Knowledge*, Berkeley, California: University of California Press, 1997, p. 148.

25. *The Spiritual Teaching of Ramana Maharshi*, Boulder, Colorado: Shambala, 2004, p. 59.

26. *Conscious Immortality—Conversations with Sri Ramana Maharshi*, recorded by Paul Brunton and Mumugala Venkataramiah, Tiruvannamalai: Sri Ramanasramam, Fifth Edition, 2015, p. 145.

27. The second *shahādah*, which together with first constitutes the creed of Islam, is *Muhammadun Rasūl-Allāh*, Muhammad is the Messenger of God.

28. *Talks*, p. 86.

29. 'The Elevated is one of God's Beautiful Names; but above whom or what, since only He exist? More elevated than whom or what, since only He is and He is Elevated in Himself? In relation to existence He is the very essence of existing beings. [...].

Naught is except the Essence, which is Elevated in Itself, its elevation being unrelated to any other.' Muḥammad ibn 'Alī Muḥyī al-Dīn Ibn al-'Arabī, *The Bezels of Wisdom*, R.W. Austin trans, Paulist Press, 1980, p. 85.

30. 'The fundamental philosophical doctrine expounded by Āchārya Gaudapāda is known as *ajātivāda* or the Doctrine of No-origination. [...] The Absolute, the eternal non-dual Self is not subject to birth, change and death. It is *aja*, the unborn eternal, the unchanging Real.' Chandradhar Sharma, *The Advaita Tradition in Indian Philosophy*, New Delhi: Motilal Banarsidass, 1996, p. 127. Needless to say the analogy is only partial here, since the Biblical Name of God is not understood by most Jewish and Christian readings as implying the unreality of the world.

31. *Talks*, p. 276.

32. Quoted in Robert Scott and George William Gilmore, *Selections from the World's Devotional Classics, Volume 8*, New York: Funk & Wagnalls Company, 1916, p. 85.

33. 'In this connection Bhagavan again said "The Name is God," and quoted the Bible, "In the beginning was the word, and the word was with God, and the word was God". Swami Ramdas often preaches the importance of *Nama smarana*, the Name he uses being *Sri Ram Jai Ram Jai Jai Ram*. In the latest issue of Vision Swami Ramdas has written about "That thou art", and Bhagavan referred me to it.' *Day by Day*, p. 59.

34. 'Given the unique nature of Sri Ramana Maharshi within this inverted spiritual era of the Kali-Yuga, he should not be taken to be a founder of a spiritual method which bypasses the guidance of a qualified spiritual master, nor an advocate for the circumventing of spiritual practice (*sādhanā*) as many neo-advaitins or proponents of the New Age suggest.' Samuel Bendeck Sotillos, 'René Guénon and Sri Ramana Maharshi: Two Remarkable Sages in Modern Times', Part Four, *The Mountain Path*, January-March 2015, p. 10.

35. 'If he follows the rules of caste and orders of life, he does so for the good of the world. He does not derive any benefit by observing the rules. Nor does he lose anything by not observing them.' *The Spiritual Teachings of Ramana Maharshi*, p. 30.

36. 'Because they love mystery and not the truth, religions cater to them so as eventually to bring them round to the Self.' *Maharshi's Gospel—The Teachings of Sri Ramana Maharshi*, Tiruvannamalai: Sri Ramanasramam, 2012, p. 11.

37. 'The Well of Ignorance
I dip into the well of Ignorance and pull forth toads, slugs, and blind fish.
I offer them Light, and quickly they slither back into the slimy darkness.
I pour acid into the pool and hold tempting baits above its rim.
Goaded, they come forth and glimpse the bait.
I lead them to a cleaner pool and a darkness not quite so dense;
And then on to a greater cleanliness and a clearer Light.
In time, slowly they build the strength to endure the Light and desire for cleaner waters.
Finally, one here and one there ventures out of the pool into the Brilliance.
It is a long and slow labor, but in the end I will win.'
Franklin Merell-Wolff, *Experience and Philosophy*, Albany, New York: State University of New York Press, 1994, p. 98.

38.   'Regulation of life, such as getting up at a fixed hour, bathing, doing mantra, japa, etc., observing ritual, all this is for people who do not feel drawn to Self-enquiry or are not capable of it.' *Day by Day*, p. 275.

39.   '[...] Another method that is prescribed is not to bother about sleep at all. When it overtakes you, you can do nothing about it, so simply remain fixed in the Self or in meditation every moment of your waking life and take up the meditation again the moment you wake, and that will be enough. Then even during sleep the same current of thought or meditation will be working.' *Day by Day*, pp. 279–80.

40.   'Visitor: Different teachers have set up different schools and proclaimed different truths and so confused people. Why? Bhagavan: They have all taught the same truth but from different standpoints. Such differences were necessary to meet the needs of different minds differently constituted, but they all reveal the same Truth.' *Day by Day*, p. 270.

41.   David Godman, *The Power of Presence, Part Two*, p. 91.

42.   Ibid.

43.   'It appears obvious to me that: either there exists a "gap" between the individual and the Divine or there does not. Unless the individual is fully and totally Divine, some sort of gap must exist and with it comes the necessity of crossing that gap. If such a gap exists, then the Divine is an "Other", of one sort or another. This raises the philosophical and existential question of 'how does one know an "other", and "is this knowledge veridical or not?"' John A. Grimes, *Problems and Perspectives in Religious Discourse: Advaita Vedanta Implications*, Albany, New York: State University of New York Press, 1994, p. 8.

44.   Chadwick, *A Sadhu's Reminiscences*, p. 13.

45.   *Sādhanā catustaya (Four prerequisites of spiritual life)* (4.2) in *The Roots of Vedānta— Selections from Śankara's Writings*, Cyber City, India: Penguin Random House India, 2012, p. 362.

46.   *Arunachala Ramana Book 1 Biography*, p. 30.

47.   *Arunachala Śiva Aksharamanamalai*, translation by T.M.P Mahadevan, Tiruvannamalai: Sri Ramanasramam, 2014, p. 29.

48.   'The idea that "I am *Brahman*" may easily fill them [Europeans] with pride and contempt, because their ancestors have always thought: "I am a mortal, a sinner", and because their minds, unless they have been purified by severe disciplines, are not accustomed to bear *jñānic* formulas.' Frithjof Schuon, *Language of the Self*, p. 55.

49.   '[...] Vasishta told Rama that the path of Self-enquiry should not be shown to anyone who is not sufficiently qualified. In some other books it has been stated that spiritual practices should be done for several births, or for at least twelve years under a *Guru*.' Suri Nagamma, *Letters*, p. 346.

50.   Arthur Osborne, edit. *The Teachings of Ramana* Maharshi, London: Rider, 2014, p. 46.

51.   'There is a stage in the beginning, when you identify yourself with the body, when you are still having the body consciousness. At that stage, you have the feeling you are different from the reality or God, and then it is, you think of yourself as a devotee of God or as a servant or lover of God. This is the first stage. The second stage is when you think of yourself as a spark of the divine fire or a ray from the divine Sun.

Even then there is still that sense of difference and the body-consciousness. The third stage will come when all such difference ceases to exist, and you realise that the Self alone exists.' *Day by Day*, p. 343.

52. Arthur Osborne, *Buddhism and Christianity in the Light of Hinduism*, Tiruvannamalai: Sri Ramanasramam, 2016.

53. Osborne, 2016, p. 79.

54. 'A devotee named Amritanatha Yati wrote on a paper a Malayalam verse imploring Bhagavān to say whether he was Hari (Vishnu) or *Sivaguru* [...] or Yativara (Siva) or Vararuchi. Bhagavān, in his answer, wrote his reply in the same Malayalam metre on the same paper. A translation of it is given below for the benefit of the devotees. The answer speaks for it self. "In the recesses of the lotus-shaped Hearts of all, beginning with Vishnu, there shines as pure intellect (Absolute Consciousness), the Paramatman, who is the same as Arunachala Ramana. When the mind melts with love of Him, and reaches the inmost recess of the Heart wherein He dwells as the beloved, the subtle eye of pure intellect opens and He reveals Himself as Pure Consciousness." *Collected Works of Sri Ramana Maharshi*, p. 143.

55. 'Elsewhere we have told what view the Easterners take of the limitations of action and its consequences, and how for them, in this respect, knowledge is the opposite of action: the Far-Eastern theory of "non-action" and the Hindu theory of "deliverance" are inaccessible to the ordinary Western mind, which cannot conceive that a man may dream of freeing himself from action, still less that he may actually come to do so.' René Guénon, *East and West*, Hillsdale, New York: Sophia Perennis, 2004, p. 59.

56. Osborne, 2014, p. 47.

57. Osborne, 2014, p. 46.

58. 'The German word "*Gelassenheit*" comes from the verb "*lassen*" meaning "leaving" or "letting". It refers to the state of "empty and free" mind without any self-attachment or self-will to achieve something, a purposive act. Thus a life lived in it would be a life "without a why" (*ohne Warum*), to use the Dominican's felicitous expression.' Kee-Sung Keel, *Meister Eckhart: An Asian Perspective*, Grand Rapids, Michigan: Eerdmans Publishing, 2007, p. 173.

59. *Arunachala Śiva*, 2014, pp. 54, 60, 65.

60. It is so true that some devotees have even proposed that Ramana was indeed initiated by hearing the Name of Arunachala: 'After having studied the lives and ways of teachings of saints and sages of the world, it strikes one that Sri Ramana falls into a class of his own. No one has achieved God-Realisation merely by hearing a name of God. Sri Ramana received "initiation" by merely hearing the name of Arunachala, pronounced only for the purpose of conveying information about a journey.' Sadhu Ekarasa, *Face to Face*, p. 25.

61. Bhagavān Sri Ramana Maharshi, *Arunachala Śiva*, translation and commentary by T.M.P. Mahadevan, Tiruvannamalai: Sri Ramanasramam, Sixth Edition, 2004, p. 3.

6. WORLD AND MIND, WORLD IN MIND

1. In his *Summa Theologiae* Saint Thomas Aquinas refers to true cognition as '*adaequatio rei et intellectus.*' *Summa Theologiae: Volume 4, Knowledge in God*: 1a. 14-18, Cambridge University Press, 2006, p. 80.

2.   In a way, the Einsteinian theory of relativity can be understood in these terms. It goes beyond a Galilean model of knowledge that entails the duality and independence of subject and object.

3.   'The symbolic universe of the post-modern subject is not that of the modern subject: without a big Subject—that is, without a marker by which symbolic anteriority and exteriority may be grounded—the subject is unable to create for itself sufficiently broad spatial and temporal coordinates. It remains fixed in a present which is its only dimension.' Dany-Robert Dufour, 'Modern subjectivity/post-modern subjectivity' in Kieran Kehoane, Anders Petersen, Bert van den Bergh, *Late Modern Subjectivity and its Discontents: Anxiety, Depression*, New York: Routledge, 2017, p. 16.

4.   Thus, the French critic Julia Kristeva refers to 'a zerological subject, a non-subject who comes to assume the thought that cancels itself'. Jean Baudrillard, *Symbolic Exchange and Death*, London: SAGE Publications, 1993, p. 256.

5.   *Anatta-Lakkhana Sutta: The Discourse on the Not-Self Characteristic*, 22.59, p. 28. https://www.accesstoinsight.org/tipitaka/sn/sn22/sn22.059.nymo.html

6.   On this important point see, for instance, James Schroeder, *Skillful Means: The Heart of Buddhist Compassion*, Honolulu, Hawaii: University of Hawaii Press, 2001.

7.   'Reconstructivists are trying to make the transition from Eurocentric, patriarchal thinking and the "dominator" model of culture toward an aesthetics of interconnectedness, social responsibility and ecological attunement', Suzi Gablik, *The Reenchantment of Art*, London: Thames and Hudson, 1991, p. 22. The idea that the metaphysics of Advaita would be akin to postmodern interconnectedness is both plausible inasmuch as it fosters unity over diversity, and not receivable since the very idea of an essential or ultimate connection is foreign to non-dualism.

8.   'This holistic paradigm defines consciousness and language, subject and object in terms derived from both quantum physics and Eastern philosophy. From the viewpoint of quantum unified field theory and Advaita (nondual) Vedanta, subject and object comprise a unified whole.' William S. Haney II, *Globalization and the Posthuman*, Newcastle upon Tyne, United Kingdom: Cambridge Scholars Publishing, 2009, p. 29.

9.   This creation is, in Hinduism, envisaged as a sacrificial begetting, or as the emergence of energy and desire to create. Thus the principle, the *Purusha*, is sacrificed or self-sacrifices to create the world: 'The All is for the present impounded in the first principle, which may be spoken of as the Person, Progenitor, Mountain, Tree, Dragon or endless Serpent. Related to this principle by filiation or younger brotherhood, and alter ego rather than another principle, is the Dragon-slayer, born to supplant the Father and take possession of the kingdom, distributing its treasures to his followers. [...] This can be done in accordance with the Father's will or against his will; he may "choose death for his children's sake," or it may be that the Gods impose the passion upon him, making him their sacrificial victim.' *The Essential Ananda K. Coomaraswamy*, edited by Rama P. Coomaraswamy, Bloomington: World Wisdom, 2004, p. 267. 'A more speculative treatment of the topic of creation is found in the *nāsadīya sūkta*, in the last book of the Veda: [...] "There was at first darkness, by darkness hidden; without distinctive marks, this all was water. That

which, becoming, was covered by the void, that One by force of heat came into being. Desire entered the One in the beginning: it was the earliest seed, the product of thought". Klaus K. Klostermaier, *A Survey of Hinduism*, Albany, New York: State University of New York Press, 1994, p. 114.

10. It bears stressing that the Maharshi's teachings are not a philosophy, but conceptual and verbal pointers designed to orient toward Reality.
11. *Ulladu Nārpadu, Arunachala Ramana. Teachings. Book 2*, pp. 298–9.
12. *Day by Day*, pp. 328–9.
13. *Poems*, p. 44.
14. Mahadevan, p. 41.
15. *The Complete Mystical Works of Meister Eckhart*, translated by Maurice O'C. Walshe, New York: Crossroad Publishing, 2009, p. 421.
16. *Letters*, p. 339.
17. Among scriptural accounts of the *gunas* probably the most famous are those included in the *Bhagavad Gītā: 'Sattva, rajas, tamas,* thus, the qualities born of material nature, bind fast in the body, O Arjuna, the imperishable embodied One [...]' Winthrop Sargeant, p. 567.
18. Georges Dicker has proposed that 'a more accurate summary of his (Berkeley's) would be "*esse est percipi aut percipere*" position, which means "to be is to be perceived or to perceive." This would be a concise way of saying that to be is to be an idea or a mind, which is Berkeley's view.' *Berkeley's Idealism—A Critical Examination*, Oxford University Press, 2011, p. 3.
19. T.M.P. Mahadevan, *Ramana Maharshi and his Philosophy of Existence*, Tiruvannamalai, Sri Ramanasramam, 2015, p. 50.
20. Cf. Shuchita C. Diviata, *Idealistic Thought in Indian Philosophy*, D.K. Printworld, 1994.
21. *Brahma-Sūtras According to Sri Shankara,* translation and commentary by Swami Vireswarananda, Kolkata: Advaita Ashrama, 1936, 2-2-28, p. 218.
22. David Godman (1986), *Be As You Are: The Teachings of Sri Ramana Maharshi*, London: Arakana, pp. 181–3, p. 184.
23. *Lankāvatāra Sūtra*, edit. Daisetz Teitaro Suzuki, New Delhi: Motilal Banarsidass, 2009, pp. 273–4.
24. In *Guru Vachaka Kovai*, we read,
   'To meet the needs of various seekers
   Master Ramana did expound
   Various doctrines. But we have
   Heard him say that his true teaching,
   Firmly based on his own experience,
   Is *Ajātavada*.' p. 19.
25. *Sat-Darshana Bhashya*, p. 99.
26. Ibid.
27. Nagamma, p. 163.
28. Mahadevan, p. 96.
29. René Guénon, *Man and His Becoming According to the Vedānta*, Hillsdale, New York: Sophia Perennis, 2001, p. 86.

30. 'In the dream state the individual "living soul" (*jīvatma*) "is to itself its own light" and it produces, through the action of its own desire (*kama*) alone, a world issuing entirely from itself, in which the objects consist exclusively of mental conceptions, that is to say of combinations of ideas clothed in subtle forms, depending substantially upon the subtle form of the individual himself, of which they are merely so many secondary and accidental modifications.' René Guénon, *Man and His Becoming According to the Vedānta*, Hillsdale, New York: Sophia Perennis, 2001, p. 91.

31. Ibid.

32. Tayeb Chouiref, *Spiritual teachings of the Prophet*, Louisville, Kentucky: Fons Vitae, 2011, p. 118.

33. *Day by Day*, p. 41.

34. Sri Vasishtha Ganapati Muni, *Sri Ramana Gita*, Tiruvannamalai: Sri Ramanasramam, 2016, p. 37.

35. 'Did I ever say that the world is there because of you? But I have put to you the question what is there without your *self*? You must know that by the self the body, subtle or gross, was not meant.' *Sat-Darshana Bhashya and Talks with Maharshi, by K.*, Tiruvannamalai: Sriramanasramam, 1953, p. vii.

36. *Arunachala Ramana - Eternal Ocean of Grace - Teachings - Book 2*, Tiruvannamalai: Sri Ramanasramam, 2018, p. 257.

37. *The Bhagavad Gītā*, translated by Winthrop Sargeant, Albany, NY: State University of New York Press, 1994, pp. 579–80.

38. 'Just as the screen is lit up by the rays of light focused by the lens, even so the insentient world of matter is illuminated through the mind, (which passes on the light or conscious principle arising from the *Ātman* or Self which is compared to the lamp with the machine.)' *Arunachala Ramana—Eternal Ocean of Grace—Teachings—Book 2*, p. 258.

39. 'It is known that the manifoldness of knowledge is brought about solely by the tendencies, since one might easily assume the existence of manifold knowledge originated by the tendencies even in the absence of the object, for instance, in dreaming and other similar states, but one cannot assume the existence of manifold knowledge only from objects in the absence of tendencies.' Natalia Isayeva, *Shankara and Indian Philosophy*, Albany, New York: State University of New York Press, 1993, p. 181.

40. 'And even if these tendencies are beginningless, this infinite regress would be devoid of foundation, just like a blind man, who is being led by another blind man, so that ordinary human practice becomes completely shattered.' Ibid.

41. Isayeva, p. 182.

42. *Gems from Bhagavān*, p. 3.

43. *Day by Day*, p. 44.

44. 'He Opened My Heart,' *Arunachala Ramana, Book 7*, p. 90.

45. The *Taittirīya Upanishad* states the matter as follows: 'it is inexplicable (*anirvachanīya*), as the *śruti* has described it in the words "Then it was not '*asat*', it was not '*sat*'. 'We cannot say that it is "*a-sat*", that it does not exist: because it is present before consciousness. Neither can we say that it is "sat", that it exists: because it is denied in the *śruti* in the words "there is no duality whatever here".

Māyā is inexplicable from another point of view. In the state of dreamless sleep there is in us no other light than the self-luminous *Chit* or Consciousness, and *Māyā* is experienced as inhering in that pure Consciousness, as we have already seen. We are at a loss to explain how the insentient *Māyā* can thus inhere in pure Consciousness (Chit).' *The Taittirīya Upanishad with the Commentaries of Sri Shankarāchārya, Sri Suresvaracharya, Sri Vidyarania,* Delhi: Samata Books, 2007, https://www.wisdomlib.org/hinduism/book/the-taittiriya-upanishad/d/doc79805.html

46.   '1.   What is *Māyā*? The answer is: It is *anirvachanīya* or indescribable.

2.   "To whom does it come? The answer is: To the mind or ego who feels that he is a separate entity, who thinks 'I do this' or 'This is mine.'" *Gems*, p. 5.

47.   *Gems*, p. 7.

48.   Ramana Maharshi, *Day by Day*, p. 1.

49.   'Where can you go, fleeing from the world or objects? They are like the shadow of a man, which the man cannot flee from.' *Day by Day*, p. 1.

50.   'Let the world bother about its reality or falsehood. Find out first about your own reality,' *Day by Day*, p. 81.

51.   *Sat-Darshana Bhashya*, p. 120.

52.   'The materialistic attitude, whether it be a question of explicit and formal materialism or of a simple "practical" materialism, necessarily imposes on the whole "psycho-physiological" constitution of the human being a real and very important modification. [...] Thus arises the idea of what is commonly called "ordinary life" or "everyday life"; this is in fact understood to mean above all a life in which nothing that is not purely human can intervene in any way, owing to the elimination from it of any sacred, ritual, or symbolical character (it matters little whether this character be thought of as specifically religious or as conforming to some other traditional modality, because the relevant point in all cases is the effective action of "spiritual influences"), the very words "ordinary" or "everyday" moreover implying that everything that surpasses conceptions of that order is, even when it has not yet been expressly denied, at least relegated to an "extra-ordinary" domain, regarded as exceptional, strange, and unaccustomed.' *The Reign of Quantity and The Signs of the Times,* Hillsdale, New York: Sophia Perennis, 2001, pp. 101–2.

53.   'The whole thing centers around the total nullification of individual things in Nothingness and their rebirth from the very bottom of Nothingness again into the domain of empirical reality as concrete individuals, but completely transformed in their inner structure.' Toshihiko Izutsu, Boulder, Colorado: Prajñā Press, 1982, *Toward a Philosophy of Zen Buddhism*, p. 30.

54.   *Gems*, p. 4.

55.   It is worth stressing, however, that appearance is here to be distinguished both from reality and unreality. The latter is typically referred to through the example of the 'son of a barren mother,' whereas the former pertains to all phenomena of experience *qua* superimpositions upon the Self.

56.   The Advaitin philosopher Franklin Merrell-Wolff refers to spiritual 'somnambulism' as the fundamental problem of human existence: 'Dreaminess is the great barrier. But most of human consciousness even in this world is in a sort of waking-dreaming or somnambulistic state. [...] The real difficulty is the almost universal somnambulism

in which men pass the bulk of their lives, some spending many lives without leaving that state at all.' Franklin Merrell-Wolff, *Pathways Through To Space - An Experiential Journal*, Julian Press, 1973, p. 110.

57. While the Supreme Lord is the creator of the world '(the dream world is) mere illusion, on account of its nature not being manifest with the totality (of attributes of the waking state.)' (3.2.3) *Brahma Sūtras According to Śrī Śankara*, edited by Swami Vireswarananda, Kolkata, 2014, p. 285.

58. 'Sankara's meaning seems to be that while dream-objects and illusory contents *vanish* altogether as soon as the person experiencing them comes back to *normal* condition, the objects of normal cognition *do not vanish* all together but are simply understood as *appearances*, as *mere appearances* to be precise.' Shyama Kumar Chattopadhyaya, *The Philosophy of Sankara's Advaita Vedanta*, New Delhi: Sarup and Sons, 2000, p. 269.

59. *Aranuchala Ramana Book 7*, p. 212.

60. '[Shankarian *Advaita*] is realist because it asserts that the cognitive life can be explained only through the conception of an extrinsic, rather than a cognitively intrinsic, order. It is idealist because it holds that there is no proof that there must be an extrinsic order in whose absence there would be no cognitive life. Instead, it asserts that the existence of a systematic cognitive order can be ascertained only because there are, in general, objects of cognition.' Chakravarthi Ram Prasad, 'Dreams and Reality: The Śankarite Critique of *Vijñānavāda*', *Philosophy East and West*, July, 1993, Volume 43, Number 3 (Jul., 1993), p. 447.

61. *Aranuchala Ramana Book 7*, p. 212.

62. Ibid.

63. 'How can the mind which has itself created the world accept it as unreal? That is the significance of the comparison made between the world of wakeful experience and the dream world. Both are but creations of the mind, and so long as the mind is engrossed in either, it finds itself unable to deny the reality of the dream world while dreaming and of the waking world while awake.' *The Spiritual Teachings of Ramana Maharshi*, p. 88.

64. *Aranuchala Ramana Book 7*, p. 213.

65. 'Once Chuang Chou dreamt he was a butterfly, a butterfly flitting and fluttering around, happy with himself and doing as he pleased. He didn't know he was Chuang Chou. Suddenly he woke up and there he was, solid and unmistakable Chuang Chou. But he didn't know if he was Chuang Chou who had dreamt he was a butterfly, or a butterfly dreaming he was Chuang Chou. Between Chuang Chou and a butterfly there must be some distinction! This is called the Transformation of Things.' Translation by Burton Watson, quoted in Yu-shih Chen, *Images and Ideas in Chinese Classical Prose*, Stanford University Press, 1988, p. 148.

66. 'Publisher's Note' in Sri Muruganar, *The Garland of Guru's Sayings - Guru Vachaka Kovai*, Sri Ramanasramam, 2016, p. v.

67. Sri Muruganar, *The Garland of Guru's Sayings - Guru Vachaka Kovai*, Sri Ramanasramam, 2016, p. 5.

68. *Garland*, p. 5.

69. Ibid.

70. *Garland*, p. 6.

71. *Arunachala Ramana, Book 5*, p. 58.
72. Quoted in Grimes, p. 65.
73. David Godman, *The Power of the Presence, Part Three*, Boulder, Colorado: Avadhuta Foundation, 2008, p. 115.

7. THE EYE OF THE SELF

1. It must be added, however, that mystical currents in the three Abrahamic traditions provide doctrines of the soul that distinguish between different degrees of the human selfhood, from the lower, vegetative soul to the highest intellective core of the self that is sometimes even identified with the Divine Immanence within.
2. 'The Penumbra said to the Umbra, "At one moment you move: at another, you are at rest. At one moment you sit down: at another, you get up. Why this instability of purpose?" "Perhaps I depend," replied the Umbra, "upon something which causes me to do as I do, and perhaps that something depends in turn upon something else which causes it to do as it does. Or perhaps my dependence is like (the unconscious movements) of a snake's scales or of a cicada's wings. How can I tell why I do one thing, or why I do not do another?"' Herbert, A. Giles, *Chuang Tzu Taoist Philosopher and Chinese Mystic*, London and New York: Routledge, 2013, p. 47.
3. 'Bhagavan frequently used the Sanskrit phrase *aham sphurana* to indicate the "I-I" consciousness or experience. *Aham* means "I" and *sphurana* can be translated as "radiation, emanation, or pulsation". When he explained what this term meant, he indicated that it is an impermanent experience of the Self in which the mind has been temporarily transcended.' David Godman, https://www.davidgodman.org/i-and-i-i-a-readers-query/
4. '*Deus est sphaera infinita cujus centrum est ubique, circumferentia vero nusquam*', *The Book of the Twenty-Four Philosophers*, Juan Acevedo, edit., Cambridge, UK: The Martheson Trust for the Study of Comparative Religion, 2015, p. 4. https://www.themathesontrust.org/papers/metaphysics/XXIV-A4.pdf
5. 'Since Derrida wants to capture the sense of "differing" as spacing and temporalizing and to indicate the sameness that is non-identical, he uses the term *différance* to point to a necessarily finite movement that precedes and structures all opposition. The *ance* ending of *différance*, marked by a silent *a* suggests that it is not simply a word or a concept; it is neither existence nor essence, and is neither active nor passive because the perceiving subject is similarly constituted. *Différance*, a necessarily finite movement, is what precedes and structures all opposition. In other words, it originates before all differences, and represents the play of differences. It is impossible for it to be exposed because it cannot reveal itself in the present moment and never produces presence itself, whose structure is constituted by difference and deferment.' Carl Olson, *Indian Philosophers and Postmodern Thinkers: Dialogues on the Margins of Culture*, Oxford University Press, 2002, pp. 182–3.
6. Carl Olson, p. 145.
7. *The Collected Works of Ramana Maharshi*, p. 86.
8. 'It is only after seeing the Self within that one will be able to see the Self in everything. One must first realise there is nothing but the Self and that he is that Self, and then only he can see everything as the form of the Self.' *Day by Day*, p. 205.

9.   'There must first be the seer before anything could be seen. You are yourself the eye that sees. Yet, you say you don't know the eye that sees, but know only the things seen. But for the Self, the Infinite Eye, referred to in the stanza in *Ulladu Narpadu* (*Reality in Forty Verses*), what can be seen?' *Day by Day*, p. 328.

10. Grimes, p. 93.

11. *The Garland*, p. 166.

12. *The Poems of Sri Ramana Maharshi*, A.W. Chadwick translator, Tiruvannamalai: Sri Ramanasraman, 2015, p. 19.

13. *Day by Day*, p. 193.

14. 'Do not hang back then, but labour in it until you experience the desire. For when you first begin to undertake it, all that you find is a darkness, a sort of cloud of unknowing; you cannot tell what it is, except that you experience in your will a simple reaching out to God. This darkness and cloud is always between you and your God, no matter what you do, and it prevents you from seeing him clearly by the light of understanding in your reason, and from experiencing him in sweetness of love in your affection.' *The Cloud of Unknowing*, Chapter 3, edited by James Walsh, SJ, Ramsey, New Jersey: Paulist Press, 1981, pp. 120–1.

15. 'When one realises the Truth and knows that there is neither the seer nor the seen, but only the Self that transcends both, that the Self alone is the screen or the substratum on which the shadow both of the ego and all that it sees, come and go, the feeling that one has not got eyesight, and that therefore one misses the sight of various things, will vanish. The realised being, though he has normal eyesight, does not see all these things.' *Day by Day*, p. 336.

16. *The thirteen principal Upanishads*, F. Max-Müller translator, Ware, Hertfordshire, United Kingdom: Wordsworth Classics, 2000, p. xxiv.

17. 'When earnest self-enquiry strikes
     The mind against the flint-stone heart,
     The bright sparks shine, one sees the light
     Of true Awareness whose name is
     An-al-Haq or "That am I".'
         The Garland of Guru's Sayings, p. 185.

18. This is the way Muruganar, with the Maharshi's approval, addressed the question of a Muslim about Self-realization:
     'Those who daily worship Allāh
     Gain all joy and peace at once,
     Attaining calm serenity
     By putting out the raging flames
     Of anguish for life's sins and sorrows.'
         The Garland of Guru's Sayings, p. 126.

19. 'Talking of the "witness" should not lead to the idea that there is a witness and something else apart from him that he is witnessing. The "witness" really means the light that illumines the seer, the seen and the process of seeing. Before, during and after the triads of seer, seen and seeing, the illumination exists. It alone exists always.' *Ramana Maharshi Day by Day*, p. 276.

20. *The Garland*, p. 165.

225

21. *Collected Works*, Arthur Osborne edit., Rider, 1959, p. 72.
22. *Day by Day*, p. 2.
23. *Day by Day*, p. 81.
24. 'The visitor also asked, "When a man realises the Self, what will he see?" Bhagavan replied, "There is no seeing. Seeing is only Being. The state of Self-realisation, as we call it, is not attaining something new or reaching some goal which is far away, but simply being that which you always are and which you always have been." *Day by Day*, p. 342.
25. *Face to Face with Ramana Maharshi*, p. 102.
26. 'Etymologically, it [the word *darshan*] is derived from Sanskrit root, *drish. Darshan* means that which enables us to experience reality, a direct contact with or realization of what in fact "is".' R.P. Pathak, *Philosophical and Sociological Perspectives in Education*, New Delhi: Atlantic, 2007, p. 34.
27. *Arunachala Śiva*, p. 23.
28. *Arunachala Śiva*, p. 24.
29. *Kena Upanishad* in *The Golden Book of Upanishads,* Mahendra Kulasrestha, translated by F. Max Muller, New Delhi: Lotus Press, 2006, p. 34.
30. The *Sri Arunāchala Ashtakam* was jotted down on paper by Pazhani Swami in 1916 while he was accompanying the Maharshi in his circumambulation (*giripradakshina*) around the hill. These Tamil verses are said to have welled up from Ramana on this occasion. *Arunachala Ramana, Book 2*, p. 116.

EPILOGUE

1. Itsuki, Hiroyuki, *Tariki: Embracing Despair and Discovering Grace*, 2001, pp. xvi–xvii.
2. Here is the way Osborne expresses this view: 'The Sages have always agreed that the type of *sādhanā* suited to the Kali-Yuga is pre-eminently *Nama-Japa*, the invocation of the Divine Name. They have agreed also that the *Jñana-Marga*, the "direct path" is not suited to the Kali-Yuga. The task undertaken by Bhagavān Sri Ramana was to reopen the *Jñana-Marga* to mankind.' *The Call Divine*, Volume 3, January 1955, p. 264.
3. 'When in thy heart thou sayest: "Who am I"? there is only the Name that answers thee. When in thy heart thou sayest: "Who am I"? Let Me Alone answer thee.' Jean-Marie Tresflin, *Alone with the Alone in the Name*, Louisville: Fons Vitae, 2004, p. 89.
4. 'A notable facet of the Maharshi's teaching is that it was available to all who sought him out, which was exemplified by all of diverse individuals who came to him from all parts of the world, who had different faiths other than Hinduism, including some without a religious affiliation. This remarkable feature of the Maharshi's teaching also presents some challenges regarding the ability of these different types of individuals to assimilate his teaching devoid of ritual and doctrinal support [...]' Bendeck Sotillos, p. 11.
5. *Living by the Words of Bhagavan*, p. 356.
6. Sri Swami Rajeswarananda, *The Call Divine*, January 1954, *Arunachala Ramana Book 7*, p. 199.

BIBLIOGRAPHY

Acevedo, Juan, (ed.), *The Book of the Twenty-Four Philosophers*. Cambridge, UK: The Matheson Trust for the Study of Comparative Religion, 2015. https://www. themathesontrust.org/papers/metaphysics/XXIV-A4.pdf

Adiswarananda, Swami, *Meditation and Its Practices: A Definitive Guide to Techniques and Traditions of Meditation in Yoga and Vedanta*. Woodstock, VT: SkyLight Paths Publishing, 2007.

Aiyer, N.R. Krishnamoorthi (trans.), *The Essence of Ribhu Gita*. 8th ed. Tiruvannamalai, India: Sri Ramanasramam, 2018.

Almond, Philip C., *Mystical Experience and Religious Doctrine: An Investigation of the Study of Mysticism in World Religions*. Berlin: Mouton, 1982.

Aquinas, Thomas, *Summa Theologiae: Volume 4, Knowledge in God: 1a. 14-18*. Edited by Thomas Gornall. Cambridge, UK: Cambridge University Press, 2006.

Arunachala Ramana – Eternal Ocean of Grace. 7 volumes. Tiruvannamalai, India: Sri Ramanasramam, 2018.

Baudrillard, Jean, *Symbolic Exchange and Death*. Translated by Iain Hamilton Grant. London: SAGE, 1993.

Be as You Are: the Teachings of Sri Ramana Maharshi. Edited by David Godman. London: Penguin Books, 1991.

Bendeck Sotillos, Samuel. 'René Guénon and Sri Ramana Maharshi: Two Remarkable Sages in Modern Times: Part Four.' *The Mountain Path* 52, no. 1 (Jan 2015): 93–104.

Bhagavān Ramana The Friend of All Creation, Offerings by the Devotees of Bhagavān at His Lotus Feet. Tiruvannamalai, India: Sri Ramanasramam, 2008.

Bhushan, Nalini, and Jay L. Garfield, *Minds without Fear: Philosophy in the Indian Renaissance*. New York: Oxford University Press, 2017.

Bloom, Alfred, (ed.), *The Essential Shinran: A Buddhist Path of True Entrusting*. Bloomington, IN: World Wisdom, 2007.

Brunton, Paul, and Munagala S. Venkataramiah, *Conscious Immortality: Conversations with Ramana Maharshi*. 5th ed. Tiruvannamalai, India: Sri Ramanasramam, 2015.

Burckhardt, Titus, *An Introduction to Sufism*. San Francisco, CA: Thornsons, 1995.

Chadwick, A.W., *A Sadhu's Reminiscences of Ramana Maharshi*. Tiruvannamalai, India: Sri Ramanasramam, 2012.

Chadwick, A.W., 'Sri Dakshinamurti and Sri Ramana.' In *Arunachala Ramana – Eternal Ocean of Grace: The Guiding Presence (Book 7)*. Tiruvannamalai, India: Sri Ramanasramam, 2018.

Chadwick, Alan W. (trans.), *The Poems of Sri Ramana Maharshi*. Tiruvannamalai, India: Sri Ramanasramam, 2015.

Chattopadhyaya, Shyama Kumar, *The Philosophy of Sankar's Advaita Vedanta*. New Delhi: Sarup & Sons, 2000.

Chen, Yu-shih, *Images and Ideas in Chinese Classical Prose: Studies of 4 Masters*. Stanford, CA: Stanford University Press, 1988.

Chodkiewicz, Michel, *The Spiritual Writings of Amir 'Abd Al-Kader*. Translated by James Chrestensen and Tom Manning. Albany, NY: State University of New York Press, 1995.

Chouiref, Tayeb (ed.), *The Spiritual Teachings of the Prophet: Hadith with Commentaries by Saints and Sages of Islam*. Louisville, KY: Fons Vitae, 2011.

Cohen, Sulaiman Samuel, *Guru Ramana*. Tiruvannamalai, India: Sri Ramanasramam, 2009.

Comans, Michael, *The Method of Early Advaita Vedānta: A Study of Gauḍapāda, Śaṅkara, Sureśvara and Padmapāda*. New Delhi, India: Motilal Banarsidass Publishers, 2000.

Coomaraswamy, Rama P. (ed.), *The Essential Ananda K. Coomaraswamy*. Bloomington, IN: World Wisdom, 2004.

Corbin, Henry, *En Islam Iranien: Aspects Spirituels et Philosophiques*. Vol 1. Paris: Gallimard, 1971.

Cowell, Edward Byles (trans.), *The Maitri or maitráyaníya Upanishad: With the Commentary of Rámatírtha*. London: W.M. Watts, 1870.

Delisi, Darlene, 'Conversation with Sri Kunju Swamigal.' In *Arunachala Ramana – Eternal Ocean of Grace: The Guiding Presence (Book 7)*. Tiruvannamalai, India: Sri Ramanasramam, 2018.

Dicker, Georges. *Berkeley's Idealism: A Critical Examination*. New York: Oxford University Press, 2011.

Duerlinger, James, *The Refutation of the Self in Indian Buddhism: Candrakirti on the Selflessness of Persons*. New York: Routledge, 2013.

Dumont, Louis, *Essays on Individualism: Modern Ideology in Anthropological Perspective*. Chicago: University of Chicago Press, 1992.

Dyczkowski, Mark S.G., *The Doctrine of Vibration: an Analysis of the Doctrines and Practices of Kashmir Shaivism*. Albany, NY: State University of New York Press, 1987.

Ebert, Gabriele, *Ramana Maharshi: His Life: A Biography*. Stuttgart: Lüchow Verlag, 2015.

Eck, Diana L., *Banaras: City of Light*. New Jersey: Princeton University Press, 1982.

Eckhart, Meister, *The Complete Mystical Works of Meister Eckhart*. Translated by Maurice O'C. Walshe. New York: Herder & Herder, 2009.

Elizarenkova, Tatyana J., *Language and Style of the Vedic Ṛṣis*. Albany, NY: State Univ. of New York Press, 1995.

Flint, Thomas P., 'Two Accounts of Providence.' In *Oxford Readings in Philosophical Theology Volume II: Providence, Scripture, and Resurrection*, edited by Michael C. Rea, Volume 2. Oxford: Oxford University Press, 2009.

Forman, Robert K. C. (ed.) *The Problem of Pure Consciousness: Mysticism and Philosophy*. New York: Oxford University Press, 1990.

Forsthoefel, Thomas A. 'Weaving the Inward Thread to Awakening – The Perennial Appeal of Ramana Maharshi.' Essay. In *Gurus in America*, edited by Thomas A. Forsthoefel and Cynthia Ann Humes, 37–38. Albany, NY: State University of New York Press, 2005.

Forsthoefel, Thomas A., and Cynthia Ann Humes (eds.) *Gurus in America*. Albany, NY: State University of New York Press, 2005.

Fort, Andrew O., and Patricia Y. Mumme, *Living Liberation in Hindu Thought*. Albany: NY: State University of New York Press, 1996.

Fox, Matthew, *Meister Eckhart – A Mystic-Warrior for Our Times*. Novato, CA: New World Library, 2014.

French, R.M., *The Way of a Pilgrim: And the Pilgrim Continues His Way*. London: SPCK, 2012.

Gablik, Suzi, *The Reenchantment of Art*. London: Thames and Hudson, 1991.

Gabriel, Theodore, 'Muni.' Essay. In *Encyclopedia of Hinduism*, edited by Denise Cush, Catherine Robinson, and Michael York, 513. London: Routledge, 2008.

Geoffroy, Éric, *Introduction to Sufism: The Inner Path of Islam*. Translated by Roger Gaetani. Bloomington, IN: World Wisdom, 2010.

Giles, Herbert Allen (trans.), *Chuang Tzu: Taoist Philosopher and Chinese Mystic*. London: Routledge, 2013.

Glassé, Cyril, *The New Encyclopedia of Islam*. Lanham, MD: Altamira Press, 1989.

Godman, David (ed.), *Be as You Are: The Teachings of Sri Ramana Maharshi*. London: Arkana, 1986.

Godman, David, 'Bhagavan and the Politics of His Day' July 12, 2019. https://www.davidgodman.org/bhagavan-and-the-politics-of-his-day/2/

Godman, David, "I' And 'I-I', a Reader's Query.' David Godman. DavidGodman.org, July 12, 2019. https://www.davidgodman.org/i-and-i-i-a-readers-query/.

Godman, David. *Living by the Words of Bhagavān*. Tiruvannamalai, India: Sri Annamalai Swami Ashram Trust, 1995.

Godman, David, 'Talks on Sri Ramana Maharshi: Narrated by David Godman – The Power of the Guru (Part I)' YouTube video, 26:21. Posted by David Godman. September 13, 2015. https://www.youtube.com/watch?v=v8wDe4ngpDw&ab_channel=DavidGodman.

Godman, David (ed.), *The Power of the Presence: Transforming Encounters with Sri Ramana Maharshi (Part 1)*. Boulder, CO: Avadhuta Foundation, 2005.

Godman, David (ed.), *The Power of the Presence: Transforming Encounters with Sri Ramana Maharshi (Part 2)*. Boulder, CO: Avadhuta Foundation, 2005.

Godman, David (ed.), *The Power of the Presence: Transforming Encounters with Sri Ramana Maharshi (Part 3)*. Boulder, CO: Avadhuta Foundation, 2005.

Goodall, Dominic (ed.), *Hindu Scriptures*. New Delhi, India: Motilal Banarsidass, 1996.

Grimes, John, *Problems and Perspectives in Religious Discourse: Advaita Vedānta Implications*. Albany, NY: State University of New York Press, 1994.

Grimes, John, *Ramana Maharshi: The Crown Jewel of Advaita*. Varanasi, India: Indica, 2010.

Guénon René, *East and West*. Translated by Martin Lings. Hillsdale, NY: Sophia Perennis, 2004.

Guénon, René, *Initiation and Spiritual Realization*. Edited by S. D. Fohr. Translated by Henry D. Fohr. Hillsdale, NY: Sophia Perennis, 2004.

Guénon, René, *Man and His Becoming According to the Vedānta*. Translated by Richard C. Nicholson. 3rd ed. Hillsdale, NY: Sophia Perennis, 2001.

Guénon, René, *The Crisis of the Modern World*. Hillsdale, NY: Sophia Perennis, 2001.

Guénon, René, *The Reign of Quantity and the Signs of the Times*. Translated by Lord Northbourne. 4th ed. Hillsdale, NY: Sophia Perennis, 2001.

Hallstrom, Lisa Lassell, *Mother of Bliss – Ānandamayī Mā*. New York: Oxford University Press, 1999.

Hamilton, Victor P., *Exodus: an Exegetical Commentary*. Ada, MI: Baker Academic, 2011.

Haney, William S., *Globalization and the Posthuman*. Newcastle upon Tyne, UK: Cambridge Scholars, 2009.

Herrera, Robert (ed.) *Mystics of the Book: Themes, Topics, and Typologies*. New York: Peter Lang, 1993.

Hess, Linda Beth, *Studies in Kabir: Texts, Traditions, Styles and Skills*. Berkley, CA: University of California Press, 1980.

Ibn al-'Arabī Muhammad ibn 'Alī Muḥyī al-Dīn, *The Bezels of Wisdom*. Translated by Ralph W. J. Austin. New York, NY: Paulist Press, 1980.

Isaeva, Natalia, *Shankara and Indian Philosophy*. Albany, NY: State University of New York Press, 1993.

Itsuki, Hiroyuki, *Tariki: Embracing Despair, Discovering Peace*. Translated by Joseph Robert. Tokyo: Kodansha, 2001.

Izutsu, Toshihiko, *Toward a Philosophy of Zen Buddhism*. Boulder, CO: Prajñā Press, 1982.

James, Michael, *Happiness and the Art of Being: An Introduction to the Philosophy and Practice of the Spiritual Teachings of Bhagavan Sri Ramana*. Self-published,

2006. https://www.happinessofbeing.com/wp-content/uploads/2020/09/ Happiness_and_the_Art_of_Being_1st_edition-4.pdf

Jaoudi, Maria, *Christian Mysticism East and West: What the Masters Teach Us.* Mahawah, NJ: Paulist Press, 1998.

Johnson, Richard L. (ed.) *Gandhi's Experiments with Truth: Essential Writings by and about Mahatma Gandhi.* Lanham, MD: Lexington Books, 2006.

Keel, Hee-Sung, *Meister Eckhart: an Asian Perspective.* Grand Rapids, MI: Eerdmans Publishing, 2007.

Kehoane, Kieran, Anders Petersen, and Bert Van den Bergh, *Late Modern Subjectivity and Its Discontents: Anxiety, Depression and Alzheimer's Disease.* New York: Routledge, 2017.

Kelley, C. F., *Meister Eckhart on Divine Knowledge.* Cobb, CA: Dharma Café, 2009.

Klostermaier, Klaus K., *A Survey of Hinduism.* Albany, NY: State University of New York Press, 1994.

Kulasrestha, Mahendra, 'Kena Upanishad.' In *the Golden Book of Upanishads: Humanity's Earliest Philosophical Compositions: Eleven Major Upanishads,* translated by Müller F. Max, 34–7. New Delhi, India: Lotus Press, 2006.

Le Saux, Henri, *Souvenir d'Arunāchala: Récit d'un ermite chrétien en terre indoue.* Paris: Epi-Desclée de Brouwer, 1978–80.

Lings, Martin, *A Sufi Saint of the Twentieth Century: Shaikh Aḥmad Al-'Alawī: His Spiritual Heritage and Legacy.* Cambridge: Islamic texts Society, 1993.

Lott, Eric, *Vedantic Approaches to God.* London: Palgrave Macmillan, 1980.

Lusthaus, Dan, *Buddhist Phenomenology: A Philosophical Investigation of Yogācāra Buddhism and the Ch'eng Wei-Shih Lun.* New York: Routledge-Curzon, 2002.

Mahadevan, T.M.P. (trans.), *Arunachala Siva: Arunachala Aksharamanamalai (Bridal Garland of Letters for Arunachala).* 6th ed. Tiruvannamalai, India: Sri Ramanasramam, 2014.

Mahadevan, T.M.P., *Ramana Maharshi and His Philosophy of Existence.* Tiruvannamalai, India: Sri Ramasramam, 2015.

Maharshi, Ramana, *Maharshi's Gospel – The Teachings of Sri Ramana Maharshi.* Tiruvannamalai, India: Sri Ramanasramam, 2012.

Maharshi, Ramana, *Talks with Ramana Maharshi: On Realizing Abiding Peace and Happiness.* Carlsbad, CA: InnerDirections Pub., 2001.

Maharshi, Ramana, *The Collected Works of Ramana Maharshi.* Edited by Arthur Osborne. San Rafael, CA: Sophia Perennis, 2006.

Maharshi, Ramana, *The Song Celestial (Verses from Sri Bhagavad-gītā): Selected and Reset by Bhagavān Ramana Maharshi.* Tiruvannamalai, India: Sri Ramanasraman, 2018.

Maharshi, Ramana, *The Spiritual Teaching of Ramana Maharshi.* Boulder, CO: Shambhala, 1998.

Max-Müller, F. (trans.), *The Thirteen Principal Upanishads.* Hertfordshire, UK: Wordsworth Editions Limited, 2000.

Mercadante, Linda A., *Belief without Borders: Inside the Minds of the Spiritual but not Religious*. New York: Oxford University Press, 2014.

Merrell-Wolff, Franklin, *Franklin Merrell-Wolff's Experience and Philosophy: A Personal Record of Transformation and a Discussion of Transcendental Consciousness*. Albany, NY: State University of New York Press, 1994.

Merrell-Wolff, Franklin, *Pathways through to Space: A Personal Record of Transformation in Consciousness*. New York: Julian Press, 1973.

Mohanty, J. N., *Classical Indian Philosophy*. Lanham, MD: Rowman & Littlefield Publishers, 2000.

Mudaliar, A. Devaraja, *Day by Day with Bhagavan: from a Diary of A. Devaraja Mudaliar*. Tiruvannamalai, India: V.S. Ramanan, 1995.

Mudaliar, A. Devraja, 'God and Destiny.' *The Mountain Path* 4, no. 2 (April 1967): 113–15.

Muller, Max (trans.), 'Chandogya Upanishad, 6,9,4.' `In *the Upanishads: Part I*. New York: Oxford University Press, 1900.

Muni, Vasishtha Ganapati, *Forty Verses in Adoration of Sri Ramana*. Tiruvannamalai, India: Sri Ramanasramam, 2012.

Muni, Vasistha Ganapati, *Sri Ramana Gita: Being the Teachings of Bhagavan Sri Ramana Maharshi*. Tiruvannamalai, India: Sri Ramanasramam, 2016.

Muruganar, Sri, *The Garland of Guru's Sayings: Guru vāchaka kōvai*. Translated by K. Swaminathan. 4th ed. Tiruvannamalai, India: Sri Ramanasramam, 2016.

Muruganar, *Padamalai: Teachings of Sri Ramana Maharshi*. Edited by David Godman. Translated by T. V. Venkatasubramanian and Robert Butler. Boulder, CO: David Godman, Avadhuta Foundation, 2003.

Nagamma, Suri, *Letters from Sri Ramanasramam,* 8th ed. Tiruvannamalai, India: Sri Ramanasramam, 2014.

Nair, Shankar, *Translating Wisdom: Hindu-Muslim Intellectual Interactions in Early Modern South Asia*. Oakland, CA: University of California Press, 2020.

Narain, Laxmi (ed.), *Face to Face with Sri Ramana Maharshi: Enchanting and Uplifting Reminiscences of 202 Persons*. Hyderabad, India: Sri Ramana Kendram, 2009.

Naṭanānanda Sadhu, T. V. Venkatasubramanian, and David Godman, *Sri Ramana Darsanam*. Edited by David Godman. Tiruvannamalai, India: Sri Ramanasramam, 2002.

Nelson, Lance E., 'Krishna in Advaita Vedānta: The Supreme Brahman in Human Form.' In *Krishna: A Sourcebook*, edited by Edwin F. Bryant, 309–28. New York: Oxford University Press, 2007.

Nikhilananda, Swami, *The Upanishads*. New York: Harper and Row, 1964.

Olson, Carl, *Indian Philosophers and Postmodern Thinkers: Dialogues on the Margins of Culture*. New Delhi, India: Oxford University Press, 2002.

Osborne, Arthur (ed.), *The Teachings of Bhagavan Sri Ramana Maharshi in His Own Words*. Tiruvannamalai, India: Sri Ramanasraman, 2002.

Osborne, Arthur (ed.), *The Teachings of Ramana Maharshi*. London: Rider, 2014.

Osborne, Arthur, *Buddhism and Christianity in the Light of Hinduism*. 5th ed. Tiruvannamalai, India: Sri Ramanasramam, 2016.

Osborne, Arthur, *Ramana Maharshi and the Path of Self Knowledge*. San Rafael, CA: Sophia Perennis, 2006.

Osborne, Lucia, 'Arunachala.' In *Arunachala Ramana – Eternal Ocean of Grace: The Guiding Presence (Book 7)*. Tiruvannamalai, India: Sri Ramanasramam, 2018.

Pathak, Ramesh Prasad, *Philosophical and Sociological Perspectives in Education*. New Delhi, India: Atlantic Publishers, 2007.

Plato, *Phaedrus*. Translated by Benjamin Jowett. New York: Cosimo, 2010.

Prasad, Chakravarthi Ram, 'Dreams and Reality: The Śaṅkarite Critique of Vijñānavada.' *Philosophy East and West* 43, no. 3 (July 1993): 405-55.

Radhakrishnan, Sarvepalli and Charles A. Moore (eds), *A Source Book in Indian Philosophy*. New Jersey: Princeton University Press, 1967.

Rajeswarananda, Sri Swami, 'The Call Divine.' In *Arunachala Ramana – Eternal Ocean of Grace: The Guiding Presence (Book 7)*. Tiruvannamalai, India: Sri Ramanasramam, 2018.

Rajeswarananda, Sri Swami, *The Call Divine*, January 1954, *Arunachala Ramana Book 7*, p. 199.

Ramamoorthy, H., and Nome (trans.), *The Song of Ribhu: the English Translation of the Tamil Ribhu Gītā*. Santa Cruz, CA: Society of Abidance in Truth, 2000.

Raman, Srilata, *Self-Surrender (Prapatti) to God in Śrīvaisnavism: Tamil Cats and Sanskrit Monkeys*. London: Routledge, 2007.

Ramanujan, A. K. (trans.), *Speaking of Siva*. Baltimore, MD: Penguin Books, 1973.

Rambachan, Anantanand, *The Advaita Worldview: God, World, and Humanity*. Albany, NY: State University of New York Press, 2006.

Rangaswami, Sudhakshina (ed.), 'Sādhanā Catustaya (Four Prerequisites of Spiritual Life).' Essay. In *the Roots of Vedānta: Selections from Śaṅkara's Writings*. Cyber City, India: Penguin Random House India, 2012.

Roy, Olivier, *Holy Ignorance: When Religion and Culture Part Ways*. London: Hurst & Company, 2010.

Sargeant, Winthrop (trans.), *The Bhagavad Gītā*. Albany, New York: State University of New York Press, 1994.

Sastri, Alladi Mahadeva, *Dakshinamurti Stotra of Sri Sankaracharya*. Chennai, India: Samata Books, 2001.

Sastri, S. N., *Hastamalakiyam of Hastamalaka, Disciple of Sri Shankara,* Turlock, CA: Dennis B. Hill, 2007.

Sastriar, Kapali, *Sat-Darshana Bhashya and Talks with Maharshi by K*. 11th ed. Tiruvannamalai, India: Sri Ramanasramamam, 2015.

Satchidānandendra, Sri Swami, *The Method of the Vedānta: A Critical Account of the Advaita Tradition*. Translated by A. J. Alston. New Delhi, India: Motilal Banarsidass, 1997.

Schimmel, Annemarie, *A Two-Colored Brocade: The Imagery of Persian Poetry*. Chapel Hill, NC: The University of North Carolina Press, 2004.

Scholl, Edith, *Words for the Journey: A Monastic Vocabulary*. Collegeville, MN: Liturgical Press, 2009.

Schroeder, John W., *Skillful Means: The Heart of Buddhist Compassion*. Honolulu HI: University of Hawaii Press, 2001.

Schuon, Frithjof, *Language of the Self*. Translated by Margo Pallis and Macleod Matheson. Madras, India: Ganesh and Co, 1959.

Schuon, Frithjof, *Light on the Ancient Worlds: A New Translation with Selected Letters*. Edited by Deborah Casey. Bloomington, IN: World Wisdom; 2006.

Schuon, Frithjof, *Spiritual Perspectives and Human Facts: a New Translation with Selected Letters*. Edited by James S. Cutsinger. Translated by Mark Perry, Jean-Pierre Lafouge, and James S Cutsinger. Bloomington, IN: World Wisdom, 2007.

Schuon, Frithjof, *The Feathered Sun: Plains Indians in Art and Philosophy*. Bloomington, IN: World Wisdom Books, 1990.

Scott, Robert, and George W. Gilmore (eds.), *Selections from the World's Devotional Classics*. Volume 8. New York: Funk & Wagnalls Company, 1916.

Shankaranarayanan, S., *Bhagavan and Nayana*. 3rd ed. Tiruvannamalai, India: Sri Ramanasramam, 2014.

Sharma, Arvind, *Our Religions*. New York: HarperOne, 1993.

Sharma, Arvind, *Sleep as a State of Consciousness in Advaita Vedānta*. Albany, NY: State University of New York Press, 2004.

Sharma, Arvind, *The Experiential Dimension of Advaita Vedanta*. New Delhi: Motilal Banarsidass Publishers, 1993.

Sharma, Chandradhar, *The Advaita Tradition in Indian Philosophy: A Study of Advaita in Buddhism, Vedanta and Kashmira Shaivism*. 1st ed. New Delhi, India: Motilal Banarsidass, 1996.

Shigaraki, Takamaro, *Heart of the Shin Buddhist Path: A Life of Awakening*. Translated by David Matsumuto. Boston, MA: Wisdom Publications, 2013.

Shikūh, Dārā, *Majma'-Ul-baḥrain, or, The Mingling of the Two Oceans*. Edited and translated by M. Mahfuz-ul-Haq. Kolkata, India: The Asiatic Society, 2015.

Singh, Jaideva, *Śivas Sūtras – The Yoga of Supreme Identity*. New Delhi: Motilal Banarsidass, 1979.

Subbalakshmiamma, Varanasi, 'My Life, My Light.' In *Arunachala Ramana - Eternal Ocean of Grace: The Guiding Presence (Book 7)*. Tiruvannamalai, India: Sri Ramanasramam, 2018.

Suzuki, D. T., *The Zen Koan as a Means of Attaining Enlightenment*. Boston, MA: Charles E. Tuttle, 1994.

Suzuki, Daisetz Teitaro (ed.), *The Lankāvatāra sūtra: A Mahayana Text*. New Delhi, India: Motilal Banarsidass, 2009.

Swami, Vishwanata, 'Activity, Help not Hindrance.' In *Arunachala Ramana – Eternal Ocean of Grace: The Guiding Presence (Book 7)*. Tiruvannamalai, India: Sri Ramanasramam, 2018.

Tattvālokah. Volume 26. Sri Abhinava Vidyatheertha Educational Trust, 2003.

Sastry Alladi Mahadeva (trans.), *Taittiriya Upanishad: With the Commentaries of Sri Sankaracharya, Sri Suresvaracharya, Sri Vidyaranya*. New Delhi, India: Samata, 2007.

Tigunait, Rajmani, *The Himalayan Masters: A Living Tradition*. Honesdale, PA: Himalayan Institute Press, 2002.

Tresflin, Jean-Marie, *Alone with the Alone in the Name*. Louisville, KY: Fons Vitae, 2004.

Tzu, Lao, *Tao Te Ching: the Definitive Edition*. Translated by Jonathan Star. New York: Jeremy P Tarcher/Putnam, 2001.

Upadēśa Sāram: The Complete Version in Four Languages Composed by Sri Bhagavan. Tiruvannamalai, India: Sri Ramanasraman, 2011.

Varghese, I.S., 'Light on the Path.' In *Arunachala Ramana – Eternal Ocean of Grace: The Guiding Presence (Book 7)*. Tiruvannamalai, India: Sri Ramanasramam, 2018.

Vijnanananda, Swami (trans.), *The Srimad Devi Bhagawatam*. New Delhi, India: Oriental Books Reprint Co., 1977.

Vireswarananda, Swami, *Brahma-Sūtras: According to Sri Sankara*. Calcutta, India: Advaita Ashrama Publication Department, 1936.

Walsh, James (ed.), *The Cloud of Unknowing*. Ramsey, NJ: Paulist Press, 1981.

Weil, Simone, *Gravity and Grace*. London and New York: Routledge, 2003.

Welter, Albert. *The Linji Lu and the Creation of Chan Orthodoxy: The Development of Chan's Records of Sayings Literature*. Oxford, NY: Oxford University Press, 2008.

Williams, Alison, 'Sunk in an Ocean of Bliss: Learning from Ramana.' *The Mountain Path* 40, no. 3 (July 2003): 9–22.

INDEX